Manifesting Destiny

Manifesting Destiny

Will Stickle

CONTENTS

Introduction: The Inevitable Absorption of Canada

The U.S. has always viewed Canada as unfinished business—annexationist ambitions stretch back centuries.

The United States has always seen Canada as unfinished business. The border, as it exists today, was never meant to be permanent—not in the minds of the men who built America. From the Revolution onward, American expansionist ambitions toward Canada have been a constant undercurrent in U.S. policy, sometimes overt, sometimes disguised under economic treaties and trade arrangements, but always present. The push for annexation didn't start with high-level policy—it started with a mindset, a belief that North America belonged to the United States by virtue of destiny, military might, and economic dominance.

The earliest documented case of direct U.S. annexationist ambitions came as early as 1775, before the United States was even formally independent. The logic was simple: the American colonies were in rebellion against Britain, and if they were breaking away, why shouldn't the northern colonies join them? The Invasion of Canada during the Revolutionary War—a calculated but ultimately disastrous attempt to seize Quebec and Montreal—was the first real attempt at expansion. The Continental Congress had already assumed that French Canadians, still bitter from British rule, would eagerly rise up and join the Revolution. It was a fatal miscalculation. The invasion failed. Quebec held, the Americans retreated, and Canada remained under British control. But the idea didn't die. It merely shifted from military conquest to long-term strategic pressure.

After the Revolution, U.S. ambitions toward Canada didn't wane—they evolved. The War of 1812 was the next major push. This wasn't just about trade disputes and impressment of American sailors. It was about Manifest Destiny before the term even existed. The War Hawks in Congress—Henry Clay, John C. Calhoun, the usual suspects of early American expansionism—pushed for war under the pretense of punishing Britain, but the real objective was territorial. They wanted Canada. Invasion attempts were launched across the Great Lakes, up the St. Lawrence, into what is now Ontario. The belief was that Canadians, just like in 1775, would welcome American "liberators" and join the union. Again, a fundamental miscalculation. British forces, reinforced by local militias and Indigenous allies, repelled the American attacks. Another failure. But another lesson learned.

After 1814, open warfare was no longer viable. Britain wasn't going to give up Canada, and the U.S. wasn't strong enough to take it outright. So the strategy shifted. Economic infiltration, settlement expansion, and soft annexation. The Monroe Doctrine (1823) declared the entire Western Hemisphere off-limits to European powers, a veiled warning that British North America wouldn't be tolerated indefinitely. The Oregon boundary disputes in the 1840s saw U.S. settlers flooding into disputed regions, forcing diplomatic confrontations with Britain, and securing American control over the Pacific Northwest. The same tactic could have worked in Canada—flood it with American settlers, tilt the demographics, and let the rest fall into place. But Britain held firm, reinforcing borders and strengthening economic ties to prevent Canadian drift into American influence.

By the time the U.S. annexed Texas (1845) and half of Mexico (1848), the writing was on the wall. Expansion wasn't a theory—it was policy. The belief was that Canada would fall into line eventually. Many Americans assumed it was only a matter of time before British disengagement or economic hardship made annexation inevitable. There were factions in Canada—especially in the business class—who openly discussed the advantages of joining the U.S. market. Why be shackled to Britain when the future was American?

Then came the Civil War. The U.S. was too busy tearing itself apart to pursue expansion, but the moment it ended, the conversation started again. The Fenian Raids (1866-1871)—Irish-American militias launching cross-border attacks into Canada—were an explicit attempt to provoke war and force U.S. annexation under the guise of an Irish rebellion. Meanwhile, Britain, weary of the cost of defending its North American territories, moved to consolidate power. That's how Confederation happened in 1867—not because Canadians organically decided to form a country, but because Britain needed a stronger, more centralized buffer state against American expansion. Confederation wasn't about Canadian identity. It was about survival.

Through the late 19th and early 20th centuries, the U.S. played a long game. It moved from military confrontation to economic control, cultural influence, and the steady erosion of Canadian autonomy. By the time NAFTA was signed in 1994, it was clear that the old game of annexation had simply evolved into something subtler. Why invade when you can buy? Why fight when you can integrate? The end goal never changed—only the methods. Canada was always meant to be part of the American empire. It just didn't realize it was being absorbed one treaty, one corporation, one industry at a time.

Manifest Destiny wasn't just an ideology—it was a justification, a guiding principle that shaped U.S. expansionism and foreign policy for over a century. It was never a passive belief. It was an active force, a mission to absorb and control everything within reach. The idea was simple: America was divinely ordained to rule from coast to coast, and anything standing in the way—whether Indigenous nations, European colonial powers, or reluctant neighbors—was merely an obstacle to be overcome. Canada was one of those obstacles. Unlike Mexico or the western frontier, it was never seen as an enemy to be conquered by force, but rather as a wayward territory that would inevitably be pulled into the fold. America didn't just want Canada. It believed Canada belonged to it.

From the earliest days of U.S. independence, there was an assumption—sometimes subtle, sometimes explicit—that British North America was unfinished business. The War of 1812 proved it. The invasion of Canada wasn't a defensive measure or a secondary front. It was a direct expression of expansionist ambition. The belief among many in Washington was that Canada would naturally fall in line, that British rule was weak, and that American values of liberty and democracy would win over the local population. The failure of that war didn't erase the idea—it simply pushed it into a different form. Instead of outright conquest, the U.S. turned to economic infiltration, settlement expansion, and long-term strategic pressure.

By the mid-19th century, Manifest Destiny had become the dominant ideology in American politics. James K. Polk, one of the most aggressive expansionist presidents in U.S. history, made it clear: American sovereignty over the continent was not a question of if, but when. Under his administration, the U.S. annexed Texas, went to war with Mexico to seize California and the Southwest, and negotiated a settlement with Britain that secured American control over Oregon. That last point was significant because it highlighted an important shift in American strategy—diplomatic expansion backed by the threat of force. The Oregon boundary dispute was settled without war, but only because Britain knew the U.S. was willing to fight for it. The message was clear: America's patience was not infinite. The same logic applied to Canada.

Even after the Civil War, as the U.S. recovered from its internal divisions, expansionist rhetoric didn't fade. If anything, it became sharper. The Fenian Raids of the 1860s, where Irish-American militias attempted to invade Canada in hopes of sparking a broader war, reflected this lingering belief that Canada was a natural extension of the U.S. It didn't matter that the raids were unofficial. What mattered was that they were tolerated, even encouraged, by elements within the American government. The notion that Canada was an inevitable part of the American empire persisted, even if military conquest had proven unfeasible.

By the early 20th century, Manifest Destiny had evolved into something more refined. The U.S. no longer needed to send troops to expand its influence—it had Wall Street, Hollywood, and multinational corporations. The real annexation didn't happen through war, but through economics and culture. The U.S. didn't need to fire a shot to control Canada; it just had to make sure Canada's industries, policies, and markets were tied so tightly to Washington that sovereignty became a technicality. The country would eventually fold—not by force, but by inertia.

That's the final evolution of Manifest Destiny. The U.S. no longer talks about annexing Canada because it doesn't need to. It's already happening, piece by piece, one trade agreement, one military pact, one corporate takeover at a time. The belief that North America should be governed as a single entity never disappeared—it just became more efficient. The American empire no longer expands through war. It expands through inevitability.

From the very beginning, the United States saw Canada not as a sovereign neighbor but as an unfinished territorial acquisition. If one strategy failed, another took its place. When military force didn't work, economic entanglement became the weapon. When annexationist rhetoric lost its edge, cultural and corporate influence did the heavy lifting. The goal was always control, whether through direct conquest, economic leverage, or political alignment.

The first and most obvious strategy was military invasion. The Revolutionary War (1775-1783) saw an early attempt when the Continental Army invaded Quebec, assuming French Canadians would join the rebellion. They didn't. The War of 1812 followed, with U.S. forces making multiple attempts to seize Canada outright. That failed too. British-backed Indigenous resistance, loyalist forces, and better logistical planning left the Americans outmatched. After 1814, the U.S. abandoned direct military campaigns but never abandoned the objective.

Instead, Washington turned to diplomatic and economic pressure. The Monroe Doctrine (1823) was the first official warning shot, signaling that European colonial rule in North America had an expiration date. The U.S. secured Oregon in 1846, making it clear that Britain's hold over Canadian territories was not untouchable. Annexationist sentiment surged again after the U.S. Civil War, when American officials debated whether to push northward, taking advantage of British disengagement. Then came the Fenian Raids (1866-1871), Irish-American militia attacks on Canada meant to provoke war and force Washington to step in. The U.S. didn't directly support them, but it didn't stop them either. The message was clear: Canada was vulnerable.

When military aggression failed, economic infiltration took over. The Reciprocity Treaty (1854-1866) created free trade ties that made Canada's economy increasingly dependent on the U.S., a pattern that has only deepened over time. NAFTA (1994) and USMCA (2018) reinforced this structure, ensuring that Canada's industries, exports, and financial system would remain locked into the American sphere. Meanwhile, defense agreements like NORAD (1958) placed Canada under U.S. military command in all but name. If Canada's security is dictated by Washington, is it really independent?

This strategy continues today. The U.S. no longer needs to push for annexation because it's already happening through economic, political, and military integration. There's no need for another invasion when trade policies, defense pacts, and corporate takeovers do the same job without firing a shot.

How economic dependency, political pressure, and global realignments are eroding Canadian sovereignty.

Canada's economy isn't just linked to the U.S.—it's effectively under its control. Over 75% of Canadian exports go directly to the U.S., making it clear that Canada doesn't operate as an independent economy but as an extension of the American market. When Washington shifts trade policies, Canada scrambles to adjust. When U.S. interest rates rise, the Canadian dollar takes a hit. The so-called "special relationship" isn't one of partnership—it's one of dependency, and dependency is just another word for control.

Industry is no different. The Canadian energy sector, particularly oil and natural gas, is at the mercy of U.S. corporations and regulatory decisions. Alberta's economy lives or dies based on whether Washington wants Canadian crude. Keystone XL was killed not by a Canadian decision but by an American president, showing just how little autonomy exists in Canada's most valuable resource sector. The auto industry follows the same pattern—most Canadian vehicle production is just a spoke in the wheel of American supply chains. The moment Detroit shifts strategies, Ontario's manufacturing sector is forced to follow.

The financial system? Even worse. Major Canadian banks are deeply intertwined with Wall Street, to the point where economic shifts in the U.S. have a direct impact on Canadian lending, mortgage rates, and investment flows. The Bank of Canada takes its cues from the Federal Reserve, whether it admits it or not. When the Fed hikes rates, Canada has no choice but to follow, or risk capital flight. U.S. hedge funds and private equity firms own massive shares in Canadian corporations, meaning that key sectors—from real estate to telecom to retail—are shaped by American financial interests, not Canadian policy.

At this point, it's not about whether American influence exists—it's about whether Canada has any control left at all. Washington doesn't need to pass a law or send troops to dictate the direction of the Canadian economy. It just needs to adjust interest rates, shift trade agreements, or let U.S. investors call the shots. Canada is already integrated into the American empire; the question is whether there's any way out.

Canada's economy doesn't operate independently—it moves when Washington pulls the strings. Over 75% of Canadian exports go directly to the U.S., making the country's financial health completely reliant on decisions made in Washington, not Ottawa. Trade agreements like NAFTA and its replacement, USMCA, were never about mutual benefit—they were about ensuring that Canada's economy remained locked into the American orbit. If the U.S. imposes tariffs or rewrites trade rules, Canada has no choice but to comply or risk economic collapse. That isn't a partnership; it's economic subjugation.

The energy sector is a prime example. Canada is one of the world's largest oil producers, yet it can't even build pipelines without U.S. approval. When Joe Biden killed Keystone XL, it wasn't Canada that made the decision—it was an American president, prioritizing American politics. The oil itself? Shipped south to be refined and sold back at a higher price. The same applies to natural gas and electricity, with massive U.S. control over pricing, production, and distribution. Canada may have the resources, but Washington controls the market.

Manufacturing follows the same pattern. The auto industry in Ontario is little more than a branch plant operation for Detroit. If the U.S. shifts production priorities, Canada follows or gets left behind. Canadian steel and aluminum industries are subject to American tariffs on a whim, despite being essential to U.S. supply chains. When Trump slapped tariffs on these industries in 2018, Canada's economy took a hit. The message was clear: Canada doesn't set the terms—Washington does.

Finance is no different. Wall Street owns a massive share of Canadian banking, real estate, and corporate assets. The Bank of Canada may pretend to act independently, but when the Federal Reserve raises interest rates, Canada has no choice but to follow or risk capital flight. Major Canadian companies—including those in telecom, mining, and retail—are either directly controlled by U.S. investors or heavily dependent on American markets. Private equity firms in New York own large portions of the Canadian housing market, driving up prices while keeping policy dictated by foreign capital.

The reality is clear: Canada doesn't run its own economy. U.S. policies, corporations, and financial institutions dictate trade, industry, and monetary policy. At this point, Canada's economic sovereignty is little more than a legal fiction—a thin layer of bureaucracy disguising the fact that Washington, not Ottawa, calls the shots.

Global institutions—IMF, WEF, WTO—aren't neutral arbiters of international cooperation. They function as instruments of economic control, shaping policies in ways that align with American geopolitical and corporate interests. Canada, despite its veneer of sovereignty, operates within a framework dictated by these institutions, each of which reinforces U.S. dominance over its economy, trade policies, and financial system. These organizations don't force Canada's hand explicitly; they simply make sure that the only choices available lead back to Washington.

Take the International Monetary Fund (IMF)—a so-called lender of last resort that dictates economic policy under the guise of "stabilization." While Canada isn't an active recipient of IMF bailouts like debt-ridden developing nations, its financial system is directly shaped by IMF policy frameworks that promote privatization, deregulation, and fiscal austerity whenever it suits U.S. corporate interests. More importantly, the IMF's real power lies in its influence over global markets. It sets the economic "rules," and Canada plays by them, not because it has to, but because deviation means punishment in the form of capital flight, currency devaluation, or investment blacklisting.

Then there's the World Trade Organization (WTO), the global enforcer of so-called "free trade." In reality, the WTO exists to make sure that smaller nations like Canada remain structurally dependent on U.S.-dominated global markets. Any attempt by Canada to enact protectionist policies to safeguard its own industries is met with WTO litigation, where the U.S. holds disproportionate influence. If American corporations want access to Canadian markets, WTO rules guarantee they get it—while Canada, locked into USMCA and other trade agreements, has little room to maneuver. The moment Canada tries to play hardball, the WTO ensures that it falls back in line.

The World Economic Forum (WEF) is even more insidious. It doesn't operate through direct financial mechanisms like the IMF or trade rulings like the WTO. Instead, it functions as a globalist policy factory, setting the ideological framework that guides national governments into alignment with U.S.-led corporate interests. Canada's leadership—particularly under Trudeau—has fully embraced WEF-driven policies on climate change, digital finance, and global governance, all of which serve to integrate Canada into the broader structure of U.S.-centric globalization. The result? Canada's natural resources, industries, and financial systems are slowly being absorbed into a supranational corporate order where American firms and investors dictate the rules.

These institutions don't need to explicitly demand Canada's compliance. They create a system where compliance is the only viable option. If Canada ever attempted to break free—say, by nationalizing key industries, imposing serious trade barriers, or creating financial independence from U.S. markets—the IMF would cut access to liquidity, the WTO would launch retaliatory trade rulings, and the WEF-aligned elite class would manufacture a political crisis. The U.S. wouldn't even need to intervene directly. The system is designed to enforce itself.

In the end, these global institutions exist not to promote fair economic policy, but to ensure that nations like Canada never become truly sovereign. The illusion of national control remains intact, but the decisions are already made—not in Ottawa, but in Washington, New York, and Davos.

The United States doesn't need a war to annex Canada—it has far more effective tools at its disposal. Tariffs, energy dependency, and financial instability are modern weapons of economic coercion, designed to weaken Canadian sovereignty and push the country toward deeper integration with the U.S. These aren't just theoretical tactics; they've already been deployed in various forms. The question isn't if Washington will use them again, but when and to what extent.

Tariffs: The Economic Squeeze
Trade is the foundation of Canada's economy, and 75% of its exports

go directly to the United States. That's leverage—leverage the U.S. has used before and will use again. Trump's 2018 tariffs on Canadian steel and aluminum weren't about protecting American industry; they were about testing how much economic pressure Canada could handle before it broke. The result? Ottawa scrambled to impose retaliatory tariffs, but the damage was already done. U.S. markets could adapt, but Canada took the bigger hit. The lesson was clear: Canada doesn't set the rules, Washington does.

If a U.S. administration wanted to force deeper integration, targeted tariffs would be an easy first step. A sudden increase in tariffs on autos, lumber, or agriculture—three industries vital to Canada's economy—would cause immediate financial distress. American companies would absorb the disruption, but Canadian firms would struggle to survive. With supply chains already tied to the U.S., Ottawa would be left with two options: accept economic decline or negotiate even closer ties with Washington to regain stability.

Energy Dependency: The Pipeline Trap

Canada produces oil, but the U.S. controls how it moves. Keystone XL wasn't canceled by Canada—it was killed by Biden. Alberta's economy hinges on energy exports, yet over half of Canadian crude is shipped to U.S. refineries, where pricing and distribution are dictated by American interests. If Washington decided to weaponize energy policy, it could choke off Canada's most valuable export overnight. A single executive order limiting U.S. refinery access to Canadian oil would send energy markets into a tailspin. Alberta would collapse, and with it, the country's already fragile economy.

If Canada tried to retaliate—say, by diverting oil exports to China or other buyers—the U.S. could respond with sanctions, regulatory blockades, or even national security threats, citing the need to "protect North American energy stability." The reality? Canada would have no choice but to comply, and likely under new conditions even more favorable to U.S. interests.

Financial Instability: Controlling the Currency

The Bank of Canada follows the Federal Reserve's lead, whether it admits it or not. If the Fed raises interest rates, Canada has to follow or risk currency devaluation and capital flight. This dependency is a ticking time bomb. The U.S. could trigger a financial crisis in Canada without lifting a finger—simply by adjusting its own policies in a way that destabilizes Canadian markets. A rapid interest rate hike, a shift in capital investment priorities, or a regulatory move against cross-border banking would send shockwaves through the Canadian economy.

If a financial crisis struck, Washington could position itself as the "solution", offering economic stability in exchange for political concessions. This could mean anything from a shared currency (effectively erasing Canada's financial sovereignty) to deeper trade integration that forces Ottawa to align completely with U.S. economic policy. In the worst-case scenario, a Canadian government—desperate to prevent economic collapse—could accept U.S. financial oversight as a temporary emergency measure, only to find out later that it was permanent.

The Long Game

None of these moves would happen overnight, and none would need to be framed as an explicit takeover. The strategy is slow, deliberate, and effective. First, apply pressure—tariffs, energy restrictions, financial stress. Then, offer solutions that look like "partnerships" but function as deeper integration into the American system. Finally, leave Canada with no real alternatives. By the time full absorption is on the table, it won't feel like an invasion. It'll feel like the only rational choice. That's the real play.

Is unification by consent, coercion, or collapse?

Canada's unity is a fragile illusion, fraying under the weight of unchecked immigration, demographic shifts, and growing separatist movements. A divided country is easy to manipulate, and whether by incompetence or design, Ottawa's policies are accelerating the fractures.

The weaker Canada becomes internally, the easier it is for outside forces—namely the United States—to exert control.

Immigration isn't just changing Canada's economy; it's reshaping its identity. The country is absorbing over 500,000 new permanent residents annually, a rate that outpaces infrastructure, housing, and the job market. Past waves of immigration had a common thread: they assimilated into a broader Canadian identity. That isn't happening now. Instead, new arrivals settle into self-contained enclaves in cities like Toronto, Vancouver, and Montreal, creating disconnected populations with little incentive to integrate. Officially, Canada celebrates this as diversity. In reality, it means there is no longer a shared national identity, just a government that manages separate groups under a single legal system. That makes national cohesion impossible. A country with no strong common culture is a country without resistance.

Mass immigration also fuels regional divides. Quebec, always fiercely protective of its Francophone identity, now faces a new demographic battle as immigration shifts the linguistic balance. Every non-French speaker settling in the province brings it closer to the tipping point where French is no longer dominant, accelerating resentment toward federal immigration policies dictated from Ottawa. Meanwhile, in Western Canada, where cultural differences with Central Canada are already pronounced, immigration policies from the East are seen as another reason to reject federal control.

Demographic change is reshaping more than just language. With Canada's aging population and low birth rates, the government relies on immigration to keep the economy moving. But this new population is fundamentally different from the older generations it replaces. The divide between rural and urban Canada has never been sharper. The political and cultural power centers—Toronto, Vancouver, Montreal—push progressive policies that don't reflect the values of rural Canada, small towns, or resource-producing provinces. The urban elite make decisions, while the energy-rich West foots the bill. Alberta and Saskatchewan are expected to fuel the economy while being ignored politically. Quebec is given special protections while rejecting full national integration. Meanwhile, rural and small-town Canadians are dismissed as an afterthought in a country supposedly built on their industries. What, if anything, still holds the country together?

Separatist movements aren't fringe ideas anymore. Quebec has been fighting for its distinct status for decades, and federal governments have consistently caved to its demands, reinforcing the idea that it is already separate in all but name. Western Canada, particularly Alberta, has a growing movement that is far past simple frustration. This isn't just economic discontent; it's the realization that the federation offers no benefit to those outside the power centers. Carbon taxes, pipeline blockades, and federal hostility toward resource extraction all send the same message: the West exists to be taxed and regulated for the benefit of Central Canada. The rise of Wexit isn't just empty rhetoric. If Alberta and Saskatchewan decide they've had enough, Canada's economy collapses. If Quebec follows suit, the national identity dissolves.

A fractured Canada is a controlled Canada. A country pulled in multiple directions—separated by language, by culture, by economic resentment—is a country incapable of resisting outside influence. It can't act in its own interest because it no longer has a singular identity, just competing groups forced into a legal framework that grows weaker by the year. If separatist movements continue to grow, if demographic shifts accelerate the erosion of national unity, and if mass immigration continues without integration, Canada will become a state in name only—directionless, dependent, and ripe for absorption into a larger North American framework.

Economic collapse is the fastest route to political surrender. Canada already sits in a precarious position—record-high household debt, skyrocketing government spending, and an over-leveraged housing market propping up an illusion of stability. The entire system is a house of cards, and when it falls, Canada won't have the tools to rebuild on its own. A full-blown economic depression or fiscal insolvency wouldn't just weaken Canada—it would leave it begging for a lifeline, and there's only one country that can provide it. A U.S.-led "rescue" wouldn't be charity. It would be a negotiation, with terms that leave Canada with nothing but the illusion of sovereignty.

The warning signs are already flashing. Canada's federal debt is well over $1.2 trillion, doubling in just a few years as the government sinks deeper into deficit spending with no plan to reverse course. Provincial debt adds another trillion. The Bank of Canada has been artificially propping up the economy with low interest rates and money printing, but inflation is catching up, forcing rate hikes that are breaking households drowning in debt. Over 70% of the economy is tied to consumer spending, but that spending is built on credit, not productivity. If the housing market crashes, if interest rates spike beyond what households can afford, or if the U.S. economy falters and takes Canada down with it, there will be no buffer. The collapse will be swift, and the government will have only one option: bailout or bankruptcy.

And who would offer that bailout? The United States. Not the IMF, not China, not Europe. The U.S. Federal Reserve, U.S. Treasury, and American financial institutions would be the only realistic backstop to prevent total economic implosion. But it wouldn't come free. A "rescue" package would come with conditions, just like every other economic intervention in history. The U.S. would demand concessions—currency integration, trade alignment, deeper military coordination, or even full financial oversight from Washington.

There's precedent for this. Argentina has spent decades falling into economic crisis, only to be "rescued" by foreign creditors who impose conditions that strip it of autonomy. Greece, after its 2008 financial meltdown, effectively lost control of its own economy to the European Union and the IMF. The playbook is always the same: financial collapse creates an opportunity for external control disguised as assistance. If Canada collapses, Washington wouldn't need to force annexation—it would be the natural outcome of a country unable to stand on its own.

Would Canadians resist? Maybe. But resistance doesn't matter when the alternative is total financial ruin. If the only way to keep the banking system afloat, maintain essential services, and prevent mass unemployment is to accept U.S. financial control, Ottawa would have no choice but to comply. It wouldn't happen overnight. The first step would be increased financial integration—perhaps a move toward a shared North American currency, a policy dictated by Washington but dressed up as a "mutual agreement." Then, deeper trade concessions, permanent military coordination, and an eventual political realignment where annexation is simply a formality.

If Canada experiences a full economic depression or insolvency, the choice won't be between independence or annexation. It will be between starvation and submission—and history has shown how that story always ends.

Trump was never subtle about Canada's place in the American orbit. Unlike past U.S. leaders who masked their annexationist ambitions under diplomatic niceties, Trump spoke in blunt terms—Canada is dependent, weak, and should fall in line. His trade war rhetoric, tariffs on steel and aluminum, and open disdain for Trudeau weren't just political theater; they were a demonstration of power. Trump made it clear that Canada was not an equal partner, but an appendage of the U.S. economy—a country that exists at America's discretion, not as an independent force.

In 2019, during his renegotiation of NAFTA into USMCA, Trump openly mocked Canada's vulnerability. "We're letting Canada and Mexico continue as independent countries, but they're lucky we are." It was meant as a joke—except it wasn't. His administration had already strong-armed Ottawa into a new trade agreement on America's terms, cutting off Canada's ability to negotiate separate deals with China and forcing it into a 16-year renewal clause that keeps U.S. economic dominance locked in. Trump's tariffs on Canadian steel and aluminum in 2018 were another economic pressure tactic, signaling that if Canada didn't fall in line, Washington could easily cripple its industries overnight.

When asked whether Canada could ever be part of the U.S., Trump smirked and said, "It would be a great place. A lot of people are asking that. We'll see what happens." That's all it took. No formal policy, no legislation—just a casual remark that implied inevitability. It was enough to send the media into a frenzy while his administration continued laying the groundwork for deeper economic and military integration. The message was clear: Canada's fate was never its own to decide.

This isn't new. U.S. presidents have toyed with the idea of absorbing Canada since the 19th century, often using economic crises or military pressure as justification. James K. Polk, the man who aggressively expanded U.S. territory through war and diplomacy, considered Canada unfinished business, much like Texas and Oregon before they were absorbed. William Seward, Lincoln's Secretary of State, openly stated that "Canada will fall to us, as a ripe apple from a tree." The logic was always the same—Canada lacks the strength to resist forever, and when the right moment comes, Washington will make its move.

Trump didn't invent this thinking. He just said out loud what has been policy in everything but name for decades. The strategy has evolved from military conquest to economic coercion, from outright annexation to slow-motion integration under the guise of trade and defense agreements. If Trump had won a second term, would he have pushed the issue further? Maybe. But it hardly matters—the trajectory is already set, and whether it's under a Republican or Democrat, Canada's absorption is simply a matter of when, not if.

A 25% tariff isn't just a trade policy—it's a weapon. When Trump slapped steep tariffs on Canadian steel and aluminum in 2018, it wasn't about protecting American industry. It was a deliberate move to test how much economic pressure Canada could handle before it buckled. The tariffs were framed under the pretense of "national security," a flimsy excuse given that Canada is supposedly America's closest ally. But the real objective was clear: leverage.

Canada's economy is already heavily dependent on U.S. trade, with over 75% of exports going south of the border. Targeting key industries with tariffs was a way to remind Ottawa who holds the power. The Trudeau government, predictably, scrambled to retaliate with counter-tariffs on American products. The problem? The U.S. economy could absorb the hit—Canada couldn't. Washington knew it. The markets knew it. The only people pretending it was a fair fight were in Ottawa.

A 25% tariff on steel and aluminum was a precision strike. These industries aren't just economic pillars—they're national security assets. By destabilizing them, the U.S. created uncertainty in Canada's supply chains and put pressure on its already fragile manufacturing sector. The longer the tariffs stayed in place, the clearer it became that the U.S. wasn't negotiating—it was dictating terms. The eventual renegotiation of NAFTA into USMCA was proof of that. The new deal restricted Canada's ability to negotiate trade agreements with non-U.S. partners, essentially locking the country into Washington's economic grip for the foreseeable future.

This wasn't just a one-off strategy under Trump. The U.S. has a long history of using tariffs and trade wars to force weaker nations into economic submission. It's how Washington squeezed Japan in the 1930s, how it punished Cuba for decades, and how it strong-armed Latin American economies into dependence through debt manipulation and trade policies. Canada may not have been treated as an enemy, but it was certainly treated as an asset being brought to heel.

If tariffs on key industries can be turned on and off at will, how independent is Canada, really? When Washington wants something, all it has to do is turn up the pressure. Maybe next time, it won't just be steel and aluminum. Maybe it'll be agriculture. Maybe it'll be energy. Or maybe it'll be a package deal: deeper integration, a shared currency, or U.S. military oversight in exchange for economic stability.

Call it what it is—economic warfare. Not with bombs or tanks, but with trade policy, financial leverage, and regulatory choke points. Canada doesn't need to be conquered when it can be economically coerced into compliance. The 25% tariff was a warning shot. The question is whether Ottawa even understood the message.

Resistance requires identity, and Canada has spent decades eroding its own. A nation that sees itself as distinct, independent, and worth fighting for will resist absorption into a larger power. But when the economic, cultural, and political ties to that larger power are already entrenched, resistance becomes unlikely, if not impossible. The question isn't whether Canadians would fight integration with the U.S.—it's whether they'd even recognize it as something to resist.

Economically, Canada is already an extension of the U.S. market. Over 75% of exports go south, meaning American policy decisions dictate Canadian economic stability. The Bank of Canada follows the Federal Reserve, U.S. hedge funds own massive portions of Canadian industries, and trade agreements like USMCA lock Canada into long-term economic dependency. If integration ever became an official policy discussion, the business class—the most influential sector of any country's power structure—would almost certainly push for it, citing stability, economic growth, and currency security. Politicians would follow, as they always do, framing it as an inevitable evolution rather than a hostile takeover. And the public? They'd be given a choice between economic crisis or a "pragmatic solution." Most would take the latter.

Culturally, the divide between Canada and the U.S. is almost non-existent. Hollywood, Big Tech, corporate America, and political activism flow seamlessly across the border, shaping Canadian thought as much as, if not more than, domestic influences. Canadian media outlets rely heavily on American narratives, often recycling U.S. political and social issues as if they were homegrown. The younger generations, growing up consuming the same content, trends, and ideologies as their American counterparts, have no strong attachment to the idea of Canadian exceptionalism—because they were never given one. The concept of a "unique Canadian identity" has been replaced by a North American corporate monoculture.

Politically, the infrastructure for resistance doesn't exist. Canada's military is underfunded, with its defense policies largely dictated by the U.S. through NORAD and NATO. Ottawa operates less like the capital of an independent country and more like a regional branch of the Washington-led global order. Every major policy decision—whether on energy, defense, trade, or finance—aligns with U.S. priorities. Resistance to integration would require a nationalist movement willing to push back against this alignment, but none currently exists at any serious level. Separatist sentiments in Quebec and Western Canada may create regional resistance, but even those movements would struggle to rally against something that has already happened in practice, even if not in name.

The truth is, the U.S. doesn't need to propose annexation. It just needs to wait. Canada is already deeply entangled, and when the next economic or geopolitical crisis forces the issue, the choice won't be framed as sovereignty vs. absorption—it will be sold as an economic safeguard, a security measure, a natural progression. And by then, the majority of Canadians won't resist. They'll already be used to it.

Part I: The Expansionist Drive

Part I: The Expansionist Drive – North America as America's Domain

Chapter 1: Manifest Destiny

M anifest Destiny – The Continent as the U.S.'s Birthright

The Religious and Ideological Underpinnings of Manifest Destiny

Manifest Destiny didn't emerge as a formal policy—it evolved as a belief system, rooted in the idea that the United States was destined to expand across North America, not just by right, but by divine will. It was an ideology that fused religious conviction, Enlightenment rationalism, and raw geopolitical ambition into a single guiding principle: expansion wasn't just possible—it was inevitable, necessary, and morally justified.

At its core, Manifest Destiny was fueled by a religious narrative. The U.S. was seen as a new Israel, a chosen nation meant to spread civilization, democracy, and Protestant Christianity across the continent. Ministers and political leaders alike framed expansion as a moral duty, arguing that the U.S. had been blessed with superior governance, values, and an obligation to uplift the "lesser" peoples who stood in the way—whether Indigenous tribes, Mexicans, or even British-controlled Canada. This belief was deeply tied to Puritan exceptionalism, the idea that America was founded not just as a nation, but as a divine experiment, an earthly representation of God's will. Expansion wasn't theft; it was salvation.

But Manifest Destiny wasn't just religious—it was also a product of Enlightenment rationalism and political philosophy. Thinkers like John Locke and Thomas Jefferson had laid the groundwork for a worldview in which land, liberty, and self-determination were inseparable. The idea that people had a right—perhaps even a duty—to expand into open lands and develop them wasn't seen as controversial. To the American mind, territory was meant to be settled, resources were meant to be used, and stagnation was an obstacle to progress. Any resistance—whether from Indigenous nations, the Mexican government, or British colonial authorities in Canada—was framed as backwardness, standing in the way of human advancement.

By the 19th century, Manifest Destiny had become a political doctrine, shaping policy at every level. Presidents like Andrew Jackson, James K. Polk, and even Abraham Lincoln embraced versions of it, using it to justify war, territorial acquisitions, and the forced removal of native populations. The Louisiana Purchase, the annexation of Texas, the Oregon Treaty, and the Mexican-American War were all products of this ideology in action. The expansion wasn't random—it followed the belief that the U.S. was meant to dominate the continent and that any other arrangement was unnatural.

Canada was always part of this vision, even if it wasn't as aggressively pursued. Many U.S. leaders assumed that British North America would eventually fall into American hands, either through diplomacy, economic absorption, or the simple pull of progress. The idea was that Britain would eventually lose interest, and Canada, recognizing its natural destiny, would align with the U.S. The fact that this didn't happen through war, as it did with Mexico, didn't mean the ambition wasn't there. It just meant the strategy changed.

Manifest Destiny never really disappeared—it simply adapted. By the 20th century, military conquest had been replaced by economic dominance, cultural assimilation, and strategic agreements that ensured the U.S. would remain the central force shaping North America. The old religious rhetoric faded, but the core idea remained: America expands, America absorbs, and resistance is either futile or temporary.

Manifest Destiny didn't begin as an official doctrine but as a deeply ingrained belief—a fusion of religion, political philosophy, and raw expansionist ambition that framed the United States as a nation destined to dominate the North American continent. It was more than just a justification for territorial conquest; it was a worldview, a self-fulfilling prophecy that combined theological conviction, Enlightenment rationalism, and geopolitical opportunism into a single force that would shape U.S. policy for over a century.

Religiously, Manifest Destiny was rooted in Puritan exceptionalism, the belief that America was divinely chosen as a "New Israel," a nation set apart to fulfill God's will on Earth. This idea stretched back to the earliest colonial settlers, who saw themselves as pioneers of Christian civilization, spreading their faith and values into untamed lands. By the 19th century, this evolved into an explicitly Protestant mission, reinforced by revivalist preachers and political leaders who framed expansion as both a moral duty and a divine right. The U.S. was not merely acquiring land—it was bringing civilization, democracy, and Christianity to peoples who, in the eyes of expansionists, lacked them.

But Manifest Destiny wasn't just a religious belief—it was also a product of Enlightenment rationalism and Lockean philosophy, which positioned land, labor, and self-governance as the natural rights of free men. John Locke's theories on property and government provided the intellectual foundation for the belief that land, if undeveloped or "underutilized," was not being used to its fullest potential. To the American mind, expansion wasn't theft—it was progress. Lands controlled by Indigenous nations, Mexico, or even Britain weren't being used "properly," and it was the duty of an enlightened, democratic nation to put them to productive use.

This philosophical argument was reinforced by the American Revolution and the democratic ideals of the early republic. Americans viewed themselves as radically different from the Old World—not a stagnant, hierarchical society like Britain, but a dynamic, expansionist power that would spread liberty as it grew. The Louisiana Purchase in 1803, the annexation of Texas in 1845, and the war with Mexico in 1846 were all framed not as acts of aggression, but as necessary steps in fulfilling the nation's destiny.

Politically, Manifest Destiny became the foundation for territorial expansion policies under leaders like James K. Polk, who aggressively pursued the idea that the U.S. must extend from the Atlantic to the Pacific. The war with Mexico wasn't just about border disputes—it was about securing the future of American expansion. The Oregon boundary negotiations with Britain in the 1840s reflected the same mindset—America was entitled to the land, and any compromise was simply a delay in the inevitable.

Even Canada wasn't exempt from this thinking. While military conquest of British North America proved too costly, many U.S. leaders assumed that economic and political realities would eventually pull Canada into the American sphere. If Britain weakened or disengaged, the logic of Manifest Destiny suggested that Canada would naturally gravitate toward the U.S., either through economic dependency, voluntary annexation, or sheer inevitability.

Though the religious rhetoric of Manifest Destiny faded in the 20th century, the underlying philosophy never disappeared. The U.S. no longer expands through war, but through economic dominance, cultural hegemony, and trade agreements that effectively achieve the same result. The belief that America is the natural leader of the continent persists—only now, annexation is achieved through financial leverage and corporate control rather than cavalry charges and bayonets. The spirit of Manifest Destiny never died—it just evolved.

Manifest Destiny wasn't born in a single moment, but John L. O'Sullivan's 1845 essay gave it a name and a rallying cry. His editorial in the Democratic Review laid out the case that the United States was divinely and historically destined to expand across the North American continent. It wasn't just a policy suggestion—it was a moral imperative, a force of nature, an unstoppable historical truth that justified the annexation of Texas and foreshadowed further expansion. He wrote:

"Our manifest destiny is to overspread the continent allotted by Providence for the free development of our yearly multiplying millions."

That single phrase—manifest destiny—captured the mindset of American expansionists. It was no longer a question of whether the U.S. should expand, but how fast it could do so. O'Sullivan wasn't inventing the idea; he was articulating a belief that had already taken hold in the American political and cultural consciousness.

O'Sullivan doubled down later in 1845 when he argued that the U.S. had a right to claim Oregon without British interference, stating:

> "And that claim is by the right of our manifest destiny to overspread and to possess the whole of the continent which Providence has given us for the great experiment of liberty and federated self-government."

This wasn't just about territorial ambition—it was about ideology. Expansion wasn't framed as conquest but as the spread of liberty, democracy, and civilization. It was a mission, ordained by Providence, to remake the continent in America's image.

Other key writings reinforced and expanded on O'Sullivan's declaration. Senator Thomas Hart Benton gave speeches in the 1840s describing American expansion as an inevitable march toward dominance, stating that "the white race" was chosen to spread across the land and bring enlightenment to lesser peoples. William Gilpin, another prominent expansionist, argued that the U.S. was at the center of global destiny and that its growth was both a geographical and spiritual necessity.

The theological justification came from ministers like Reverend Josiah Strong, whose 1885 book Our Country: Its Possible Future and Its Present Crisis pushed the idea that the U.S. had a religious duty to spread Protestant Christianity and Anglo-American values. This blended Manifest Destiny with the later American imperialist projects, stretching beyond North America into overseas territories.

Politically, James K. Polk's speeches during his presidency (1845-1849) turned O'Sullivan's words into government policy. Polk aggressively pursued expansion, using the idea of Manifest Destiny to justify the war with Mexico, the annexation of Texas, and the push for Oregon. Every land acquisition was framed as inevitable, just, and in service of American greatness.

Even Abraham Lincoln, despite opposing the Mexican-American War, was shaped by the logic of Manifest Destiny. His vision of a transcontinental railroad, the Homestead Act, and the opening of the West were all built on the same foundation—America's future was to expand, occupy, and develop the land, ensuring that nothing stood in the way of its continental dominance.

By the late 19th century, the language of Manifest Destiny had changed, but the concept remained intact. The Turner Thesis (1893)—historian **Frederick Jackson Turner's argument that the frontier shaped American identity—was a direct intellectual descendant of O'Sullivan's vision. When the continental frontier closed, America looked outward, using the same logic to justify interventions in Cuba, the Philippines, and beyond.

O'Sullivan gave the movement its name, but Manifest Destiny had always been there, lurking in the American mind. His words merely crystallized what politicians, businessmen, and expansionists already believed—that the United States was not just a country, but a force of history, unstoppable and inevitable.

Early American Leaders' Visions of a U.S.-Dominated North America

Thomas Jefferson

Thomas Jefferson saw the United States not as a fixed nation but as a living, expanding republic, destined to grow across the continent. His vision of expansion was rooted in both political philosophy and practical strategy—he believed that territorial growth was essential to maintaining a free and agrarian society, while also ensuring that the U.S. would never be boxed in by European powers. To Jefferson, the American experiment was unfinished as long as vast, unsettled lands remained outside its reach.

His most famous territorial acquisition, the Louisiana Purchase in 1803, was proof of this belief in action. Jefferson was willing to bend his own constitutional principles to buy the land from France, arguing that securing the Mississippi River and opening new territory for American settlers was too important to pass up. But Louisiana was never the final goal—it was just the beginning. Jefferson envisioned a republic that would extend all the way to the Pacific, with self-governing states gradually joining the Union as settlers moved west.

And Canada? He absolutely saw it as part of this vision. During his presidency, Jefferson actively encouraged the idea that Canada would one day join the U.S., whether through voluntary annexation or conquest. He believed that French Canadians under British rule would naturally prefer to be part of the United States rather than remain under a monarchy. This assumption mirrored the later U.S. miscalculations during the War of 1812, when American leaders falsely believed Canadians would welcome them as liberators.

Jefferson's aggressive expansionist policies toward British North America were most evident in his embargoes and trade wars with Britain, which were designed to weaken British influence in the region and open the door for U.S. dominance. In 1807, his Embargo Act sought to strangle British trade, but instead, it hurt American merchants and failed to achieve its goal of forcing Britain to back down. Yet Jefferson's hostility toward Britain—and his belief that Canada should be part of the American sphere—never wavered.

Even after leaving office, Jefferson continued to push the idea that Canada's future was tied to the United States. He predicted that British North America would eventually separate from Britain and that when it did, it would naturally align with the U.S. rather than remain independent. In private letters, he speculated that Canada might eventually join the Union through economic pressure, migration, or even rebellion against British rule.

Jefferson's vision of U.S. expansion set the stage for everything that followed—Manifest Destiny, the Monroe Doctrine, and later U.S. attempts to control Canada through economic and political means. While he didn't live to see the War of 1812, it was his expansionist mindset that inspired many of its architects, who believed that Canada was unfinished business.

He was wrong, at least in the short term—Canada remained under British control, and its leaders resisted integration into the American system. But Jefferson's long-term vision? That's still playing out. While the U.S. never took Canada by force, it slowly absorbed its economy, culture, and strategic resources. If Jefferson were alive today, he might argue that Canada is already part of the American system—just without the official statehood.

Andrew Jackson

Andrew Jackson saw expansion as the lifeblood of American strength—a continuation of the fight for independence, a means of securing economic dominance, and a way to ensure that the United States remained a nation of self-reliant, landowning citizens. His vision was built on three pillars: military aggression, territorial acquisition, and economic supremacy. He wasn't interested in diplomacy or gradual influence—he believed that land was taken, not negotiated. His presidency was defined by an aggressive expansionist mindset, and while his primary focus was on removing Indigenous resistance and pushing westward, he absolutely saw British North America as part of the greater U.S. destiny.

Jackson was an old soldier, a man who had fought against both the British and Indigenous nations in the War of 1812. To him, Canada was unfinished business from that war—a territory that should have fallen into American hands had the invasion been handled properly. Like Jefferson before him, he viewed British control of Canada as an unnatural holdover from the colonial era, something that would eventually be rectified either by war or political realignment. His hatred of the British was legendary, and he saw any British influence in North America as a direct threat to U.S. sovereignty.

Though he didn't launch an official campaign for Canada, Jackson's policies laid the groundwork for future American dominance. His economic warfare against British influence in North America—through aggressive tariffs and trade policies—was designed to weaken Canada's economic ties to Britain and force greater dependence on the U.S. His use of military force to claim Florida from Spain in 1819 showed exactly how he viewed expansion: if a territory was weak, if its colonial ruler couldn't hold it, the U.S. had a right to take it. This same logic was applied to Texas, where Jackson covertly supported American settlers rebelling against Mexico, knowing full well that the region would eventually be absorbed into the U.S.

If Jackson had been in power during a time of greater British weakness, there's little doubt he would have pushed for an annexation attempt in Canada, likely under the pretense of "liberating" it from monarchy. His presidency came just a little too early—British power was still strong, and the U.S. was still consolidating its hold over new western territories. But the legacy of his expansionism lived on in the leaders who followed. James K. Polk, a Jacksonian Democrat, took Jackson's philosophy and ran with it—using war, diplomacy, and economic leverage to fulfill what Jackson had started.

Jackson's real impact on Canada wasn't through direct action but through the precedent he set: American land acquisition was a right, and any foreign power in North America was living on borrowed time. He helped entrench the belief that the U.S. was destined to dominate the continent, whether by war, by trade, or by slow economic absorption. If he were alive today, he wouldn't be surprised to see Canada economically tied to the U.S., dependent on American trade and policy decisions. He might even argue that annexation is already happening—not with muskets, but with markets.

James K. Polk

James K. Polk was the most aggressive expansionist president in U.S. history, the man who took Manifest Destiny from theory to reality. Under his leadership, the U.S. annexed Texas, seized California and the Southwest from Mexico, and secured Oregon, effectively fulfilling the long-held vision of a continental empire. Polk believed that U.S. expansion was inevitable and justified, and while his primary focus was on the west, he certainly saw Canada as part of the broader American destiny.

Polk's administration was obsessed with securing land, and British North America was no exception. His biggest move regarding Canada was in the Oregon boundary dispute, where he pushed for full American control over the territory, using the slogan "Fifty-Four Forty or Fight!" The idea was to take everything up to the 54°40' latitude, which would have included much of present-day British Columbia. Though Polk ultimately settled on the 49th parallel in a treaty with Britain, it wasn't because he lost interest in expansion—it was because he was preparing for war with Mexico and needed to prioritize. The compromise was practical, but it also reinforced the idea that U.S. territorial expansion into British North America was negotiable rather than impossible.

If Polk had had more time, or if the Mexican-American War hadn't consumed his presidency, it's likely he would have pursued Canadian territory more aggressively. He viewed British presence in North Amer-

>rary obstacle, not a permanent reality. He knew Britain ₃ to fight a war over Oregon, and he likely assumed that, same would be true for the rest of British Canada. Polk wasn ι ιᴄᴄ⎽ess—he was strategic. He picked fights he knew he could win, avoided unnecessary distractions, and understood that the U.S. could absorb land in stages rather than all at once.

His vision of Manifest Destiny wasn't just about borders—it was about economics and influence. Even though he didn't push for an outright invasion of Canada, he supported the idea that British North America would eventually fall under American control through trade, migration, and political alignment. He saw British rule in Canada the same way he saw Mexican rule in Texas—weak, unsustainable, and destined to fail against the economic and demographic force of the U.S.

Polk's legacy in relation to Canada is one of missed opportunity, not lack of ambition. If the U.S. had been in a stronger position, or if Britain had shown signs of weakening, he almost certainly would have pressed further north. His administration was the high-water mark of territorial expansion, and after him, U.S. annexationist ambitions shifted from direct conquest to economic and cultural absorption—a strategy that continues to this day.

The Monroe Doctrine (1823)

The Monroe Doctrine (1823) was a direct warning to European powers, but beneath the surface, it was also an implicit claim over all of North America, including Canada. While James Monroe framed it as a policy of protecting the Western Hemisphere from further European colonization, the real message was clear: North America was America's domain, and any foreign influence was unwelcome. It was the first formal declaration that the U.S. saw itself as the dominant power in the New World, a position that would only grow stronger over time.

At its core, the doctrine had two major components. First, it declared that European nations could no longer establish new colonies in the Western Hemisphere. Second, it warned that any interference in the political affairs of the Americas would be seen as a direct threat to the United States. While Monroe was primarily concerned with Latin America, where newly independent nations were emerging from Spanish rule, the doctrine had clear implications for British North America as well. The U.S. wasn't just drawing a line between the Old World and the New—it was setting the stage for eventual dominance over the entire continent.

Britain was the only European power left with significant holdings in North America, and while the U.S. wasn't yet strong enough to challenge it directly, the Monroe Doctrine signaled that British rule in Canada was an anomaly, not a permanent reality. Monroe and his advisers believed that over time, British North America would either drift toward the U.S. economically and politically or be abandoned by Britain altogether. The doctrine didn't call for immediate annexation, but it created a framework where Canada's separation from Britain—and eventual absorption into the American sphere—was seen as inevitable.

This wasn't just theoretical. In the decades following the doctrine, U.S. expansionist policies repeatedly pushed against British interests in North America. The Oregon boundary dispute (1840s) saw the U.S. claim vast amounts of land controlled by Britain, with President James K. Polk pushing aggressively for full American control. The Reciprocity Treaty (1854-1866) attempted to tie Canada's economy more closely to the U.S., making economic dependence the first step toward political realignment. Even the War of 1812, which predated the Monroe Doctrine, had been an early attempt to force British North America into submission, and the desire to complete that unfinished business never fully disappeared.

By the late 19th and early 20th centuries, the Monroe Doctrine had evolved into a justification for economic and military intervention across the Americas, reinforcing the idea that North America—and by extension, Canada—was part of the U.S. sphere of influence. The British presence remained, but U.S. trade, migration, and cultural influence slowly eroded Canada's distinctiveness. Today, Canada may still have its own flag and government, but its economy, military strategy, and political direction remain deeply tied to the U.S. In many ways, Monroe's vision has already been fulfilled—not through war, but through slow, relentless integration.

The 19th century was filled with American ambitions to annex Canada, both through military action and political maneuvering. From the War of 1812 to secret expansionist plots, there were multiple attempts to pull British North America into the U.S. orbit. None succeeded, but not for lack of trying. The failures weren't due to a lack of American desire but rather a combination of British resistance, Canadian pushback, and shifting U.S. priorities.

The War of 1812 was the most overt military attempt. American leaders, including President James Madison and War Hawks like Henry Clay, believed that taking Canada would be easy—that British rule was weak and that Canadians, many of whom were former American colonists, would welcome the U.S. as liberators. This assumption was fatally incorrect. The invasion was poorly planned, Canadian militias fought back harder than expected, and Indigenous resistance, led by figures like Tecumseh, turned the war into a disaster for the U.S. The British burned Washington, D.C., in retaliation, and by the time the war ended in 1814, the U.S. had gained nothing.

Despite that failure, expansionist sentiment didn't disappear. The Rebellions of 1837-1838 in Upper and Lower Canada—uprisings against British rule—briefly revived American hopes that Canada would be destabilized enough for annexation. American militias, known as the "Patriot Hunters," launched cross-border attacks to support the rebels, believing they could trigger a pro-U.S. revolution. The British crushed the rebellion, and the U.S. officially distanced itself, though the annexationist spirit remained strong.

By the 1840s, President James K. Polk, the most aggressive expansionist president in history, briefly considered pushing northward. His administration's focus, however, was on Texas, Oregon, and the war with Mexico, leading to the 1846 compromise with Britain that established the U.S.-Canada border at the 49th parallel. Polk was pragmatic—he wanted Canada, but he prioritized land grabs that were easier to take.

The Fenian Raids (1866-1871) were another serious, if unofficial, attempt. Irish-American militias—many of whom were Union Army veterans—believed they could invade Canada, weaken British control, and use it as leverage to free Ireland from British rule. With the U.S. government looking the other way, the Fenians launched multiple cross-border attacks. While disorganized, these raids revealed the lingering American belief that Canada was vulnerable and could be absorbed given the right conditions. The British, however, responded swiftly, and Canadian militias once again held the line.

The most serious political move came in the aftermath of the U.S. Civil War (1861-1865). With a battle-hardened army and a belief in Manifest Destiny stronger than ever, some in Washington believed that British North America should be the next target. Many Northern politicians blamed Britain for indirectly supporting the Confederacy and saw annexing Canada as revenge. However, by this point, Britain was fully committed to defending its colony. The U.S., still recovering from civil war, wasn't ready for another fight. Instead, British fears of American aggression pushed Canada toward Confederation in 1867, creating a unified defense against future U.S. incursions.

By the late 19th century, military annexation became less practical. The U.S. had expanded westward, its focus shifting to global influence rather than continental conquest. Instead of trying to conquer Canada militarily, the U.S. turned to economic dominance, trade agreements, and cultural absorption—methods that have proven far more successful in the long run.

Manifest Destiny never ended—it evolved. The days of military conquest may be over, but the ideology behind Manifest Destiny—the belief that the United States is destined to dominate North America—never disappeared. Instead of outright wars of expansion, the U.S. has used economic leverage, military integration, and political influence to achieve what 19th-century expansionists sought with rifles and bayonets. The goal remains the same: total continental control, whether through direct governance or functional dependency.

The clearest evolution of Manifest Destiny is in economic dominance. The U.S. no longer needs to annex territory when it can own the industries, dictate the trade policies, and control the financial systems of its neighbors. Canada, once seen as a land to be conquered, has become an economic satellite of the U.S. Over 75% of Canadian exports go south, and major industries—energy, banking, telecom, and manufacturing—are deeply tied to American investors and corporations. NAFTA and its successor, USMCA, weren't about free trade; they were about ensuring permanent economic integration that makes Canadian sovereignty little more than a formality.

Militarily, Manifest Destiny has adapted into strategic control through alliances. The old vision of American troops marching into Canada has been replaced by NORAD, NATO, and joint military operations that place Canada under de facto U.S. command. Washington doesn't need to seize Canadian military bases when it can simply dictate Canadian defense policy through shared intelligence, weapons agreements, and operational dependence. If a crisis erupted tomorrow, Canada wouldn't act independently—it would follow Washington's lead, as it always has.

Politically, the U.S. no longer needs to install governors or claim provinces as states—it exerts influence through cultural hegemony, diplomatic pressure, and economic coercion. Canadian leaders, regardless of party, must always consider American interests first, whether on trade, foreign policy, or even domestic regulation. The Bank of Canada mirrors the Federal Reserve, Canadian media mirrors American narratives, and Canadian political movements mirror U.S. ideological shifts. The integration is so deep that most Canadians don't even recognize it as annexation—because it doesn't look like the textbook definition. But it is.

The truth is, Manifest Destiny was never just about land—it was about dominance. Today, that dominance is achieved not through military conquest but through economic entanglement, cultural absorption, and strategic dependency. The U.S. doesn't need to wave a flag over Ottawa. It already owns the market, dictates the security framework, and shapes the political landscape. The vision of 19th-century expansionists has been realized—not with a declaration, but with a slow, methodical integration that ensures America's control over North America without the need for a single shot.

Chapter 2: President James K. Polk

P resident James K. Polk – The Architect of American Expansion

James K. Polk wasn't just a believer in Manifest Destiny—he was its most ruthless executor. More than any other president, Polk turned the ideology from a vague national ambition into a concrete reality, seizing more territory in four years than any U.S. leader before or after him. His presidency redrew the map of North America, adding over a million square miles to the United States through war, diplomacy, and sheer force of will.

Polk came into office in 1845 with three clear territorial objectives:

Annex Texas—which had declared independence from Mexico in 1836 but was still contested.

Settle the Oregon boundary—where Britain and the U.S. both claimed the Pacific Northwest.

Take California and the Southwest—which belonged to Mexico but was seen as rightfully American land.

Polk pursued these goals with no hesitation and no concern for international consequences. He embodied the most aggressive ideals of Manifest Destiny, believing that the U.S. was not only entitled to these lands but morally obligated to take them.

The annexation of Texas was his first major victory. Mexico had warned that it would consider the move an act of war, but Polk ignored the threats and pushed forward, knowing full well that war would give him an excuse to take even more. He provoked a border skirmish in disputed territory, then used it as justification to launch the Mexican-American War (1846-1848). That war, which was framed as a defensive struggle, was in reality a blatant land grab. By the time it ended, the U.S. had taken California, Arizona, New Mexico, Utah, and parts of Colorado, Nevada, and Wyoming—nearly half of Mexico's territory. It was the largest forced territorial expansion in American history.

At the same time, Polk negotiated a treaty with Britain to secure Oregon, using the threat of war to push for U.S. control of the region. The slogan "Fifty-Four Forty or Fight!" summed up the aggressive sentiment—though in the end, Polk settled for the 49th parallel. He was willing to fight Mexico but knew Britain would require a more strategic approach. It wasn't about recklessness; it was about maximizing gains while minimizing risks.

Polk's view of expansion wasn't just about seizing land—it was about securing America's dominance over the continent. He didn't see U.S. expansion as a possibility; he saw it as a historical inevitability. In his mind, it wasn't a question of whether America would take the land—it was simply a question of when and how.

And what about Canada? If Polk had had more time, British North America might have been next. His administration had already pushed the British to compromise on Oregon, proving that the U.S. was willing to challenge European rule in North America. Had Mexico not been the immediate target, it's likely that further pressure would have been applied to British Canada, either diplomatically or militarily.

Polk's expansionism was so aggressive that he burned himself out after one term, choosing not to seek re-election in 1848. But by then, his work was done. The U.S. had stretched from the Atlantic to the Pacific, fulfilling the dream of Manifest Destiny. His actions ensured that America, not Britain or Mexico, would dominate the continent—a reality that shaped the future of North America permanently. If Manifest Destiny had a single champion, it was James K. Polk—the president who made it happen by force, by strategy, and by sheer, unrelenting ambition.

James K. Polk's expansionist policies weren't just about ideology or national pride—they were driven by economic ambition. He understood that territorial expansion meant economic dominance, and every move he made was calculated to secure trade routes, natural resources, and control over strategic land. Manifest Destiny wasn't just about spreading democracy—it was about securing wealth, trade power, and long-term economic supremacy for the United States.

One of the biggest economic motivators behind Polk's land grabs was access to the Pacific Ocean. In the 1840s, global trade was shifting, and the Pacific was the next frontier. The U.S. was still a relatively young power, but its leaders saw the economic potential of controlling ports that could open direct trade with Asia, particularly China and Japan. However, at the time, the U.S. had no major Pacific coastline beyond a small stretch of the Oregon Territory. California was the real prize—it had deep-water ports like San Francisco, which could turn the U.S. into a dominant Pacific trading power. But there was a problem: Mexico owned it.

Polk's solution? War. His administration provoked conflict with Mexico, using a border skirmish in Texas as a pretext. The Mexican-American War (1846-1848) ended with the Treaty of Guadalupe Hidalgo, which forced Mexico to hand over California, Arizona, New Mexico, and much of the modern Southwest. The U.S. didn't just acquire land—it acquired direct access to the Pacific, setting the stage for America's rise as a global trading power. The importance of this cannot be overstated: within a few decades, the U.S. was dominating Pacific trade, reaching into Asia and securing its place as an emerging global superpower.

Beyond trade, Polk also sought fertile agricultural land. The U.S. economy was still heavily agrarian, and controlling vast, resource-rich territories meant long-term prosperity. The land acquired in Texas, California, and Oregon wasn't just about expanding borders—it was about securing millions of acres for farming, ranching, and settlement. This was especially critical as cotton and other cash crops fueled the Southern economy. Expansion meant more land for plantations, more exports, and more economic influence over global markets.

The Oregon boundary dispute with Britain was another example of economic ambition. Polk wanted full control of Oregon because of its rich farmland and valuable timber resources. The territory was already seeing an influx of American settlers via the Oregon Trail, and Polk knew that securing it would further expand the U.S. economy westward. While the U.S. didn't get all of Oregon, the eventual compromise with Britain in 1846 (establishing the 49th parallel as the border) ensured that America gained a huge swath of prime land, setting up future economic expansion.

Polk's vision was relentlessly strategic—he didn't just want land, he wanted land that could be economically exploited, tied into trade networks, and turned into long-term financial power for the U.S. His expansionist policies secured coast-to-coast trade routes, deepened agricultural dominance, and gave the U.S. the territorial foundation to become a global economic force.

His legacy? The U.S. went from a regional power to a continental empire under his leadership, and his acquisitions set the stage for America's rise as an economic superpower. While later presidents would use different methods—corporate influence, trade agreements, and military bases instead of outright annexation—the economic motivations behind U.S. expansion never changed. Polk just did it more directly, aggressively, and successfully than anyone before or after him.

James K. Polk's pledge to serve only one term gave his presidency an unprecedented sense of urgency. Unlike most politicians, who often tempered their actions to secure re-election, Polk had no interest in long-term political maneuvering. He entered office with a clear agenda: expand U.S. territory, secure American dominance over the continent, and fulfill the promises of Manifest Destiny. With only four years to achieve his goals, Polk approached the presidency with ruthless efficiency, pursuing land acquisitions at any cost—diplomatic, military, or political.

His one-term promise was not an empty campaign tactic. It was a strategic decision that allowed Polk to focus entirely on ambitious, high-stakes territorial expansion without worrying about how it might affect his popularity in the next election. This freed him from the usual constraints of political compromise. His mission wasn't about legacy-building through diplomacy or moderation—it was about immediate action. Polk believed that the window of opportunity for U.S. expansion was limited, and he was determined to capitalize on it before European powers or domestic instability could undermine American dominance.

This urgency was evident in how he handled his three key territorial goals: the annexation of Texas, the Oregon boundary dispute, and the conquest of California and the Southwest. Rather than pursuing these objectives one at a time, Polk pursued them simultaneously, taking on multiple international conflicts in quick succession. Within months of taking office, he was embroiled in a standoff with Mexico over Texas, aggressive negotiations with Britain over Oregon, and military preparations for a potential war in the West.

The Texas annexation, which had already been set in motion before Polk's presidency, quickly escalated into a provoked war with Mexico under his leadership. Polk knew that conflict was inevitable and saw it as an opportunity to seize not just Texas, but California and the entire Southwest. His actions—deploying U.S. troops to disputed territory along the Rio Grande and framing the Mexican response as an act of aggression—were deliberate steps to trigger war and justify large-scale territorial conquest. This war, fought and won in less than two years, resulted in the Treaty of Guadalupe Hidalgo (1848), which added over 500,000 square miles of land to the U.S., including modern-day California, Arizona, New Mexico, and more.

Polk applied the same aggressive approach to the Oregon boundary dispute with Britain. While many American expansionists demanded the entire Oregon Territory up to the 54°40′ parallel, Polk prioritized results over rhetoric. Knowing that war with Britain would be far riskier than war with Mexico, he settled for the 49th parallel, securing a significant territorial gain without distracting from his larger goal of defeating Mexico. This pragmatic compromise reflected Polk's sense of urgency—he wasn't interested in symbolic victories; he wanted land, fast.

Polk's one-term pledge also meant that he had no interest in maintaining long-term alliances or appeasing political factions. He clashed with members of his own Democratic Party, including powerful figures like Martin Van Buren and John C. Calhoun, and alienated many of his Whig opponents. But Polk didn't care. His sole focus was on achieving his expansionist agenda before his time in office ran out, regardless of the political fallout.

By the time Polk left office in 1849, he had accomplished everything he set out to do—and more. He had expanded U.S. territory by nearly a third, fulfilled the promises of Manifest Destiny, and reshaped the geopolitical map of North America. His relentless drive to acquire land at all costs was a direct result of his one-term pledge. He wasn't building a political dynasty or courting public favor—he was executing a mission, one that fundamentally transformed the United States from a regional power into a continental empire.

Polk's legacy is one of efficiency, aggression, and results. His one-term promise allowed him to act with a level of urgency and decisiveness rarely seen in American politics, and by the time he left office, the U.S. had achieved territorial dominance from the Atlantic to the Pacific—a feat that cemented Polk as the most effective expansionist president in U.S. history.

James K. Polk's success in expanding U.S. borders wasn't just about his relentless ambition—it was also about timing. The geopolitical landscape of the 1840s created a perfect storm that allowed him to push U.S. territory farther than any president before him. His expansionist policies were made possible by a combination of British pragmatism, Mexican instability, European distractions, and a growing American military advantage.

One of the biggest factors in Polk's success was Britain's weakened grip on North America. The Oregon boundary dispute had been simmering for years, with both the U.S. and Britain claiming vast portions of the Pacific Northwest. Earlier American leaders had been hesitant to push too hard, fearing British retaliation. But by the 1840s, Britain was stretched thin globally—it was dealing with colonial conflicts in India, navigating political instability at home, and focusing more on economic influence than territorial expansion. Polk knew that Britain, despite its military power, wasn't willing to go to war over Oregon—especially not against a rising U.S. determined to settle the West. So he pushed hard, knowing that Britain would rather negotiate than fight.

Mexico, meanwhile, was a collapsing power. The Mexican government was politically unstable, broke, and still recovering from its independence from Spain. It had little ability to defend its northern territories, which were sparsely populated and largely ignored by Mexico City. By 1845, Texas had already been effectively lost, and California—Polk's true target—was vulnerable. The Mexican military was ill-equipped, disorganized, and no match for the highly motivated, expansionist U.S. forces. Polk understood this weakness and used it to his advantage, deliberately provoking war by stationing troops in disputed territory to force Mexico into a response. When Mexican troops engaged, Polk had his excuse—the war began on his terms.

Another key factor was European distraction. The 1840s were a turbulent period for Europe, with growing revolutionary movements across the continent. By 1848, major uprisings broke out in France, Germany, Italy, and Austria, keeping European powers focused on their own affairs. With Britain preoccupied and other major powers in turmoil, no European nation was in a position to challenge U.S. expansion. Unlike earlier decades, when European intervention could have threatened American land grabs, Polk had a free hand to reshape North America without external interference.

At the same time, the United States had a growing military and economic edge. The country's population was booming, industry was expanding, and the rail network was beginning to take shape, making westward expansion more viable. The U.S. Army, battle-hardened from conflicts with Indigenous nations and the War of 1812, was now more organized and better equipped than ever before. The Mexican-American War showcased how quickly and decisively U.S. forces could seize territory, with victories in Texas, California, and deep into Mexican territory within months. By the time the Treaty of Guadalupe Hidalgo was signed in 1848, Polk had forced Mexico to cede over half its territory without any significant threat from foreign powers.

The final piece of the puzzle was Manifest Destiny itself—not just as an ideology, but as a unifying national movement. The 1840s saw a surge in American expansionist sentiment, with settlers flooding into Texas, Oregon, and California. Public support for expansion was high, and Polk used that momentum to justify rapid, aggressive territorial acquisition. The political climate of the U.S. favored growth, and opposition to expansion was weak. Congress, despite occasional resistance, ultimately backed Polk's land grabs because they aligned with the national mood and economic interests.

Polk didn't just take advantage of geopolitical conditions—he understood them better than anyone and exploited them to their fullest. Britain was willing to compromise, Mexico was too weak to resist, Europe was too distracted to interfere, and the U.S. was stronger, richer, and more determined than ever to fulfill its expansionist destiny. He saw the moment for what it was—a rare chance to redraw the map of North America—and he seized it.

The Annexation of Texas, the Oregon Boundary Dispute, and the U.S.-Mexico War—His Triple Land Grab

TEXAS

Polk didn't just annex Texas—he ensured it was unavoidable. For nearly a decade, U.S. leaders hesitated, fearing war with Mexico and the political fallout of expanding slavery. Texas had declared independence in 1836, but its status remained in limbo. Northern politicians resisted annexation, worried it would tilt the balance of power toward the South. Mexico had never recognized Texas independence and warned that any attempt to bring Texas into the U.S. would be treated as an act of war. Britain had also taken an interest, seeing an opportunity to weaken U.S. expansion by supporting an independent Texas. Every factor that had made annexation difficult still existed when Polk took office in 1845, but unlike his predecessors, he didn't hesitate. He saw Texas as an economic and strategic necessity, and he acted quickly to secure it.

Rather than risk a treaty battle in the Senate, where a two-thirds majority would have been required, Polk used a joint resolution in Congress to pass annexation with a simple majority. It was a bold maneuver that ensured Texas would be absorbed into the U.S. without further delay. But annexation wasn't just about adding a new state. It was a provocation designed to push Mexico into war, setting the stage for even greater territorial expansion. The border dispute between Texas and Mexico gave Polk the opening he needed. He ordered General Zachary Taylor to move U.S. troops into contested land between the Nueces River and the Rio Grande, knowing full well that Mexico would see it as an invasion. When Mexican forces attacked, Polk declared that American blood had been spilled on American soil and used it to justify full-scale war.

There was never any doubt about the outcome. Mexico was politically unstable, militarily weak, and no match for the expanding U.S. war machine. The war Polk had engineered ended in total American victory. The Treaty of Guadalupe Hidalgo in 1848 forced Mexico to surrender not just Texas but also California, Arizona, New Mexico, and vast portions of the modern Southwest. Polk had done in four years what previous administrations had failed to do in decades. He didn't just secure

Texas—he used it as a stepping stone to complete the U.S. push to the Pacific. His tactics were aggressive, calculating, and ruthless, but they worked. The map of North America was redrawn, and Manifest Destiny became reality.

OREGON

Polk came into office with a clear goal: secure the Oregon Territory and extend U.S. control to the Pacific. Expansionists had rallied around the slogan "54°40' or fight!", demanding the entire territory up to the southern border of Russian Alaska. It was a bold stance, meant to pressure Britain into giving up its claim to the region. Polk, always strategic, let the rhetoric build but had no real intention of going to war over Oregon—not when a much bigger prize was within reach in the South. The real fight Polk wanted was with Mexico, and he couldn't afford to take on Britain at the same time. His genius lay in making Britain believe he was willing to fight while quietly preparing to settle for less.

The Oregon Territory had been jointly occupied by the U.S. and Britain for decades, but with tens of thousands of American settlers pouring into the region via the Oregon Trail, the balance was shifting. Polk understood that Britain had economic interests in Canada and global priorities elsewhere, and that a prolonged conflict over Oregon wasn't in their best interest. He played on these realities, keeping his public position aggressive while signaling to British diplomats that a negotiated settlement was possible.

His timing was perfect. Britain, already stretched thin with colonial concerns in India and rising tensions in Europe, wasn't eager for another conflict, especially not with an increasingly powerful and expansionist U.S. The British had also come to realize that their control over Oregon was slipping—American settlers outnumbered British subjects in the region, and the U.S. was clearly committed to long-term occupation. Polk used this leverage masterfully, waiting for Britain to blink first.

When negotiations finally took place, Polk accepted the 49th parallel as the dividing line, securing the bulk of the Oregon Territory while avoiding an unnecessary war. Britain, recognizing that holding on to the land wasn't worth the fight, agreed to the Oregon Treaty in 1846. Polk walked away with a major territorial victory, adding a vast expanse of land to the U.S. while keeping Britain at bay. The agreement also freed him to turn his full attention to the real war he wanted—Mexico.

Polk had outmaneuvered Britain without firing a shot. He let the public believe he was ready for war, forced Britain into a position where compromise was the only logical outcome, and secured U.S. control over the Pacific Northwest on his terms. It was a textbook example of how Polk operated: maximum pressure, calculated risk, and strategic retreat when necessary to secure the larger goal.

MEXICO

Polk didn't wait for a justification to go to war with Mexico—he created one. Texas had already been annexed into the U.S. in 1845, but the border was still disputed. Mexico claimed it ended at the Nueces River, while Texas and the U.S. insisted on the Rio Grande. This strip of land, largely uninhabited and strategically meaningless, became the perfect excuse for war. Polk sent General Zachary Taylor into the contested region, fully aware that his presence would provoke a Mexican response. When Mexican troops clashed with Taylor's forces in April 1846, Polk immediately went to Congress, declaring that Mexico had "shed American blood upon American soil." It was a blatant distortion of reality—the U.S. had entered disputed land, and Mexico had merely defended what it still considered its own territory. But it didn't matter. Congress authorized war, and the U.S. military mobilized to seize not just Texas, but California, New Mexico, and everything in between.

Polk used a two-pronged approach—aggressive military action combined with diplomatic pressure. Militarily, the U.S. had every advantage. Superior artillery, better-trained troops, and a rapidly expanding navy allowed the U.S. to dominate the battlefield. General Winfield Scott captured Mexico City after a brilliant amphibious landing at Veracruz, following the same route Hernán Cortés had taken centuries earlier. Taylor won decisive victories in northern Mexico, while in the West, John C. Frémont led U.S. forces into California, securing it with minimal resistance. Every major Mexican stronghold fell quickly, exposing just how weak and unprepared Mexico was for war.

Diplomatically, Polk played hardball. Mexico's government was in chaos, cycling through multiple leaders during the war, making it easier for Polk to pressure the regime into surrender. He sent Nicholas Trist to negotiate peace but kept him under strict orders—no half-measures, no minor concessions. Mexico would have to give up everything Polk wanted, or the war would continue. When Trist initially failed to secure enough land, Polk nearly fired him. But Trist, sensing that the war had reached a point where Mexico had no choice, pressed forward and secured the Treaty of Guadalupe Hidalgo in 1848.

The treaty was a complete victory for the U.S. Mexico was forced to cede nearly half its territory, including California, Arizona, New Mexico, Utah, Nevada, and parts of Colorado and Wyoming—over 500,000 square miles. The U.S. agreed to pay $15 million, a token sum meant to maintain the illusion of a fair deal. In reality, it was conquest disguised as diplomacy.

Polk had achieved exactly what he set out to do. He had expanded the U.S. to the Pacific, secured massive new territories, and completed the vision of Manifest Destiny. The war had been engineered from the start, and in less than two years, the U.S. had redrawn the map of North America. The sheer scale of what Polk accomplished was staggering—no other U.S. president before or after him expanded the nation's borders as dramatically. The war cemented America's status as a continental power, while Mexico was left humiliated and permanently weakened. Polk had won, and he had done it on his own terms.

CANADA?

Polk absolutely considered extending the U.S. border northward—not just in theory, but in active negotiations with Britain. While his presidency is most famous for expanding westward, there was a moment where British North America (Canada) could have become part of that expansion. The Oregon boundary dispute was the key moment where this nearly happened, and if Polk had been in a slightly stronger position—or Britain in a weaker one—the U.S. map could have looked very different.

The Oregon Territory stretched from modern-day Oregon, Washington, and Idaho up to 54°40' latitude, the southern edge of Russian Alaska. Expansionists pushed for the U.S. to take the entire region, rallying behind the slogan "Fifty-Four Forty or Fight!" The idea wasn't just to claim the Pacific Northwest—it was a broader challenge to British rule in North America. Polk let this rhetoric build, knowing that many Americans wanted the U.S. to push further north and absorb British-held lands.

Polk was pragmatic, not reckless. He understood that fighting both Britain and Mexico at the same time was too risky, so he had to decide which battle was worth pursuing. While war with Mexico was a calculated gamble that he knew the U.S. could win, war with Britain would have been a much bigger challenge. Britain was still a global superpower with a massive navy, and Polk wasn't willing to risk a two-front conflict. He used the threat of war as leverage but ultimately settled for the 49th parallel compromise, which gave the U.S. most of modern-day Washington, Oregon, and Idaho while Britain retained what is now British Columbia.

But the fact remains—if Britain had been weaker or more reluctant to defend its territory, Polk might have pushed further. The U.S. had momentum, a growing population, and an economy that was rapidly outpacing British Canada. Many Americans saw British North America as inevitably drifting toward the U.S., either through economic dependence or outright annexation. The Fenian Raids (1860s) and later U.S. expansionist movements continued this thinking, proving that Polk's era was not the last time the idea of absorbing parts of Canada was considered.

While Polk ultimately chose Mexico as his primary target, he left behind a precedent of expansionism that future American leaders would continue to pursue—through economics, trade, and influence rather than direct conquest. His negotiations over Oregon showed that the U.S. saw no permanent limit to its northern border, only temporary compromises. Had circumstances been different, the U.S. border could have stretched even further into what is now Canada.

There was absolutely political pressure within the U.S. to push farther north beyond the 49th parallel, particularly among hardline expansionists and those who saw British North America as unfinished business. The Oregon boundary dispute of the 1840s was the clearest example, with expansionist factions demanding that the U.S. claim the entire Oregon Territory up to 54°40' latitude, encompassing much of modern-day British Columbia. The slogan "Fifty-Four Forty or Fight!" wasn't just rhetoric—it reflected a widespread belief that British control over the Pacific Northwest was temporary and that the U.S. had every right to extend its reach further north.

While President James K. Polk played into this sentiment publicly, he was always more strategic than ideological. He let the aggressive rhetoric build to strengthen his negotiating position but never intended to start a war with Britain. His real priority was expansion in the South—war with Mexico was a much more viable path to territorial gain. So while there was serious political momentum for annexing more land in the north, Polk ultimately settled for the 49th parallel compromise in 1846, avoiding a costly war with Britain.

Even after the Oregon dispute was settled, expansionist sentiment toward British North America didn't fade entirely. There were Americans who believed that Canada would eventually become part of the U.S., either by economic absorption or political realignment. The Annexation Manifesto of 1849, written by Quebec-based American sympathizers, openly called for Canada to join the U.S., arguing that British rule was unnatural and that Canada would be better off as part of a growing continental power.

In the years that followed, U.S. interest in annexing parts of Canada resurfaced multiple times. During and after the U.S. Civil War (1861-1865), many Northern leaders blamed Britain for indirectly supporting the Confederacy and saw British Canada as a logical next target for expansion. The Fenian Raids (1866-1871)—cross-border attacks by Irish-American militias—were a direct attempt to destabilize British rule in Canada and provoke a U.S. takeover. While these efforts failed, they revealed that the belief in pushing northward still had traction.

The reality was that the U.S. didn't need to annex Canada militarily when it could do so economically and politically over time. The American economy quickly outpaced Canada's, trade ties deepened, and U.S. cultural influence slowly took hold. By the late 19th century, formal annexation wasn't necessary—Canada was already drifting into the American orbit. While the 49th parallel became the official boundary, the long-term goal of American dominance over North America was never abandoned—it just evolved.

A modern Polk-style expansionist policy wouldn't rely on military conquest or direct annexation—it would use economic leverage, trade dependency, corporate influence, and strategic agreements to achieve the same goal. Polk's expansionist vision was about securing long-term dominance over the continent, ensuring that the U.S. dictated the economic, political, and military direction of North America. That process hasn't stopped—it's simply evolved. Today, the U.S. doesn't need to seize land to control it; it just needs to own the markets, regulate the trade flows, and integrate Canada and Mexico into a system where Washington calls the shots.

Polk used territorial expansion to secure strategic resources, trade routes, and economic power. Today, the U.S. achieves those same ends through USMCA (the modern NAFTA), financial entanglement, and corporate control. The American economy is the gravitational force of North America—over 75% of Canadian exports go to the U.S., and key Canadian industries, from energy to banking, are deeply tied to American capital. The Bank of Canada follows the Federal Reserve's lead, meaning U.S. monetary policy indirectly controls Canada's economic stability. In a modern Polk-style approach, the goal wouldn't be to plant an American flag over Canada but to ensure that Canadian sovereignty is little more than a formality.

Instead of military incursions like the Mexican-American War (1846-1848), today's expansionism is achieved through economic pressure and trade agreements. When the U.S. wanted better terms in trade negotiations, Trump imposed tariffs on Canadian steel and aluminum, testing how much economic pain Ottawa could endure before complying. The same logic Polk used in Oregon—bluff hard, push aggressively, and force a compromise that benefits the U.S.—is still in play. Canada's supply chains are so dependent on the U.S. that if Washington wanted to force further economic integration, all it would need to do is tighten trade restrictions or impose regulatory barriers that force compliance.

Energy is another frontier of modern expansion. Instead of outright seizing land as Polk did with Texas and California, today's U.S. dominance comes from controlling pipelines, investment, and refining capacity. Canada may produce oil, but much of it is shipped south for processing, priced according to U.S. markets, and exported on American terms. When Biden canceled Keystone XL, Canada had no say—its most valuable resource sector was at the mercy of Washington. That is what modern expansionism looks like—no invasion, no war, just economic dependency so deep that resistance is impossible.

Polk's military strategy also has its modern counterpart in NORAD, NATO, and integrated defense agreements. Instead of sending U.S. troops into Canada or Mexico, Washington simply ensures that North American security is structured around U.S. command. Canada's military is so underfunded and reliant on U.S. technology that it could not operate independently in any serious conflict. The Monroe Doctrine once warned European powers to stay out of the Western Hemisphere—today, Canada doesn't even need such a warning, because its defense policy is already aligned with U.S. strategic interests.

A modern Polk-style policy wouldn't announce itself as annexation. It wouldn't be a dramatic war or a forced merger. It would simply continue what has already been happening for decades: pulling Canada further into the American economic, military, and cultural orbit until separation becomes meaningless. Where Polk used armies, today's U.S. dominance is secured through trade agreements, currency influence, corporate ownership, and security dependence. The result is the same—control without the cost of governance.

A modern Polk-style expansionist policy wouldn't rely on outright military conquest or formal annexation. It would achieve the same results through economic control, trade dependency, financial leverage, and strategic pressure. The U.S. already dominates Canada economically—over 75% of Canadian exports go south, and major industries, from banking to energy, are deeply entangled with American corporations. A U.S. leader looking to absorb Canada would only need to exploit existing vulnerabilities. Trade restrictions, selective tariffs, or regulatory barriers could cripple Canadian industries overnight, forcing Ottawa to make economic concessions that lead to deeper integration.

Monetary policy is another tool. The Bank of Canada already follows the Federal Reserve's lead, adjusting interest rates and financial policy based on American decisions. A well-timed financial crisis could push the idea of a North American currency union as a "stability measure." If the Canadian dollar collapses under inflationary pressure or economic downturn, the U.S. could offer the U.S. dollar as a solution, effectively erasing Canada's financial independence.

Energy dependence is another pressure point. While Canada is one of the world's largest oil producers, its refining capacity and export routes are largely controlled by the U.S. When Biden canceled Keystone XL, it wasn't a Canadian decision—it was an American one that immediately impacted Alberta's economy. Washington could restrict pipeline access, impose environmental regulations that strangle Canadian production, or even offer sweetheart deals to U.S. energy firms to shift development southward. The result would be Western Canada, particularly Alberta and Saskatchewan, left with few options outside of deeper integration into the U.S. economic system.

Political fractures make absorption even easier. Western Canada's resentment toward Ottawa has only grown, with Alberta increasingly frustrated over federal policies that restrict its resource sector. If economic conditions worsen, the idea of Alberta separating from Canada and aligning with the U.S. could shift from fringe rhetoric to a legitimate political movement. Quebec remains a separate issue—rather than absorbing it, a modern Polk strategy would likely encourage Quebec's independence push, knowing that a Canada without Quebec is economically unsustainable and easier to break apart.

The U.S. also controls Canadian security in all but name. NORAD already places North American defense under joint command, and Canada's military is dependent on U.S. weapons, intelligence, and logistics. A manufactured security crisis—an Arctic territorial dispute, a cyberattack, or a supposed terrorist threat—could be used to justify greater U.S. military involvement in Canadian affairs. Once Canadian defense policy is fully subordinated to Washington, sovereignty becomes meaningless.

A modern annexation wouldn't come with an official declaration or statehood process—it would come in stages, through financial dependency, trade agreements that erode autonomy, and political destabilization that weakens Ottawa's ability to resist. At some point, full absorption would be the only logical outcome. No need for war, no need for conquest—just the slow, calculated dismantling of a nation until it becomes a legal formality.

Chapter 3: The War of 1812

The War of 1812 – America's First Attempt at Canadian Annexation

Manifest Destiny existed as an idea long before it had a name. The belief that the United States was meant to expand across the continent was deeply embedded in American political thought from the country's founding. Even without a formal doctrine, early leaders saw territorial expansion as both inevitable and necessary. The Revolutionary generation had already embraced the notion that North America was destined to be controlled by a free, democratic republic rather than European monarchies. By the early 19th century, this idea took a more aggressive turn, driven by a mix of economic ambition, national security concerns, and an emerging sense of American exceptionalism.

The War Hawks of the early 1800s were among the most vocal expansionists. Led by figures like Henry Clay, John C. Calhoun, and Felix Grundy, they pushed for war with Britain under the pretext of stopping British interference in American affairs. Officially, they claimed to be responding to British violations of U.S. sovereignty—seizing American ships, impressing sailors, and stirring up Native resistance on the frontier. In reality, their motives went far beyond these grievances. The War Hawks saw war as an opportunity to eliminate British influence in North America once and for all, with the ultimate goal of annexing Canada. They believed that British control over Canada was a direct threat to U.S. security and that absorbing it into the Union would so-lidify American dominance over the continent.

Henry Clay, a leading voice in Congress, viewed expansion as both an economic and strategic necessity. He championed internal improve-ments and infrastructure projects that would facilitate westward expan-sion, and he saw war as a means to clear out foreign and Indigenous obstacles to American settlement. Clay's vision of a strong, unified, and economically self-sufficient America depended on securing more land and resources. John C. Calhoun, despite his later association with Southern sectionalism, was an equally fierce advocate for territorial growth in his early years. He saw British presence in Canada as a linger-ing colonial threat and argued that war was necessary to complete the unfinished business of the American Revolution.

These leaders helped push the United States into the War of 1812, convinced that it would end with the annexation of Canada. They as-sumed that British forces would be spread too thin fighting Napoleon in Europe and that Canadians, many of whom were former American colonists, would welcome U.S. forces as liberators. These assumptions proved disastrously wrong. The war ended in a stalemate, and the U.S. gained no new territory. However, the expansionist mentality of the War Hawks didn't fade. The war reinforced the belief that America's destiny was to dominate the continent, and that if military conquest failed, economic and political strategies would be needed to achieve the same goal.

Long before John L. O'Sullivan gave the ideology its famous name in 1845, Manifest Destiny had already shaped U.S. policy. The Louisiana Purchase, the push for control over Florida, and the aggressive settle-ment of the frontier all reflected the same underlying conviction: that America's expansion was not only desirable but inevitable. The War Hawks of the early 19th century provided the first real test of this belief, laying the foundation for the even more aggressive land grabs of the Polk era and beyond. Even in failure, they proved that expansionism was now a permanent fixture of American political thought.

American leaders justified the War of 1812 as a war of "liberation"—a continuation of the Revolutionary War to free North America from British control once and for all. To them, Canada was not just a British colony; it was an unnatural holdover from the past, a piece of the continent that rightfully belonged to the United States. Expansionists argued that British rule was oppressive and that Canadians, many of whom were of American descent, would welcome U.S. forces as liberators. In their minds, annexing Canada wasn't an act of aggression—it was completing what had already begun in 1776.

The Napoleonic Wars in Europe played a critical role in shaping this belief. With Britain engaged in a massive, existential struggle against France, American leaders assumed that London wouldn't be able to defend its North American territories effectively. The British military was stretched thin, fighting Napoleon across Europe and enforcing a global naval blockade. U.S. expansionists, led by the War Hawks, saw this as a golden opportunity—if America struck quickly, it could seize Canada before Britain had a chance to react. The assumption was that Britain would prioritize its European war over a distant colony and negotiate peace on American terms. This miscalculation would prove costly.

Beyond the ideological and strategic motives, there were clear economic incentives for targeting Canada. The region was rich in fur trade routes, which were still highly lucrative in the early 19th century. Control of Canada would allow American merchants and traders to dominate the fur industry, cutting British companies like the Hudson's Bay Company out of the market. But more importantly, Canada offered fertile farmland and control over the Great Lakes trade network. U.S. settlers, particularly in the frontier states, saw Canadian lands as ideal for expansion, while merchants in the Midwest wanted greater access to trade routes that connected to the Atlantic.

Seizing Canada would have also removed British influence over Indigenous resistance to U.S. expansion. The British had long supported Native alliances as a buffer against American encroachment, particularly in the Ohio Valley and Great Lakes region. Many U.S. leaders saw

Britain's presence in Canada as the last major obstacle preventing the complete settlement and control of the West. If Canada was absorbed, British arms and support for Indigenous nations would vanish, clearing the way for unrestricted expansion.

Ultimately, the war failed in its goal of annexing Canada. The U.S. underestimated British and Canadian resistance, misjudged the willingness of Canadians to rebel against British rule, and overestimated its own military strength. But the war cemented the idea that Canada was unfinished business, a land that should have belonged to the U.S. and, in the minds of some American leaders, eventually would. Even after the war ended in a stalemate, expansionist sentiment remained, shifting from military conquest to economic integration as the next best path to control.

The belief that Britain was arming and encouraging Indigenous resistance provided the perfect pretext for war. For years, American settlers and expansionists accused the British of using Native alliances to block U.S. control over the frontier, particularly in the Great Lakes and Ohio Valley regions. While Britain did provide weapons and limited support to Indigenous nations, the real reason U.S. leaders focused on this was because it justified expansion. By portraying Indigenous resistance as a British plot rather than an independent struggle, American leaders could frame war with Britain as a necessary step toward securing the western frontier.

Tecumseh's Confederacy was the prime example. Tecumseh, a Shawnee leader, sought to unite Indigenous nations to resist U.S. encroachment on their lands, particularly after a series of land grabs facilitated by unfair treaties. He found support among the British in Canada, who saw a strong Indigenous alliance as a buffer against American expansion. This fueled American fears that Britain was actively orchestrating resistance to U.S. settlement. Expansionists, particularly the War Hawks, seized on this as evidence that Britain was interfering in American affairs and had to be dealt with permanently.

In reality, Indigenous resistance was not simply a British proxy war—it was a direct response to relentless U.S. land seizures and broken treaties. But framing it as a British conspiracy allowed American leaders to justify an invasion of Canada. If Britain could be removed from North America, Indigenous nations would be left without powerful allies, and the U.S. would have free rein to dominate the continent.

The Louisiana Purchase in 1803 reinforced the idea that territorial expansion was not just possible but inevitable. The U.S. had acquired a massive new frontier from France with little resistance, proving that land could be absorbed without prolonged war. This emboldened expansionists, who began to see Canada as the next logical target. If France had so easily surrendered its North American claims, why wouldn't Britain do the same, especially when it was preoccupied with Napoleon?

The ease of the Louisiana Purchase led to a false sense of confidence among U.S. leaders that expansion was a matter of asserting pressure rather than engaging in prolonged conflict. The assumption that Canada would fall just as easily proved to be a costly miscalculation. Unlike the sparsely settled Louisiana Territory, Canada had an established British military presence and a population that wasn't eager to become part of the U.S. When American forces invaded, they found themselves facing not just British troops but well-organized Canadian militias and Indigenous warriors—many of whom were fighting precisely because they feared what U.S. expansion would mean for their lands.

The War Hawks had assumed that Britain's support for Indigenous nations was an act of hostility. In reality, it was a defensive measure to counter relentless U.S. expansionism. But that distinction didn't matter. The perception of British interference gave the U.S. a justification for war, a rallying cry for expansion, and an excuse to launch an invasion that had always been about land, not defense.

The Failed Invasions – Why Americans Assumed Canadians Would Welcome Them as "Liberators"

U.S. war planners in 1812 made a fatal miscalculation: they assumed that Canadians, particularly in Upper Canada (modern-day Ontario), would welcome American troops as liberators. This assumption was based on a naïve and oversimplified reading of history, shaped by early American expansionist ideology. Many American leaders believed that because large portions of Canada's population were former British colonists—just like those in the Thirteen Colonies—they would naturally want to join the United States and embrace republican government. They failed to grasp the deep Loyalist identity that had formed in Canada and the distinct cultural and political differences that separated Canadians from their southern neighbors.

American expansionists, particularly the War Hawks, viewed the Revolution as an unfinished business, believing that all of British North America was meant to break away from Britain alongside the United States. They saw Canada as an unnatural outpost of monarchy on a continent that was destined for republican rule. When American war planners looked at Upper Canada, they saw a population largely made up of British settlers and assumed that their dislike of British rule would make them natural allies. This was a dangerous misreading of the political landscape. Many of those settlers were Loyalists—people who had fled the U.S. precisely because they wanted to remain under British rule. They had no interest in switching sides again.

In Lower Canada (modern Quebec), the situation was even worse for U.S. ambitions. Many Americans assumed that French Canadians would prefer U.S. rule over British rule, given Britain's history of treating them as second-class citizens. What expansionists failed to recognize was that the British had granted French Canadians significant autonomy under the Quebec Act (1774), allowing them to keep their language, religion, and legal traditions. The idea that the United States, a predominantly Anglo-Protestant republic, would offer them the same protections was laughable to most French Canadians. Many saw the

U.S. as a greater threat than Britain, fearing they would lose their Catholic identity and French-language rights under American rule.

The U.S. also underestimated the strength of Canadian nationalism, which was still in its infancy but growing rapidly in response to the American invasion. Once war broke out, local militias—many of them made up of settlers who had every reason to resent British rule—rallied to defend their homes against the Americans. The war gave Canada an opportunity to forge a distinct identity, one that saw survival as a British colony as preferable to being swallowed up by the U.S.

American war planners had assumed that the only thing keeping Canada tied to Britain was military occupation and elite British rule, and that once American troops arrived, resistance would collapse. They completely miscalculated the population's loyalty and willingness to fight. Instead of rising up, Canadians actively fought against American forces, with British troops, local militias, and Indigenous allies all playing decisive roles in repelling the invasions.

By the time the War of 1812 ended, the U.S. had learned a painful lesson: Canada was not waiting to be liberated. The assumption that Canadians were "Americans-in-waiting" had backfired spectacularly, reinforcing Canada's separate identity and ensuring that any future U.S. attempts at annexation would have to rely on economic and political influence rather than military force.

The American invasions of Canada during the War of 1812 were a series of failures, driven by overconfidence, poor planning, and a complete misunderstanding of both the enemy and the terrain. The United States launched multiple offensives, expecting quick victories and Canadian support, only to be met with stubborn resistance from British troops, Canadian militias, and Indigenous warriors. The three most significant U.S. invasion attempts—Detroit, Queenston Heights, and Montreal—failed spectacularly, proving that American expansion into Canada would not be as easy as many had assumed.

The Detroit campaign in 1812 was one of the most embarrassing defeats in U.S. military history. General William Hull, leading a poorly trained and under-equipped force, invaded Upper Canada but quickly realized he lacked the supplies, reinforcements, and local support needed to hold territory. British forces under General Isaac Brock, along with Tecumseh's Indigenous warriors, launched a psychological and tactical assault that completely demoralized the American troops. They faked larger numbers, used the wilderness to cut off supply lines, and exploited Hull's paranoia about Native warfare. Without a single shot being fired in direct battle, Hull panicked and surrendered Detroit to a vastly outnumbered British force. This loss shattered American confidence and handed Britain a key early victory.

The Battle of Queenston Heights in October 1812 was another failure, exposing the disorganization and lack of coordination in the U.S. military. American forces attempted to cross the Niagara River and seize a strategic position in Upper Canada. They initially succeeded in landing troops and taking ground, but British reinforcements, Canadian militia, and Mohawk warriors under John Norton launched a brutal counterattack. The Americans, isolated on the heights, quickly ran out of ammunition and reinforcements. Worse, New York militia units refused to cross the river to support them, citing legal concerns about fighting outside U.S. borders. With no escape and no reinforcements, the American troops were overwhelmed and forced to surrender. This battle proved that Canada's defense wasn't just coming from British regulars but from a population actively fighting to repel American invaders.

The Montreal campaign in 1813 was supposed to be the decisive blow—if the U.S. could take Montreal, it would effectively cut off British reinforcements from the Atlantic and secure control over Lower Canada. Instead, it was a disaster of logistical failures, poor leadership, and a lack of coordination. The plan required two American armies to converge on Montreal from different directions, but they never linked up. One force was defeated at Châteauguay by a much smaller group of Canadian and Indigenous fighters, using superior tactics to hold off a force ten times their size. The other U.S. force, slowed by bad weather and supply shortages, was ambushed and turned back before even reaching the city. The entire operation collapsed before the Americans could launch a serious assault.

Indigenous alliances with the British played a decisive role in disrupting American war strategy. Tecumseh and his warriors used guerrilla tactics, ambushes, and psychological warfare to harass American forces, cutting off supplies and preventing major U.S. advances. American troops, already undisciplined and poorly supplied, were terrified of Native combatants, who fought on home terrain and understood how to use the wilderness to their advantage. U.S. leaders saw Indigenous forces as a secondary threat, but in reality, they were a crucial part of Canada's defense. Without them, British forces would have been stretched too thin to resist American advances.

Despite aggressive American rhetoric before the war, the U.S. military was completely unprepared for conflict. The country had a small, poorly trained standing army, an overreliance on untested state militias, and a leadership structure riddled with political appointees instead of competent generals. Many U.S. officers, including William Hull, were aging veterans of the Revolutionary War who were out of touch with modern warfare. There was also no clear strategy—some wanted to attack Canada in the east, while others focused on the western frontier. Instead of a coordinated campaign, the U.S. invasions were a series of disconnected, poorly executed assaults that failed to capitalize on momentum.

For the British and Canadians, these victories weren't just defensive successes—they became powerful propaganda tools. The War of 1812 is often called the war that created Canada, because it was the first time the country's settlers, Indigenous nations, and British rulers fought together as one unified force. British officials praised the bravery of Canadian militias and Indigenous warriors, reinforcing the idea that Canada was not just a British colony, but a separate nation capable of defending itself. The failure of the American invasions cemented a national identity that defined Canada in opposition to the U.S., an identity that persists to this day.

The War of 1812 was supposed to be a quick and easy conquest for the United States. Instead, it exposed deep weaknesses in American military strategy and strengthened the very Canadian nationalism that would ensure its survival as an independent nation. The dream of annexing Canada didn't die, but after the war, it became clear that it would have to be pursued through economic dominance rather than military conquest.

Had U.S. forces succeeded in taking Upper Canada during the War of 1812, Britain would not have simply accepted the loss—it would have escalated the war dramatically. The British Empire had no intention of allowing the United States to absorb its North American territories without a serious fight. While the British were preoccupied with Napoleon in Europe during the early stages of the war, by 1814 that distraction was disappearing, and Britain was already shifting resources toward crushing the American invasion. If Upper Canada had fallen, Britain would have diverted even more troops, ships, and resources to North America, potentially turning the war into an even greater disaster for the U.S.

Britain's ability to fight back was already demonstrated in the later stages of the war. Once Napoleon was defeated in 1814, Britain sent thousands of battle-hardened troops to North America, launching devastating counterattacks. British forces burned Washington, D.C., in retaliation for the U.S. invasion of York (Toronto), and they launched a full-scale invasion of New York via Lake Champlain, only to be turned back at Plattsburgh. If Upper Canada had fallen earlier in the war, it is likely that Britain would have launched an even larger counter-invasion, reclaiming lost territory and possibly pushing the U.S. back into its own borders.

The British Navy, already blockading American ports and strangling trade, would have intensified its campaign. Britain had total naval superiority and could have cut off U.S. supply lines, preventing reinforcements from reaching Canada. The Royal Navy's dominance meant that any U.S. gains in Upper Canada would have been difficult to sustain, as British forces could launch amphibious landings and retake key regions while keeping the American economy in a chokehold.

The most significant factor that would have led Britain to fight back harder is the risk to Lower Canada (Quebec). If the U.S. had successfully occupied Upper Canada, the next logical step would have been an invasion of Montreal and Quebec City. These were the gateway cities to British control of North America—if they fell, British North America would be at risk of total collapse. Britain would never have allowed this to happen without an overwhelming response.

Indigenous alliances would have also remained a major factor. Even if the U.S. had captured Upper Canada, it would have faced relentless resistance from Indigenous forces allied with Britain, who saw the war as a fight for their own survival. Tecumseh's Confederacy was already waging a brutal guerrilla war against American forces, and with British support, they could have continued attacking supply lines, ambushing American patrols, and making occupation nearly impossible. The U.S. had already struggled to control newly acquired western territories—it's unlikely it could have pacified all of Upper Canada while still facing Indigenous and British counterattacks.

If the British had lost control of Upper Canada but still retained Quebec, they might have offered temporary concessions in peace negotiations to avoid a prolonged war. However, it is far more likely that they would have poured reinforcements into North America, retaken the lost territory, and made the war even more devastating for the U.S. The British Empire was at its peak, and losing a major North American colony to a young republic was not something it would have accepted lightly.

Had the U.S. somehow managed to hold onto Upper Canada, Britain might have shifted its focus from direct military reconquest to economic warfare. The Royal Navy could have blockaded the entire eastern seaboard indefinitely, crushed American trade, and bankrupted the U.S. government. Without economic stability, holding onto Canadian territory would have been unsustainable.

The failure of the U.S. invasions ultimately prevented Britain from fully retaliating, as neither side gained enough ground to justify an all-out war effort. But if Upper Canada had fallen, Britain would have had both the motive and the means to retaliate in full force. Instead of a stalemate, the war could have ended with the U.S. not just failing to take Canada, but potentially losing territory itself.

The Treaty of Ghent and How the U.S. Shifted to Economic Annexation Instead

The Treaty of Ghent (1814) ended the War of 1812 by restoring pre-war boundaries, effectively erasing any territorial gains made by either side. For the United States, this meant it had nothing to show for its invasion attempts into Canada. The treaty did not grant the U.S. any new land, nor did it force Britain to make territorial concessions. The American dream of annexing Canada had failed, and the war concluded with the status quo firmly intact.

Britain flatly refused to cede any Canadian territory, despite American demands, for several reasons. First, Britain had successfully defended its North American holdings, repelling multiple U.S. invasions and demonstrating that Canada was not vulnerable to easy conquest. American forces had been decisively defeated at Detroit, Queenston Heights, and Montreal, proving that British and Canadian forces—along with their Indigenous allies—were fully capable of resisting American expansion.

Second, Britain had no reason to reward American aggression with territorial concessions. The war had been started by the U.S., largely on the pretext of stopping British interference in American trade and the belief that Canada could be easily taken. By 1814, the British had turned the tide, launching counteroffensives into U.S. territory, most notably the burning of Washington, D.C. and an invasion of New York. With

Britain in a stronger bargaining position, there was no reason to give the U.S. anything it had failed to take by force.

Another crucial factor was the end of the Napoleonic Wars in Europe. Britain had been preoccupied with defeating Napoleon for most of the war, but once Napoleon was exiled in 1814, Britain was free to focus more on North America. If the U.S. had continued to demand territory, Britain could have simply prolonged the war and escalated its military efforts, knowing it now had the resources to overwhelm American forces. The U.S. recognized this risk and decided to settle for peace rather than push for a fight it could not win.

Indigenous alliances also played a role in Britain's refusal to cede Canadian land. Many Native nations had fought alongside the British, seeing them as a lesser evil compared to relentless American expansion. Tecumseh's Confederacy had been devastated after Tecumseh's death in 1813, but Indigenous warriors had still been instrumental in defending Canada. Britain had promised to protect Indigenous lands from U.S. encroachment, and handing over Canadian territory to the U.S. would have betrayed those allies and further weakened British credibility.

For the U.S., the failure to gain any Canadian territory was a major disappointment. The War Hawks had sold the war as an opportunity to expand the nation, and yet the U.S. ended up exactly where it had started. The only real American "victory" was in the national myth that emerged afterward. While the war itself had been a strategic failure, the defense of New Orleans in 1815 and the survival of the young republic against the British Empire allowed the U.S. to frame the war as a patriotic struggle rather than an expansionist miscalculation.

Britain, on the other hand, had successfully protected Canada and reinforced its status as a permanent British possession. While it did not gain any new land, it ensured that the U.S. would not attempt another full-scale invasion of Canada in the future. The Treaty of Ghent made it clear: Canada would not be annexed by force. If the U.S. wanted to dominate its northern neighbor, it would have to do so through economic and political influence, not military conquest.

The War of 1812, despite being a military victory for Britain in terms of defending Canada from American invasion, had profound long-term consequences for British commitment to the colony and its relationship with the United States. While the British maintained control over Canada, the war highlighted the difficulties of managing and defending distant territories with limited resources, especially as Britain's focus shifted back to European conflicts after Napoleon's defeat in 1815. This shift left Canada more vulnerable to American influence and played a pivotal role in making the colony increasingly economically dependent on the United States.

The war drained Britain's resources, and its ability to defend and invest in Canada became increasingly strained. The Royal Navy's resources were stretched thin by global commitments, and British military forces in North America had to be scaled back after the war. Britain's focus now was on rebuilding its empire and recovering economically from the toll of the Napoleonic Wars, which meant that Canada was no longer the central priority it had once been.

This weakening of Britain's direct commitment to Canada set the stage for increased economic integration between Upper Canada (now Ontario) and the United States. As Britain moved away from actively investing in its Canadian colony, American economic power began to fill the void. The U.S. had already begun trading with Canada during the war—often bypassing British blockades—but the post-war period saw an even stronger push toward economic integration. In the years following the war, American entrepreneurs and investors flooded into Canada, particularly in Upper Canada, which was rich in natural resources and land for settlement.

The U.S. played a significant role in encouraging economic integration between Upper Canada and American markets after the war. In the early 19th century, the U.S. was one of the most dynamic economies in the world, with vast amounts of capital, rapidly expanding infrastructure, and an increasing need for raw materials. Meanwhile, Canada, particularly the fertile lands of Upper Canada, had an economy based on agriculture and the export of timber, which were in high demand south of the border. This made Canada a natural trading partner for the United States, and American businesses were eager to tap into this market.

One of the most significant drivers of economic integration came in the form of reciprocity treaties between the U.S. and Canada. The Reciprocity Treaty of 1854 was particularly important, as it allowed for free trade of many goods between Canada and the U.S., such as timber, fish, grain, and coal. This treaty significantly boosted economic ties, as it increased the flow of Canadian goods into U.S. markets while also making Canadian industries reliant on American demand. The treaty also helped foster infrastructural development, with U.S. capital being invested in Canadian railroads, canals, and other key industries. By linking Upper Canada's economy with that of the U.S., the treaty essentially deepened the economic dependency of the colony on its southern neighbor.

Moreover, American banks and financiers were increasingly involved in the Canadian economy, providing the capital needed for industrial expansion. U.S. banks financed infrastructure projects, such as the building of the Grand Trunk Railway, which connected Canada's provinces with U.S. trade routes. As more American investments flowed into Canada, the U.S. became the primary source of financial and industrial growth for Canada, turning it into a de facto economic satellite.

By the mid-19th century, Canada's economic ties to the U.S. were so deeply embedded that the threat of British withdrawal from Canada's economic sphere became increasingly clear. The British government's focus had shifted elsewhere, and its commitment to ensuring Canada's economic independence began to wane. As a result, Canada's future seemed to be inexorably linked to the United States—economically, if not yet politically. This growing reliance on American markets and investment ultimately laid the groundwork for greater political and economic integration, culminating in the eventual confederation of

Canada in 1867 and its growing dependence on U.S. trade policies in the years to follow.

In essence, while Britain may have won the war militarily, the economic consequences of the War of 1812 ensured that Canada's long-term relationship would be defined by its economic ties to the United States, not its political ties to Britain. The U.S. role in encouraging economic integration was critical to Canada's development in the 19th century and set the stage for the continued dominance of American economic influence in Canada throughout the following decades.

After 1815, trade policies between the United States and Canada laid the foundation for long-term U.S. economic dominance over Canada, shifting the focus from military conquest to economic influence. The War of 1812 had shown the limits of military expansionism, with the U.S. failing to annex Canadian territory despite aggressive attempts. The war forced the U.S. to reconsider its strategy and pivot toward a more subtle, long-term approach that would eventually achieve what military conquest could not: economic domination and eventual integration.

Post-war, the United States began shifting its focus to trade and diplomacy as the primary tools for influence. Britain's weakened commitment to Canada, following its victory over Napoleon in 1814, meant that the U.S. had greater leverage. The British Empire's reduced attention to its North American colonies made it easier for the U.S. to deepen economic ties with Canada, particularly in Upper Canada (Ontario), which had vast natural resources that were attractive to American industries.

One of the key drivers of U.S. economic influence over Canada after 1815 was the Reciprocity Treaty of 1854, which opened the door for free trade between the U.S. and Canada. The treaty allowed the exchange of products like timber, grain, coal, and fish without tariffs, which allowed both economies to become more interdependent. As a result, American businesses were able to invest heavily in Canada, especially in the areas of infrastructure (railroads, canals) and natural resource extraction (timber and minerals). American merchants and investors began to dominate Canadian markets, and the Canadian economy, reliant on exports to the U.S., became more integrated with its southern neighbor. This economic relationship fundamentally shifted the power dynamics of North America, with the U.S. in the driver's seat.

Trade policies after the war, such as tariffs on British imports and favorable terms for U.S.-Canadian exchanges, allowed the U.S. to exert growing economic control over Canada. As the United States expanded its internal markets and infrastructure, it found natural partners in Canada. The U.S. also offered Canadian industries access to its vast market, positioning itself as the primary economic partner. By the time the Transcontinental Railroad connected the U.S. from coast to coast, Canada was left increasingly isolated from other trade partners, leaving American markets as the dominant force in Canadian trade.

In terms of military strategy, the War of 1812 did indeed mark a shift from military conquest to economic domination. Prior to the war, the U.S. had believed that military power would secure Canada, but the failure of the war, combined with the realization of Britain's ability to effectively defend its colony, made it clear that conquest would not be feasible. The war, rather than achieving territorial annexation, demonstrated that Canada was a difficult and costly target, and the U.S. would have to seek alternative means to bring it under its influence. Military defeat forced the U.S. to reconsider the viability of territorial expansion and led to a strategic shift in thinking.

After the war, U.S. leaders realized that annexation through war was too costly and unlikely to succeed. The U.S. instead turned its attention to more subtle tactics: diplomacy, trade deals, and financial control. The British North American colonies were geographically close, culturally linked, and economically complementary to the United States. Rather than military conquest, U.S. policymakers increasingly focused on leveraging economic relationships to draw Canada closer. Trade agreements like the Reciprocity Treaty and later economic policies ensured that the

U.S. became Canada's primary market and financial partner, making full political integration through military force unnecessary.

Furthermore, by the mid-19th century, U.S. politicians had begun to recognize that Canadian dependency on U.S. markets was more important than formal annexation. They realized that economic control could be a more lasting form of dominance than military conquest. The development of the railroad network, growing investment in Canadian industries, and strategic control over trade routes meant that U.S. influence over Canada would only deepen without the need for formal annexation.

By the time the British Empire granted Canada dominion status in 1867, the economic and political framework for U.S. dominance was firmly in place. Canada was already deeply integrated into U.S. economic systems, with its industries and markets essentially functioning as satellites of American capitalism. The U.S. had won the war for Canada's economy, not through military conquest, but through the slow process of economic dependence, financial control, and diplomatic maneuvering. The failure of the War of 1812 and the shift toward economic dominance through trade and finance paved the way for a form of soft annexation—a reality where Canada's future was already intertwined with the U.S., even if it wasn't formally part of the Union.

Chapter 4: The Confederation of Canada

The Confederation of Canada – A British Defense Against American Takeover

How Fears of U.S. Annexation Led to Canada's Formation in 1867

The American Civil War (1861-1865) was a crucial turning point that shifted the perception of U.S. expansionism, especially among British and Canadian leaders. Prior to the war, Britain and Canada viewed the United States primarily as an economic partner and potential threat, but the Civil War made the reality of American expansionist ambitions much more apparent.

Britain, already wary of U.S. territorial ambitions, saw the Civil War as a stark warning sign that American expansionism could destabilize the continent. While Britain had been historically aligned with the United States in many respects, it understood that the U.S. was a rapidly growing power, unpredictable in its aims and more inclined toward military aggression than diplomacy. The Civil War showed Britain that, once the internal conflict was over, the U.S. would likely resume its westward expansionist agenda. If the North triumphed, the United

States would be more unified and militarily stronger, which could mean more efforts to annex lands like Canada and bring them into the Union.

For Canadian leaders, the Civil War raised alarms about the U.S. turning its attention toward British North America after the conflict. Throughout the war, there had been incidents involving U.S. support for raids into Canada (like the Fenian Raids, where Irish-American militants attempted to take Canada to use it as leverage in their struggle for Irish independence). The U.S. was seen as distracted and internally divided during the war, but once the Union victory was secured, American attention would undoubtedly turn back to territorial ambitions, especially in the North. As Canada was still under British rule, the prospect of American annexation was a real concern.

Britain, deeply engaged in maintaining its empire, was not inclined to give up Canada without a fight. Yet, it also understood the political and military risks posed by an increasingly powerful and unified United States. To mitigate these risks, British leaders strengthened their commitment to Canada, ensuring that the colony was defensible in the event of an American invasion. The creation of the Canadian Confederation in 1867 was partly an attempt to foster a more unified and resilient political entity that could better withstand U.S. expansionism. While Britain would not directly annex Canada, it encouraged a more self-sufficient and cohesive structure within the colony.

After the Civil War, the United States turned its attention back to expansion, and many politicians began openly calling for the annexation of British North America. The war had left the U.S. with a renewed sense of nationalism and unity, as well as a powerful industrial economy and a large, battle-hardened military. The idea of Manifest Destiny, which had driven U.S. territorial ambitions in the first half of the 19th century, was far from over. The war had forged a stronger, more nationalistic Union, and with slavery abolished, the focus shifted to other territorial acquisitions.

Some U.S. leaders, particularly those in the Republican Party, openly discussed annexing Canada in the wake of the Civil War. William H.

Seward, President Abraham Lincoln's Secretary of State, was one of the most prominent advocates for this idea. He believed that the U.S. should push northward and absorb British North America to create a unified continent under American rule. Seward argued that annexation would be an economic boon and further strengthen the country's strategic position. The idea wasn't universally popular, but it was part of a larger vision of American continental dominance.

While the U.S. did not pursue direct annexation immediately after the Civil War, the idea continued to circulate as part of the broader postwar expansionist sentiment. The purchasing of Alaska from Russia in 1867, while not directly related to Canada, was an important step in this broader strategy of extending American control over the northern territories. It showed that the U.S. was ready to expand and exert influence over regions that had previously been outside its control.

Thus, the Civil War effectively convinced British and Canadian leaders that U.S. expansionism was a real and present threat. It shifted the American focus back to the idea of territorial conquest, including the potential annexation of Canada, and prompted Britain to reconsider its colonial policies in North America. Ultimately, while the U.S. did not annex Canada after the Civil War, the period marked a clear moment of transition in which U.S. expansionism went from military conquest to economic, political, and diplomatic dominance over Canada, a process that would unfold in the years to come.

The Fenian Raids (1866-1871), carried out by Irish-American militants who aimed to use Canada as leverage for Irish independence from Britain, played a significant role in reinforcing the need for national unity in Canada. These raids were a direct challenge to Canadian security, demonstrating that the country was vulnerable to external threats, and they underscored the urgency of creating a stronger, more unified political entity to defend itself. Though the Fenian Raids were militarily unsuccessful, they highlighted the weaknesses of Canada's fragmented governance and spurred political leaders to seek a more coordinated defense system.

The Fenians believed that by invading Canada, they could pressure Britain into withdrawing its forces from Ireland. The raids themselves were sporadic and lacked broader strategic coordination, but they were symbolic of the growing unrest and the desire for change in the British Empire. For Canada, the Fenians were not just an external threat—they represented a larger issue. The raids underscored that Canada could not rely on Britain to defend its North American colonies indefinitely, especially as the British Empire's priorities shifted.

The Fenians' repeated attacks served as a wake-up call for Canadian leaders, who saw that their fragile, disjointed system of government made them vulnerable to external attacks. While British North America had long been composed of separate colonies—each with its own legislature, economy, and interests—the raids forced a reconsideration of Canada's political unity and defense strategy. The need for a unified Canadian defense system became clearer, and it was within this context that the idea of Canadian Confederation gained traction.

The formation of the Canadian Confederation in 1867, which unified Ontario, Quebec, New Brunswick, and Nova Scotia into the Dominion of Canada, was a direct response to the perceived threats posed by the Fenian Raids and the growing vulnerability of Canada's fragmented colonies. A united Canada would not only have more resources to defend itself but could also establish a more effective military and political structure to deal with potential threats. The Fenians, while not a significant military threat, forced Canada's leaders to realize that self-governance and unity were essential to the country's survival in a changing world.

Britain's shifting priorities also played a crucial role in Canada's path toward self-governance. After the Napoleonic Wars and with the end of the U.S. Civil War, Britain began to reevaluate its colonial holdings, particularly in North America. The British Empire had already begun a process of gradual decolonization, reducing the costs of maintaining far-flung territories, and it increasingly shifted its focus toward India and the empire's economic interests in Asia. The costs of defending

Canada—both financially and militarily—were becoming untenable, and Britain no longer saw Canada as a critical part of its global strategy.

As a result, Britain began to push for more self-governance in its North American colonies. British leaders wanted to reduce military expenditures and were increasingly reluctant to keep large garrisons in Canada. The Fenian Raids highlighted Canada's vulnerability, but Britain was no longer willing to provide military protection at the level it had in the past. The British government was more inclined to focus on maintaining control over its imperial interests, particularly in India, where British rule was under more direct threat due to growing resistance movements. This shift in priorities meant that Canada could no longer rely on Britain's military support and would have to look to its own defenses.

In response, Canadian leaders began to push for self-governance as a way to secure their own defense and economic future. The British North America Act of 1867, which created the Dominion of Canada, marked the first step in Canada's journey toward full self-governance. While Canada remained part of the British Empire, this act granted it the power to govern itself domestically, control its defense, and make decisions independently of Britain. This was a defensive measure designed to ensure that Canada could protect itself from external threats, like the Fenians, without relying on Britain's resources.

Ultimately, the Fenian Raids and Britain's shift in priorities forced Canada to confront the reality that its future lay in self-governance and unity. The raids made it clear that a fragmented colonial system would not be able to defend Canada against external threats. As a result, the move toward Confederation and the creation of a unified, self-governing Canada was not just a response to the Fenians but also a recognition that the country needed to be more self-sufficient, both politically and militarily, especially as Britain began to reduce its direct involvement in North America.

The political mood in Washington regarding Canada in the years following the Civil War was mixed but increasingly characterized by a renewed sense of expansionist ambition. While there were some serious political figures who openly advocated for the annexation of Canada, these voices were not yet mainstream, and much of the rhetoric around expansion was more about regional pride and nationalist sentiment than concrete policy. The prevailing mood in Washington was a mix of economic optimism, post-war euphoria, and a desire to further assert U.S. dominance on the continent. The U.S. was already emerging as a global economic power, and for many Americans, it was not a matter of whether the country should expand, but when and how.

In the immediate aftermath of the Civil War, there was a notable shift in focus toward territorial consolidation, especially in the West. Politicians, particularly Republicans, who had won the war, were interested in securing the economic and political future of the nation. Manifest Destiny had evolved into an economic ideology, with more interest in the potential of the American West and the Pacific Ocean than in annexing Canadian territory. Despite this, there were prominent figures, including Secretary of State William H. Seward, who pushed for a more aggressive U.S. stance toward British North America. Seward and others believed that the U.S. should use its growing strength to absorb Canada, especially as British influence waned in the region. Seward even entertained the idea of directly annexing British Columbia after the U.S. had successfully purchased Alaska in 1867.

However, these annexationist plans were never fully developed into serious action, and the rhetoric surrounding the annexation of Canada was often more symbolic than practical. Political realities—such as the complexity of dealing with Canada's diverse population, its already established systems of governance, and the risk of sparking a broader international conflict—made actual annexation highly unlikely. Instead, the rhetoric of expansion served more to inflame nationalist pride and project a sense of American destiny than to drive actual policy changes.

Canada, on the other hand, had its own pressing concerns that accelerated the process of Confederation. By the mid-19th century, it became clear that the British colonial system was no longer a sustainable model for North America. Britain had grown increasingly disengaged from its North American colonies, especially after the War of 1812, when the limits of British power in the region had been exposed. The Fenian Raids (1866-1871), though relatively small in scale, were a wake-up call for Canadian leaders. They demonstrated that the colonies were vulnerable to attacks from the United States and that relying on Britain for defense would no longer be viable in the long term.

Confederation was rushed in part because the British government had little appetite for continuing to defend and subsidize its North American colonies. The cost of maintaining a military presence in Canada was becoming more burdensome, and Britain was shifting its focus to other parts of the world, particularly India and Africa. As a result, Britain encouraged the colonies to form a union and take more control over their own defense and governance, while still maintaining a nominal connection to the British Empire.

Canadian leaders, especially in Upper Canada (Ontario) and the Maritime colonies, were also motivated by the need for economic stability and unity. The economic challenges of the individual colonies—coupled with the fear of U.S. expansionism—led to a desire for a stronger, more coordinated political system that could defend against both internal and external threats. By creating the Dominion of Canada in 1867, the colonies were able to form a united defense force, coordinate economic policies, and address many of the political tensions that had existed between them, particularly between English-speaking Ontario and French-speaking Quebec.

The rush for Confederation was not simply about American threat, but also about internal stability. The British North America Act of 1867 was an attempt to address longstanding political divisions, economic challenges, and security concerns. The Act created a self-governing federation that provided more control over domestic affairs while still preserving links to the British Empire. In short, it was a defensive measure against both American expansionism and the growing sense of Canada's need to govern itself independently.

In sum, while there was some serious annexationist sentiment in Washington, the U.S. never took any meaningful action toward annexing Canada, largely because of the political and logistical obstacles involved. Instead, expansionist rhetoric festered, but it did not translate into concrete action. On the Canadian side, the Fenian Raids, British disengagement, and internal pressures led to the formation of a unified Canada that could better defend itself and ensure its long-term security, laying the foundation for a more self-sufficient future.

British and Canadian Strategies to Resist American Economic and Military Dominance

The creation of Canada in 1867 was, in many ways, a complex balance between sovereignty and a strategic buffer against American expansionism. While the formation of the Dominion of Canada can be seen as a assertion of Canadian sovereignty, it was undeniably shaped by the broader geopolitical realities of the time—particularly the growing threat posed by the United States and its territorial ambitions following the Civil War.

On one hand, the British North America Act of 1867, which established the Dominion of Canada, marked a significant step toward Canadian sovereignty. For the first time, the provinces of Ontario, Quebec, New Brunswick, and Nova Scotia united under a single federal structure, with a degree of self-governance over domestic affairs and the ability to manage their own military and economic policies. This was a clear break from the previous colonial system, where Canada was governed directly by Britain, with British-appointed governors and limited local representation. The Act granted Canada control over most of its internal matters, leaving foreign affairs, defense, and constitutional changes under British authority, though these powers would later be relinquished. In this sense, the creation of Canada was an act of sovereignty, reflecting the growing desire among Canadian leaders to chart their own course.

However, this push for sovereignty was also closely linked to the need for security and stability in the face of external threats—primarily the United States. Following the U.S. victory in the Civil War, the U.S. had emerged as a dominant continental power, and many American leaders continued to harbor expansionist ambitions, especially toward British North America. The Fenian Raids (1866-1871), while relatively minor, demonstrated the vulnerability of Canada to U.S.-backed incursions. The American expansionist rhetoric that persisted after the Civil War—embodied in the desire to annex Canada—reinforced the need for a unified Canadian defense. By creating a federation of colonies, Canada could present a united front against potential American aggression.

For Britain, the creation of Canada served as a practical response to the costs of maintaining its colonial empire, particularly in North America. While Britain had no intention of abandoning its Canadian colonies outright, it was increasingly unwilling to spend the resources necessary to defend them against a growing and increasingly powerful United States. The push for Canadian Confederation can be viewed as a compromise: it allowed Canada to govern itself domestically, thus easing Britain's financial burden, while Britain retained control over foreign policy and defense in the short term. This arrangement made sense from a British perspective because a unified Canada would be better equipped to defend itself, making British intervention less likely and ultimately unnecessary. So, while the British allowed for greater self-governance, they also saw the formation of Canada as an act of prudence, ensuring the stability of their remaining North American colonies without having to invest in their defense.

Ultimately, Canada's formation in 1867 was driven by both a desire for greater self-determination and a pragmatic recognition of its need for security. It was an act of sovereignty, but one that was inextricably tied to the strategic reality of American territorial ambitions. The creation of Canada was as much about securing the nation from external threats, particularly from the United States, as it was about building a system of governance that could chart an independent path. Thus, while it was a step toward sovereignty, it was also a strategic decision aimed at protecting Canada's future in a rapidly changing geopolitical landscape.

British military assets and defense strategies in Canada were essential to maintaining British control over the colony and deterring American aggression. Throughout the 19th century, Britain understood that Canada's geographic position made it vulnerable to U.S. expansion, especially after the War of 1812, which had proven that American territorial ambitions toward Canada were very real. To defend Canada, the British established strategic fortifications, deployed significant military forces, and maintained naval dominance in key regions, all while fostering strong alliances with Indigenous nations as a buffer against American encroachment.

Key military installations like the fortifications at Quebec, Kingston, and Halifax played a crucial role in the defense strategy. Quebec, as the capital of Lower Canada, was heavily fortified with stone walls and reinforced after the War of 1812 to protect it from potential American assaults. Kingston, strategically located on the St. Lawrence River and near the Great Lakes, was also fortified, with British troops stationed there to control the region and ensure secure shipping routes. Halifax, as a major British naval port, provided the British with the ability to quickly deploy reinforcements and maintain control of the eastern seaboard, making it a key part of the defense strategy.

The British also relied on the presence of regular troops stationed throughout Canada. These troops were deployed at key points along the U.S. border and in areas vulnerable to attack. In addition to this, the British maintained a naval presence in Canadian waters, particularly in Halifax, which provided significant protection against American naval incursions. The Royal Navy's dominance in the Atlantic and along the St. Lawrence River allowed Britain to ensure Canadian defense and prevent U.S. expansion into these critical regions. The British were also able to deploy reinforcements quickly, maintaining control of the waters and securing Canada's trade routes and communications with Britain.

Another key aspect of the British defense strategy was their relationship with Indigenous nations. The British recognized the strategic value of these alliances, particularly in the western and frontier regions. During the War of 1812, British forces worked closely with Indigenous groups, including Tecumseh's Confederacy, to resist American invasions. Indigenous fighters played an instrumental role in disrupting American supply lines, providing crucial intelligence, and engaging in guerrilla tactics that slowed down American forces. After the war, the British continued to support Indigenous allies, ensuring that these groups remained a crucial part of the defense against U.S. expansion into Canada. British promises to protect Indigenous lands and culture from American settlers helped solidify these alliances and create a buffer against American territorial ambitions.

Together, these military strategies formed a robust defense system that, at the time, helped prevent the United States from easily overtaking Canadian territories. However, as Britain's imperial priorities shifted toward its interests in India and other parts of the world, it became increasingly clear that Canada could not rely on Britain indefinitely for military defense. This, combined with the growing sense of Canadian identity and the pressures of internal economic and political challenges, contributed to the movement toward Confederation in 1867, where Canada began taking on more responsibility for its own defense and governance. This shift marked the beginning of Canada's transition toward greater autonomy, with military and strategic decisions increasingly in the hands of Canadian leaders rather than British authorities. Despite the British military's vital role in defending Canada against American expansion during the 19th century, the creation of Canada as a self-governing entity was, in many ways, a natural progression toward sovereignty, shaped by both external threats and internal aspirations for greater control over its future.

Britain's economic policies in the 19th century played a key role in preventing Canada from becoming a satellite state of the United States. By maintaining preferential trade relationships, investing in key infrastructure, and providing military subsidies, Britain helped Canada develop its own economic and political identity, independent from U.S. influence. These strategies allowed Canada to maintain a measure of autonomy while still being tied to Britain within the broader imperial system.

One of the most significant ways Britain shielded Canada from becoming a U.S. satellite was through preferential trade policies. Canada's economy was deeply intertwined with Britain's, and the British government ensured that Canadian goods had access to British markets at favorable terms. The Navigation Acts and later policies allowed Canada to trade more easily with Britain than with any other country, which helped protect Canadian industries from the growing economic power of the United States. While the U.S. had a burgeoning economy with rapidly increasing industrialization, Canada's dependence on British markets allowed it to avoid becoming economically absorbed into the U.S. sphere. British trade preferences meant that Canada could maintain a measure of economic independence, limiting the pressure to integrate fully with the U.S. economy.

In addition to preferential trade policies, Britain also invested heavily in infrastructure projects, particularly railroads, which helped Canada avoid total reliance on American capital. The British government saw the importance of developing Canadian infrastructure as a way to ensure that Canada could maintain internal cohesion and resist American economic dominance. British investments in railroad construction—like the Canadian Pacific Railway, which was partially funded by British investors—allowed Canada to better connect its vast territories, from the Atlantic to the Pacific. This network of railways promoted economic independence by facilitating internal trade and linking Canadian markets without relying on U.S. infrastructure. Additionally, the railroad projects helped Canada consolidate its territories, making it harder for the U.S. to impose economic control over the region. British investments in Canadian industry, particularly in mining and natural resource extraction, also ensured that Canada developed its own economic strength, countering any pressure from American capital.

Britain also provided military subsidies to Canada, ensuring that it remained under British strategic control. After the War of 1812, British forces in Canada were significantly reduced, but Britain continued to provide funds for the defense of Canada. These military subsidies helped Canada maintain its military readiness and defend against potential U.S. expansionist ambitions. Canada's defense, at least initially, relied heavily on British military support, which kept U.S. military influence at bay. As Britain's global interests shifted, particularly with the end of the Napoleonic Wars, Britain maintained a military presence in Canada and offered defense subsidies as a way to ensure Canadian security against U.S. aggression. By the mid-19th century, as the U.S. became an increasingly powerful neighbor, the British government worked to ensure that Canada could defend itself militarily, rather than risk its economic and political absorption by the U.S.

Together, these British policies helped Canada build an economic and political foundation that was distinct from the United States. The preferential trade agreements prevented Canada from becoming too dependent on U.S. markets, while British investments in infrastructure and industry kept Canadian economic growth within a sphere of influence that was not dominated by American capital. Finally, military subsidies and defense strategies ensured that Canada had the ability to defend its sovereignty from American expansionism. Ultimately, these policies provided Canada with the tools to preserve its independence and avoid becoming a satellite state of the United States, even as American economic and military power grew.

Canadian leaders like John A. Macdonald, George-Étienne Cartier, and George Brown saw Confederation as a necessary step to secure Canadian autonomy and protect their young nation from the growing influence of the United States. The idea was to create a stronger, more unified political entity that could stand as a buffer against American expansionism, which had been an ongoing threat since the War of 1812. These leaders framed Confederation not just as a way to consolidate political power but as a strategic defense against U.S. territorial ambitions.

John A. Macdonald, Canada's first prime minister, played a central role in the movement toward Confederation. He was keenly aware of the U.S. expansionist mindset, which had been emboldened after the Civil War. Macdonald believed that a unified Canada would be better able to defend itself against the U.S. and would give the British Empire a stronger foothold in North America. He viewed Confederation as a way to strengthen the Canadian colonies' defenses, both militarily and economically. Macdonald was concerned that the growing U.S. influence would destabilize Canada, and that without unification, the provinces would remain vulnerable to American annexation. By bringing together the colonies into a single, self-governing federation, he could ensure a cohesive defense system, making it harder for the U.S. to divide and conquer. Macdonald and his supporters also feared the possibility of American-backed separatism in regions like Quebec and the Maritimes, which could weaken the overall structure and make Canada more susceptible to U.S. influence.

George-Étienne Cartier, a key political figure from Quebec, supported Confederation as a way to protect French-Canadian identity and ensure the continued influence of French Canadians within a new Canadian framework. Cartier framed Confederation as a way to create a stronger, more secure Canada that could resist the cultural assimilation pressures that often came with U.S. expansionism. He believed that a unified Canada would provide a political and military safeguard for French Canadians, protecting them from the fate of being absorbed into the American melting pot, which he feared would happen if Canada remained divided and weaker. Confederation, in his view, was an insurance policy against potential threats from the U.S., allowing

French-Canadians to preserve their distinct culture, religion, and language in a federal system where they would be a powerful minority.

George Brown, a prominent reformer from Ontario, viewed Confederation as a means to protect Canadian interests from U.S. dominance by fostering a more inclusive, democratic political system that would unite the colonies against external threats. Brown was particularly concerned with the threat of U.S. annexation and saw the need for a stronger federal government to better manage the growing political and economic pressures from the U.S. He believed that by forming a more centralized government, Canada could better coordinate defense efforts, manage trade relations, and leverage its resources to ensure it would not be absorbed into the U.S. like some of the smaller neighboring regions had been. Brown's vision of Confederation was one of nation-building, where Canadian prosperity and independence would be protected through the cooperation of provinces, rather than by relying on Britain, whose military presence in North America was increasingly limited.

Together, these leaders used the U.S. threat as a rallying cry for Confederation. They framed it not just as a political or economic necessity, but as a national survival strategy. They argued that Canada needed to act quickly to avoid becoming a satellite of the United States or even a target for annexation. The idea of a united Canada—with a common defense strategy, shared economic policies, and stronger internal governance—was seen as a way to fend off U.S. influence and establish a distinct Canadian identity. The success of Confederation in 1867, they believed, would solidify Canada's place in North America as a strong and independent nation, capable of standing its ground against the United States.

The Canadian Pacific Railway (CPR), completed in 1885, was a vital tool in unifying Canada both physically and economically, while also serving as a strategic response to U.S. economic influence and expansionism. The construction of the CPR was not just about improving transportation; it was about ensuring Canada's sovereignty, consolidating its national identity, and integrating its vast territories into a cohesive whole, making it much harder for the United States to exert control over Canadian lands or exploit its resources.

From a geopolitical perspective, the CPR was crucial in binding the western provinces—particularly British Columbia—to the Canadian Confederation. British Columbia had been initially hesitant to join Canada, primarily due to concerns over the lack of access to markets and trade routes. The promise of a transcontinental railway was the key concession made by Ottawa to convince British Columbia to join the Confederation in 1871. Without this railway, the provinces of British Columbia and the rest of Canada would have remained more isolated, and the western part of the country could have been more vulnerable to U.S. economic and territorial influence. The CPR effectively united the eastern parts of Canada with the western territories, creating a transcontinental connection that integrated the entire nation, from coast to coast, both economically and politically.

The CPR was strategically designed to address the economic pressures posed by the United States. The U.S. had long been Canada's largest trading partner, and the growing economic dominance of the U.S. presented a significant risk to Canadian economic independence. Before the railway, Canada's western territories were largely cut off from the central Canadian markets and the eastern seaboard. The railway allowed for efficient trade between the West and the East, reducing reliance on American markets and making Canada's internal trade more self-sufficient. This internal trade system was essential to counteracting American economic pressures by providing Canada with a viable alternative to U.S. markets.

The CPR also had defense and strategic value. In the 19th century, the United States was seen as a growing threat due to its Manifest Destiny ambitions and territorial expansion. The railway helped solidify Canadian sovereignty over its western lands, which were viewed by many as a buffer against potential U.S. encroachment. In particular, the railway made it much easier for Canada to move troops, resources, and supplies across the country in the event of a military conflict with the U.S. It essentially reinforced Canada's territorial integrity by ensuring that Canada's vast land mass was logistically connected, making it far more difficult for any foreign power to divide or isolate parts of the country. This strategic infrastructure gave Canada a greater sense of control over its national defense and security.

Economically, the CPR spurred Canadian industrialization. As the railway extended across the country, it facilitated the transportation of Canadian goods to market, increasing the export of Canadian natural resources like timber, wheat, and minerals. This allowed Canada to build a stronger, self-sustaining economy that wasn't entirely dependent on the U.S. for trade. It also helped to develop Canadian industries that were previously underdeveloped in the western provinces, promoting economic diversification. The CPR was integral to the growth of Canadian cities, like Winnipeg, Calgary, and Vancouver, which became key economic centers along the transcontinental route. This economic independence further reduced Canada's reliance on U.S. trade routes and provided Canada with the ability to manage its own economy without being overly influenced by the American market.

In conclusion, the Canadian Pacific Railway was a strategic tool that served multiple functions: it physically connected Canada from coast to coast, making the country more unified; it served as an economic lifeline that reduced Canada's dependence on the U.S.; and it acted as a defense mechanism, ensuring that Canada could maintain control over its own land and resources, countering any U.S. ambitions for expansion into the Canadian West. The CPR was a critical piece of nation-building, protecting Canadian sovereignty, and ensuring that Canada could navigate the growing economic and political pressures from the United States in the 19th century.

Was Confederation a Victory for Sovereignty or Just a Temporary Delay?

Canada's Confederation in 1867 was not a straightforward move toward full independence, but it was certainly a key step in asserting its sovereignty and protecting itself from U.S. expansionism. While the Confederation wasn't a direct declaration of independence from Britain—Canada did not achieve full autonomy until the Statute of Westminster in 1931—it was a critical measure designed to ensure the country's survival in the face of growing American power and territorial ambitions.

At the time of Confederation, the United States was seen as a major threat to Canadian security, particularly after the U.S. Civil War and its subsequent expansionism. The U.S. had long viewed Canada as unfinished business, and many American leaders continued to entertain ideas of annexing Canada into the Union. The Fenian Raids (1866-1871), led by Irish-American militants seeking to use Canada as leverage for Irish independence, reinforced the vulnerability of the British North American colonies to U.S. aggression. The raids highlighted the fact that Canada's fragmented system of governance made it an easy target for military incursions and that the colonies were not equipped to defend themselves against the threat of annexation.

Confederation was, in many respects, a response to these external pressures. By uniting the colonies of Ontario, Quebec, New Brunswick, and Nova Scotia into a single political entity, the Canadian leaders were strengthening the country's defense capabilities, ensuring that it could present a unified front against the possibility of U.S. annexation. The idea was to create a stronger, more coordinated political and military system that could better defend against external threats and maintain some level of independence from the United States. The promise of a transcontinental railway (the CPR), which would connect the Canadian colonies from coast to coast, was one of the central components of this defense strategy, as it would make it much more difficult for the U.S. to divide the country or seize land in the West.

Though Britain remained responsible for Canada's foreign policy and military defense for several more decades, Confederation was a clear step toward greater self-governance. The British government was increasingly uninterested in defending its North American colonies and wanted to reduce its financial burden in the region. In that sense, Confederation can also be seen as a strategic measure to align with Britain's shifting priorities. Britain was focused on maintaining its empire, but in an era of decolonization, it was also eager to relinquish control over its distant colonies that were increasingly capable of governing themselves. Britain's withdrawal from active involvement in North American defense meant that Canada had to take on more responsibility for its own protection—making Confederation a necessity.

However, it would be incorrect to say that Confederation was purely a last-ditch effort to stall U.S. annexation. The leaders who championed Confederation, such as John A. Macdonald, George-Étienne Cartier, and George Brown, were motivated by more than just external threats. They were also focused on building a stronger, more unified political system that would facilitate economic growth, allow for better governance, and create a more cohesive national identity. They saw the opportunity to build a country that was more than just a collection of colonies but a federation capable of managing its own affairs and standing up to external pressures.

That being said, U.S. annexation remained a very real concern, and many of the leaders involved in Confederation believed that a unified Canada was essential to keeping the United States at bay. Economic integration with the U.S. had already begun before Confederation, but these leaders understood that economic dependency alone would not be enough to maintain Canadian independence. They knew that military strength, political cohesion, and control over domestic and foreign policy would be necessary to prevent Canada from being absorbed into the U.S. over time.

In the years following Confederation, Canada's path to full independence was a gradual one. The country continued to grow economically and expand its territory westward, but it was still largely tied to Britain for matters of defense and foreign policy. It wasn't until the Statute of Westminster in 1931 that Canada was granted full legal autonomy, and only with the passage of the Constitution Act of 1982 did Canada gain complete control over its constitution, severing the final legal ties to Britain.

The fear of American dominance has been a defining factor in shaping Canada's national identity and policies for much of its history, particularly through the 20th century. From the outset of Confederation in 1867, Canadian leaders understood that the United States posed a significant threat to their sovereignty. Though military annexation was the immediate concern, the long-term impact of U.S. economic and cultural influence was just as critical. This constant fear of losing political independence spurred Canada's political development and helped define its identity as distinct from the U.S.

From the late 19th century onwards, Canada's leaders took conscious steps to ensure that their country did not fall into the economic or political orbit of the United States. The formation of the Canadian Pacific Railway, the creation of a unified defense strategy, and the push for self-governance all stemmed from a desire to prevent U.S. influence from overshadowing Canada. The need for a strong, independent identity became a cornerstone of Canadian national pride, and this sense of distinctiveness played a major role in keeping Canada separate from American cultural and political spheres. Canada increasingly defined itself not just by its ties to Britain but by its resistance to the assimilationist pressures of U.S. expansionism.

However, while Canada successfully resisted direct annexation, the U.S. did not abandon its ambitions. Instead, it shifted tactics, moving from military conquest to economic assimilation. Over time, the United States became the dominant economic force in North America. Canada's economic dependence on the U.S. grew, especially after the Civil War, as trade, capital investments, and industrial developments increasingly tied Canadian markets to American demand. The U.S. was deeply involved in Canadian industries, particularly resource extraction, and the demand for Canadian raw materials ensured that American economic influence continued to expand.

The transition from military expansion to economic dominance allowed the U.S. to exercise a different form of control over Canada. While Canada was never annexed, economic integration made the relationship between the two countries deeply interdependent. Canada's growing reliance on U.S. capital and markets shifted the balance of power, making economic decisions and cultural influences increasingly shaped by American interests. Though this assimilation was not as overt as military conquest, it has had a lasting impact on Canada's ability to control its own economic policies.

Thus, Canada's national identity has been shaped by a continuous struggle to maintain sovereignty in the face of economic pressure, all while resisting the cultural and political pull of the United States. Even today, Canada remains closely linked to the U.S. economically, but its leaders have continued to balance this relationship with efforts to preserve its independence, often through multilateral agreements, cultural distinctiveness, and political autonomy. While the U.S. may have shifted away from annexation and toward economic assimilation, the core issue for Canada remains the same: preserving its sovereignty and independence in the face of an ever-present neighbor.

Part II: Economic Warfare

Part II: Economic Warfare – The Slow Merger of the U.S. and Canada

6

Chapter 5: The Reciprocity Treaties

The Reciprocity Treaties – The First Economic Handcuffs

1854: The First Trade Deal That Made Canada Dependent on American Markets

As Britain's interest in its North American colonies began to wane in the mid-19th century, Canada found itself at a crossroads. With Britain focusing more on its imperial priorities elsewhere, particularly in Asia and Africa, and reducing its military and economic commitments to Canada, the colonies were left to confront a growing economic dependency on the United States. The British Empire, dealing with its own financial pressures and strategic realignments, became less inclined to subsidize its North American holdings. This shift meant that Canada had to find new ways to ensure its economic viability and security. As a result, Canada increasingly sought closer economic ties with the U.S.—an inevitable move given the geographic proximity and overwhelming economic power of its southern neighbor.

One of the most significant steps toward this economic integration was the Reciprocity Treaty of 1854. This agreement between the United States and the British North American colonies (primarily Canada) was designed to facilitate trade between the two regions by removing tariffs on a wide range of goods—including raw materials such as timber, fish, and grain. The treaty was a mutual economic benefit; the U.S. gained access to important Canadian resources, while Canada could sell its goods to the U.S. without the usual trade restrictions.

Canada's agreement to the treaty was motivated by several factors. First and foremost, Canada faced economic isolation from Britain. With Britain gradually reducing its role in the defense and economic affairs of the colonies, Canada was left with little choice but to turn to the U.S. to maintain its economic growth. The Reciprocity Treaty allowed Canada to tap into American markets, which were expanding rapidly as the U.S. industrialized and needed access to natural resources. For Canada, it was a way to reduce its dependence on Britain and bolster its own economy by benefiting from the burgeoning U.S. economy.

Additionally, the treaty provided Canada with a degree of protection from the economic encroachment of the U.S. while still maintaining a cooperative relationship. By aligning itself more closely with the U.S., Canada could avoid the risks of being completely economically absorbed or bypassed by American trade. The treaty helped to integrate Canadian agriculture and resource industries into the American market, strengthening Canada's economic position on the continent.

From Britain's perspective, the treaty was a pragmatic move. British North America was increasingly seen as an economic burden, and Britain was looking for ways to reduce its commitments to the colonies while still maintaining their loyalty. By allowing Canada to enter into trade agreements with the U.S., Britain could maintain some degree of economic influence in the region while slowly shifting the responsibility for the colonies onto the colonies themselves.

In summary, as Britain's economic focus shifted away from North America, Canada had no choice but to seek closer economic ties with the U.S. The 1854 Reciprocity Treaty was a direct response to this new reality, allowing Canada to increase its economic interdependence with the United States while still maintaining some degree of control over its own resources. It was a pragmatic response to the declining British commitment to its North American colonies, and it laid the groundwork for a future relationship between Canada and the U.S. that would continue to evolve over the following decades.

American policymakers viewed the Reciprocity Treaty of 1854 as more than just a trade agreement—it was framed as a step toward economic annexation, a means to deepen U.S. economic dominance over Canada. While the treaty was officially a trade agreement between the British North American colonies (primarily Canada) and the United States, it provided the U.S. with preferential access to Canadian resources, significantly strengthening the ties between the two economies. American leaders saw the treaty as a way to integrate Canadian markets into the U.S. economy, weakening the Canadian reliance on Britain and making it more difficult for Canada to resist full economic integration with the United States in the future.

For American policymakers, the treaty was part of a broader vision to expand U.S. influence in the Western Hemisphere. With the doctrine of Manifest Destiny still influencing American politics, there was a strong belief that the U.S. should dominate the continent economically, politically, and, in some cases, territorially. The Reciprocity Treaty allowed the U.S. to secure access to Canadian resources—such as timber, grain, and fish—while giving American industries a crucial economic foothold in Canada. By creating this interdependent trade relationship, the U.S. could effectively use its economic power to make Canadian businesses reliant on American markets, eventually pushing Canada into a position where it would have little choice but to align its policies with U.S. economic interests.

This shift in trade dynamics had profound effects on Canadian industries, particularly in agriculture, mining, and manufacturing. Canadian businesses, which had previously relied on British markets, began to shift their focus toward the U.S., where there was greater demand for raw materials as the U.S. economy rapidly industrialized. The Reciprocity Treaty provided Canadian businesses with direct access to a growing and more affluent market, leading many to view the United States as a more reliable and lucrative partner than Britain. For Canadian industries, especially those in the natural resource sector, it made economic sense to cater to U.S. demand, as it provided them with a larger and more stable consumer base.

The treaty encouraged Canadian industries to invest in infrastructure—such as railways and port facilities—that would better connect Canadian businesses to U.S. buyers. The construction of the Canadian Pacific Railway, for example, was driven in part by the need to facilitate trade with the U.S. and to ensure that Canadian goods could be efficiently transported to U.S. markets. Over time, this focus on trade with the U.S. deepened Canada's economic reliance on its southern neighbor, making it increasingly difficult for Canada to maintain its previous economic relationships with Britain. Canadian agricultural exports, such as grain, timber, and furs, became more directly integrated into the American economic system. Meanwhile, Canada's manufacturing sector also started to align more closely with American production, as U.S. companies became major investors in Canadian industries.

This growing dependence on American markets came with significant political and economic consequences. As Canadian businesses became more reliant on U.S. buyers, they increasingly had to adapt to American pricing structures, trade policies, and industry standards. Over time, this reliance made it harder for Canada to resist American economic influence, and it was increasingly difficult for Canada to turn to Britain for economic or political support when it had so thoroughly integrated itself into the American economic sphere.

The economic entanglement with the U.S. thus made Canada more vulnerable to U.S. political pressure, even as it formally maintained ties with Britain. As American influence expanded through these economic ties, Canada's political leaders recognized the growing reality that their economy was becoming inextricably linked to that of the United States, making them more receptive to the idea of eventual political integration, though this was not yet openly discussed at the time. Ultimately, the

Reciprocity Treaty and the economic shifts it triggered contributed to Canada's increasing economic and political autonomy from Britain, as Canada's future seemed more tied to its growing relationship with the United States.

The Reciprocity Treaty of 1854, while beneficial in the short term by opening American markets to Canadian goods, ultimately undermined Canada's negotiating power in later trade disputes. The treaty created a one-sided dependence, where Canada became increasingly reliant on the U.S. market for its raw materials, agricultural products, and resources, while the U.S. benefited from easy access to Canadian goods with minimal barriers. Over time, this economic asymmetry meant that Canada had less leverage in subsequent negotiations with the U.S., as its reliance on American markets made it more vulnerable to U.S. trade policies and demands.

When the Reciprocity Treaty was abrogated in 1866, largely due to American political pressure and changing domestic priorities, Canada found itself in a much weaker position. Canada had tied its economic fortunes to the U.S., and when the treaty ended, Canada could no longer rely on the same trade privileges. Without the preferential trade access to the U.S., Canadian industries, especially in the resource and agricultural sectors, faced new tariffs and barriers that made it harder for them to compete in American markets. This shift caused Canadian businesses to seek new trade arrangements, but it also exposed the extent to which Canada had allowed itself to become economically integrated into the U.S. system, leaving it with limited options for retaliation or alternative markets.

In the aftermath of the treaty's cancellation, Canada was at a disadvantage in future trade negotiations. The U.S. knew that Canada had few viable alternatives to American markets, and the prospect of losing access to U.S. markets was a significant threat to the Canadian economy. This made it difficult for Canada to leverage its position when seeking new trade agreements or defending its economic interests, as the U.S. held a strong economic position over Canada. Canada's over-reliance on the U.S. market meant that it had little room to maneuver, particularly when it came to negotiating favorable terms for Canadian industries.

Additionally, the loss of the Reciprocity Treaty highlighted Canada's vulnerability to U.S. economic pressures, a dynamic that persisted throughout the 20th century. The Treaty's cancellation and the subsequent economic fallout forced Canada to seek new arrangements, but the process of transitioning away from the U.S. economic sphere took time and careful negotiation. Even in the face of new trade pacts like the Canada-U.S. Free Trade Agreement (1989) and the North American Free Trade Agreement (NAFTA) in the 1990s, the historical precedent set by the Reciprocity Treaty meant that Canada's economic dependence on the U.S. remained a significant factor in its foreign policy, often limiting its negotiating power and making it difficult to strike independent trade deals without accommodating U.S. interests.

In summary, the Reciprocity Treaty ultimately weakened Canada's negotiating power by making its economy overly dependent on the U.S. This dependence left Canada vulnerable to economic and political pressure, especially when the treaty was dissolved in 1866. The economic ties created by the treaty left Canada with few alternatives to the U.S. market, leading to a loss of leverage in future trade disputes and negotiations, and contributing to Canada's continued economic integration into the American sphere of influence.

How Economic Integration Has Been the Primary Weapon in America's Annexationist Strategy

American politicians and economists did begin to recognize over time that economic control was a more effective and less costly means of expanding influence than military conquest. While early American expansionist rhetoric was heavily focused on territorial acquisition—often under the banner of Manifest Destiny—by the late 19th and early 20th centuries, the realization set in that economic domination could achieve many of the same goals without the need for military intervention. This shift was largely due to the rapid industrialization of the U.S., its growing economic might, and the realization that control over trade, investment, and markets could integrate Canada into the U.S. economic system in ways that military conquest could not.

Rather than invading Canada or seeking annexation through force, American policymakers and businessmen saw the potential for economic assimilation. The idea of economic imperialism—where U.S. businesses and investors could exert significant influence over Canadian industries, resources, and markets—became a dominant strategy. This approach was much more subtle, less overtly confrontational, and ultimately just as effective at tying Canada's economy to the U.S., making it increasingly difficult for Canada to remain fully independent in its economic policies.

U.S. businesses and investors gained disproportionate influence over Canadian industry through several key channels, particularly capital investment, trade agreements, and infrastructure development. By the time the Reciprocity Treaty of 1854 had been enacted, American companies were already beginning to flood Canadian markets with their goods and investments, particularly in resource extraction and railroad construction. With the expansion of the U.S. economy, American businesses sought to find new markets and cheap sources of raw materials. Canada, with its vast natural resources and proximity, became an ideal partner, but more importantly, it became a target for investment.

American capital poured into Canada's industries, especially in mining, forestry, and railroads. For example, U.S. financiers helped build the Canadian Pacific Railway, which was central to the unification of the country, but also tied the Canadian economy more closely to the U.S. economy. American investors were able to gain significant control over Canadian rail networks and mining operations, ensuring that Canadian industries were increasingly dependent on U.S. capital. As American businesses bought up key Canadian industries and established dominating positions in mining, forestry, and agriculture, they were able to set prices, control production, and exert influence over Canadian labor markets and the broader economy.

Through the Reciprocity Treaty, American businesses also benefited from preferential access to Canadian markets, solidifying the economic interdependence of the two nations. The treaty eliminated tariffs on many goods, allowing American products to flood into Canada and making Canadian manufacturers reliant on American supplies and customers. This reinforced the ties between the two economies, making it harder for Canada to negotiate independently or shift away from American interests.

Furthermore, American banks and financial institutions took a leading role in financing Canadian growth. By providing loans to Canadian companies and municipalities, American investors were able to dictate terms of development. The resulting debt meant that Canada was often forced to align its economic policies with U.S. interests to maintain its ability to service loans and stay economically viable. The influence of American financial institutions became so entrenched that American economic priorities began to shape Canadian policy, particularly when it came to trade and industrial development.

In the 20th century, this influence only increased, as the U.S. solidified its position as Canada's largest trading partner and a major source of investment. Through a combination of investment capital, trade relationships, and control over infrastructure, U.S. businesses gained enormous leverage over Canadian industries, ensuring that even as Canada maintained political sovereignty, it could not escape the economic orbit of the United States.

Canadian trade policy, which was once firmly controlled by Britain, gradually shifted under the pressures of U.S. economic dominance, beginning in the 19th century. With Britain increasingly disengaging from its North American colonies, Canada found itself forced to adjust its economic policies, especially as the United States emerged as the dominant economic power in North America. Over time, U.S. economic pressures and market demands began to shape Canadian trade deci-sions, fundamentally altering the nature of its relationships with both Britain and the United States.

Initially, British trade policy governed Canada's economy. Under the Navigation Acts and other imperial policies, Canada's trade was largely directed toward Britain, with British merchants and manufacturers ben-efiting from Canadian resources and goods. Canada's economy was intricately tied to British markets, with its agricultural products, raw materials, and timber largely sold to Britain. However, by the mid-19th century, Britain's imperial focus began to shift, particularly after the Napoleonic Wars, and the costs of maintaining control over distant colonies began to outweigh the benefits. As a result, Britain gradually reduced its investment in Canada and loosened its grip on Canadian trade.

The Reciprocity Treaty of 1854 marked a pivotal moment in this transition. The treaty, which removed tariffs on many goods traded be-tween the U.S. and Canada, allowed for unrestricted access to Ameri-can markets for Canadian goods like timber, grain, fish, and coal. The treaty marked a shift away from British-controlled trade and deepened Canada's economic reliance on the United States. It was the beginning of a trend where U.S. economic power began to dictate Canadian trade policy. The terms of the treaty were heavily skewed in favor of the United States, as American industries gained access to Canadian re-sources at minimal cost, and Canada became more intertwined with the U.S. economic system. This shift meant that Canada's economic future was increasingly tied to the United States, and the country could no longer rely on Britain for its trade arrangements.

The Reciprocity Treaty created a pattern of economic dependency that has persisted into modern U.S.-Canada trade agreements. Al-though the treaty was terminated by the United States in 1866, the foundation it laid for U.S.-Canada trade relations remained. The eco-nomic interdependence fostered by the treaty remained intact, even as Canada sought to diversify its economic relationships. In the years following the treaty's cancellation, Canada was forced to seek new ways to maintain its access to U.S. markets, and this continued reliance on the United States influenced subsequent trade agreements.

The pattern established by the Reciprocity Treaty carried over into later agreements, such as the Canada-U.S. Free Trade Agreement (1989) and NAFTA (1994), which further cemented Canada's economic ties to the U.S. These modern agreements, much like the 1854 treaty, were primarily aimed at opening up Canadian markets to American products and ensuring Canadian businesses continued to rely on U.S. capital and investment. With each agreement, the U.S. gained more influence over Canadian trade, gradually dictating the terms of trade policies, even as Canada pursued its own interests.

The Reciprocity Treaty's legacy of economic integration helped Canada avoid the risk of total isolation from American markets, but it also made it increasingly difficult for Canada to develop an independent trade policy. U.S. businesses, investors, and policymakers saw Canada as an integral part of their economic system, and Canadian businesses, facing greater competition in global markets, found it hard to ignore the economic weight of the United States. By relying on U.S. markets and capital, Canada became more vulnerable to shifts in U.S. trade policy, particularly as American policymakers exerted more control over the trade agenda, making Canadian businesses increasingly dependent on U.S. buyers.

In conclusion, the Reciprocity Treaty of 1854 created a pattern of economic dependency that shaped the course of Canadian trade policy well into the modern era. While the treaty initially provided Canada with access to U.S. markets, it also tied the Canadian economy closely to that of the United States, leading to a shift in power where U.S. economic interests began to dominate Canada's trade policy. This pattern continued through subsequent agreements, which ensured that Canadian trade relations were increasingly dictated by the economic forces of its southern neighbor, leaving Canada with limited room to maneuver independently in the face of U.S. pressures.

U.S. investors gained significant influence over Canadian industries, particularly in banking, railroads, and manufacturing, through a combination of economic agreements and strategic investments that tied Canada's economy more closely to the United States. These investments and economic relationships not only reshaped Canadian industries but also set the stage for a gradual erosion of Canada's economic independence from the U.S. By the late 19th and early 20th centuries, American capital was deeply embedded in Canadian economic structures, often through agreements that opened Canadian markets and industries to U.S. influence.

In banking, U.S. investors began infiltrating Canadian financial institutions as early as the mid-1800s. The Reciprocity Treaty of 1854, which removed tariffs on many goods between the U.S. and Canada, was a key moment that opened the door for American financial institutions to extend their reach into Canada. Many U.S. banks started providing capital for Canadian businesses, gaining influence over Canadian industries by funding infrastructure projects, resource extraction, and agricultural expansion. As Canada's economy grew, particularly in the West, U.S. financial institutions played a critical role in the development of Canadian industries, often setting terms and controlling credit in ways that made Canadian businesses increasingly reliant on American capital. This economic dependency made it harder for Canada to resist U.S. economic policies and opened the door for further economic and political integration.

In the railroad sector, American investment was even more pronounced. The Canadian Pacific Railway (CPR), completed in 1885, was partly funded by U.S. capital, especially after American businessmen recognized the economic potential of a transcontinental rail system. American investors not only financed the construction of the CPR, but they also gained control over key railroad assets and routes, which enabled them to dominate the transportation of Canadian goods and resources. Railroad lines became critical in connecting Canadian industries to U.S. markets, ensuring that Canada's economic growth would be closely aligned with U.S. interests. By building the rail infrastructure that connected Canada's vast territory, American investors also laid the groundwork for economic integration that would make the U.S. the dominant player in Canadian trade and resource management.

American investors also infiltrated Canadian manufacturing industries. As Canada's natural resource economy grew, particularly in mining and forestry, American businesses began to buy up Canadian resource companies. U.S. corporations sought to control key sectors such as timber, minerals, and agriculture by either directly purchasing Canadian companies or establishing joint ventures. Through these investments, U.S. businesses were able to dictate the terms of production, pricing, and trade, making Canadian industries dependent on American markets for their goods. This economic dominance also led to American companies' control over Canadian industrial output, further reducing Canada's ability to pursue independent economic policies.

In terms of political integration, while there were no direct U.S. attempts to force annexation through military or political means in the late 19th and early 20th centuries, the use of economic leverage was a more subtle but powerful form of pressure. Economic dependency on the U.S. created a situation where Canada was increasingly influenced by American interests, even without formal political integration. American policymakers understood that if they controlled the economic levers of Canadian industries, they could exert significant influence over Canadian political decisions, particularly in areas such as trade policy, infrastructure development, and defense spending.

For example, during the Alaska Boundary Dispute of the late 19th century, the U.S. used its economic and political power to push Canada into accepting a settlement that favored American interests. The U.S. was able to leverage its economic importance to Canada, making it difficult for Canada to oppose U.S. demands in an era when American markets were crucial to Canadian businesses. Additionally, American financiers and industrialists used their economic influence to ensure that

Canada's political decisions increasingly aligned with U.S. economic interests, particularly in trade agreements and resource management.

While the U.S. did not push directly for political annexation, the economic integration of Canada into the U.S. sphere served to undermine Canada's autonomy. This ongoing economic influence made it increasingly difficult for Canadian leaders to chart an independent course, as American economic priorities dictated much of the economic activity in Canada. This trend continued into the 20th century, with NAFTA and other trade agreements further cementing the U.S. as Canada's dominant economic partner, making political and economic separation ever more difficult.

In conclusion, U.S. investors, through strategic economic agreements and investments, were able to infiltrate key Canadian industries, significantly increasing their economic influence over Canada. While there were no direct American attempts to use military force to politically annex Canada, economic pressure served as a subtle but highly effective method of ensuring that Canada's policies would align with American economic interests, effectively blurring the lines between economic control and political autonomy.

The Tariffs and Trade Wars That Pushed Canada Closer to the U.S.

The United States' decision to cancel the Reciprocity Treaty in 1866 was driven by several economic and political factors, marking a significant turning point in U.S.-Canada relations. After over a decade of enjoying the benefits of the treaty, which had allowed both the U.S. and Canada to trade freely across borders without tariffs on many goods, the United States opted to end the agreement due to changing political priorities and the belief that the treaty no longer served its strategic or economic interests.

One of the primary reasons for the cancellation was the shift in U.S. domestic politics following the Civil War. The U.S. government, especially under President Andrew Johnson, turned its focus inward, aiming to rebuild the country after the war and address issues like reconstruction and economic growth. By the time the treaty came up for renewal in 1866, there was a shift in American protectionist policies, as industrial growth in the U.S. created a desire to protect domestic industries. With tariffs being a tool to boost American manufacturing, policymakers saw the Reciprocity Treaty as an impediment to imposing protective tariffs that could help U.S. industries compete with foreign markets. The U.S. also felt that its economic strength had grown to the point where it no longer needed access to Canadian resources on favorable terms to maintain its growth.

The cancellation of the treaty marked a shift toward economic self-sufficiency and protectionism for the U.S., which was also influenced by the country's desire to assert control over its economic relationships in North America. In addition, many in the U.S. believed that Canada's growing economic ties with the United States were already significant enough, and the cancellation of the treaty was not expected to dramatically disrupt the flow of trade between the two countries. This reflected the U.S.'s confidence in its own economic power, with the belief that Canada was already too economically intertwined with the U.S. to resist American influence.

For Canada, the consequences of the cancellation were significant. The Reciprocity Treaty had been vital for Canadian access to the American market, especially for Canadian agricultural products, timber, and minerals. When the treaty was terminated, Canada lost free access to the U.S. market for many goods, forcing Canadian businesses to face new tariffs and trade barriers that undermined their competitive position in American markets. This put Canadian industries at a serious disadvantage, especially in areas like timber and agriculture, which were heavily dependent on U.S. buyers. Canadian exporters were suddenly vulnerable to the high tariffs the U.S. imposed on goods that had previously been traded freely under the treaty.

Faced with this challenge, Canada had to adjust its trade strategy and, for a time, deepened its economic ties with Britain. The British, recognizing the need to counterbalance U.S. influence, agreed to provide support for Canada's economic independence, including an emphasis on trade agreements and investment opportunities that would reduce Canada's reliance on the U.S. Britain sought to maintain its economic relationship with Canada to ensure that the colonies did not become completely absorbed into the U.S. sphere. During this period, the Canadian government sought to strengthen ties with Britain, particularly through reciprocal trade agreements that would offer preferential access to British markets and reduce the immediate economic pressure caused by the end of the Reciprocity Treaty.

However, this reliance on Britain was only temporary. Britain, increasingly focused on its imperial interests elsewhere, particularly in India and Africa, had little interest in maintaining the level of economic involvement that Canada required to compete with the United States. Over time, British economic support proved insufficient to counterbalance the growing dominance of U.S. economic power in North America. Canada's dependence on Britain for economic stability was only a temporary delay in the eventual dominance of the U.S., and it was only a matter of time before Canada would have to seek a more permanent solution to its economic relationship with the United States. This would eventually lead to the formation of new trade agreements, such as the Canada-U.S. Free Trade Agreement in the 20th century, which re-established strong economic ties between the two nations, though under more balanced terms.

In conclusion, the cancellation of the Reciprocity Treaty in 1866 fundamentally reshaped U.S.-Canada relations by forcing Canada to seek alternative economic partnerships, particularly with Britain, to mitigate the consequences of losing access to the U.S. market. The U.S. shifted from its initial policy of economic cooperation with Canada to one of economic self-interest and protectionism, leaving Canada to navigate its future without the same free access to American markets. Although the shift temporarily delayed American economic dominance, it also set the stage for the eventual deepening of economic ties between the U.S. and Canada, particularly in the context of the 20th-century global economy.

In 1879, John A. Macdonald's National Policy introduced a system of protective tariffs aimed at promoting Canadian economic independence, stimulating domestic industries, and reducing reliance on U.S. trade. At the time, Canada faced growing economic pressures from the United States, as the U.S. economy expanded rapidly and American industries sought to dominate Canadian markets. Macdonald's National Policy was designed to address these issues by using tariffs to protect Canadian manufacturers from cheaper American goods, foster economic growth in the country's industrial sectors, and promote a more self-sufficient Canadian economy.

The core goals of the National Policy included:

Protecting Canadian industries: By imposing high tariffs on imported goods, particularly manufactured goods, Canada could shield its emerging industries from the dominant American industrial sector. The goal was to encourage the growth of Canadian manufacturing by making imported goods more expensive, thus stimulating demand for domestically produced items.

Promoting westward expansion: A key part of Macdonald's plan was to build the Canadian Pacific Railway (CPR), which would connect Canada's eastern markets to the western frontier. The railway would not only open up new agricultural and resource-rich regions to development but also create a domestic market for Canadian goods.

Reducing Canadian dependency on the U.S.: By imposing tariffs on American goods, Macdonald hoped to reduce Canada's economic dependence on the United States, which had grown steadily after the cancellation of the Reciprocity Treaty in 1866. The tariff system was viewed as a way to weaken American economic control and foster stronger ties between Canadian provinces.

The success of the National Policy was mixed. On one hand, it helped foster the growth of Canadian industry, particularly in the manufacturing sector, by encouraging the production of goods that were previously imported from the U.S. Over time, industries like textiles, steel, and agriculture in Canada grew more robust, and many Canadian cities began to industrialize more rapidly. The construction of the Canadian Pacific Railway, which was funded in part by protective tariffs, played a critical role in integrating Canada's national economy and encouraging settlement in the West. Additionally, the policy helped establish a stronger sense of Canadian national identity, as it was seen as an effort to assert economic autonomy from the United States.

However, while the National Policy achieved some of its goals, it also provoked retaliatory measures from the United States, which had significant consequences for Canadian trade. U.S. politicians, particularly those in the industrial and manufacturing sectors, viewed the Canadian tariffs as an unfair trade barrier that undermined the benefits of previous trade agreements. In response to the National Policy, the U.S. imposed higher tariffs on Canadian goods, especially agricultural products like grain, which had previously been able to flow into U.S. markets with relative ease. This retaliatory move harmed Canada's ability to access the lucrative American market, particularly for agricultural exports. While Canada had hoped to shield its industries with the tariffs, the retaliation showed the extent to which Canada's economic relationship with the U.S. was deeply intertwined—and how difficult it was to make independent policy decisions without facing U.S. repercussions.

This cycle of retaliatory tariffs deepened the tension between the two countries and highlighted Canada's vulnerability to U.S. economic pressures. While the National Policy stimulated industrial growth within Canada, it also made clear that Canada's economic policy could not entirely escape U.S. influence. Over time, Canada was forced to negotiate new trade agreements with the U.S. in the 20th century, such as the Canada-U.S. Free Trade Agreement (1989) and NAFTA (1994), which would again reshape the economic relationship between the two nations.

In conclusion, Macdonald's National Policy was a significant step toward economic independence for Canada, but it also revealed the complexities of resisting U.S. economic control. While it promoted domestic industries and allowed for greater Canadian economic growth, it also provoked retaliatory U.S. tariffs, which highlighted the difficulties Canada faced in balancing protectionism with trade relationships. The policy's effectiveness was limited by the broader reality that Canada's economic fate was still heavily influenced by the economic power and market demands of the United States, and its efforts to reduce reliance on U.S. markets were met with significant challenges.

Over the course of the 19th and 20th centuries, major U.S. trade wars have played a significant role in shaping Canadian economic policy, forcing Canada into economic concessions and contributing to a pattern of increasing dependency on U.S. markets. From the Reciprocity Treaty in the 19th century to the North American Free Trade Agreement (NAFTA) in the 20th, the economic dynamics between the U.S. and Canada have consistently favored American economic interests.

One of the earliest and most impactful U.S. trade wars was the cancellation of the Reciprocity Treaty in 1866, which had given Canada preferential access to U.S. markets. In response to increased U.S. tariffs following the end of the treaty, Canada was forced to implement protective tariffs in an effort to shield its industries and maintain access to its own economic markets. However, the cancellation of the treaty was a significant blow, as it reduced Canada's market access to the United States, and Canadian exporters faced higher tariffs on goods entering the U.S. This forced Canada to not only raise its own tariffs but also to rely more on British trade. In the long term, the cancellation of the treaty only increased Canadian economic dependence on the U.S., as it made it harder for Canadian businesses to diversify their export markets and find alternative trading partners.

In the early 20th century, as U.S. industry expanded and American tariffs became more aggressive, Canadian industries were once again faced with economic pressure. The Smoot-Hawley Tariff Act of 1930, passed by the U.S. Congress, raised tariffs on a wide range of imported goods, including Canadian products. This tariff act led to a severe drop in Canadian exports to the U.S., forcing Canada to seek new trade arrangements. This period of economic turmoil highlighted Canada's vulnerability to U.S. tariffs, as the U.S. held the dominant position in trade with Canada and had a powerful influence over Canadian economic decisions. As a result, Canada had little choice but to make economic concessions to the U.S., including lowering tariffs on American products and aligning its economic policies more closely with American interests.

The U.S. continued to use tariffs as a tool to shape Canadian economic policy, and Canada's retaliatory tariffs often proved ineffective. In the post-World War II era, Canada sought to implement its own trade policies to protect domestic industries, including higher tariffs on U.S. imports. However, U.S. retaliation was swift and decisive, and Canadian businesses often faced the consequences of being locked out of the U.S. market. Canadian retaliatory tariffs were generally seen as a losing battle, as the U.S. could exert far more economic leverage due to its larger market and more robust industrial capacity.

For example, in the 1950s and 1960s, Canada attempted to counter American tariffs with its own retaliatory measures, but these often resulted in limited success. The U.S. had an overwhelming economic advantage and could afford to impose tariffs without significantly harming its own economy, while Canada, heavily reliant on the U.S. as its largest trading partner, was hurt more by these trade barriers. Even when Canada was able to negotiate some tariff reductions or limited trade access, the U.S. could always use its economic size to continue asserting its dominance over Canada's markets.

The 1970s and 1980s saw continued U.S. economic pressure through the use of tariffs and trade barriers, forcing Canada into a series of trade negotiations and agreements with the United States. The Canada-U.S. Free Trade Agreement (FTA), signed in 1987 and fully implemented in 1989, marked a major shift in Canadian trade policy, as Canada had little choice but to enter into a trade agreement that favored the U.S. economy. The agreement reduced or eliminated most tariffs between the two countries and allowed the U.S. to expand its market influence in Canada even further. This agreement was framed as a victory for Canada, but in many ways, it marked a deepening economic integration with the U.S., and effectively neutralized Canada's ability to impose its own tariffs or assert a truly independent economic policy.

Canada's retaliatory tariffs during the NAFTA negotiations and beyond continued to reflect the reality that the U.S. had the upper hand in trade relations. While Canada could impose counter-tariffs or seek legal action through international bodies like the World Trade Organization (WTO), these actions were rarely decisive and often resulted in limited victories. In the end, the U.S. consistently retained control over the broader trade agenda, shaping agreements and negotiations to its advantage.

In conclusion, U.S. tariffs repeatedly forced Canada into a pattern of economic concessions, making it increasingly dependent on American markets and rendering retaliatory tariffs ineffective in many cases. Canada's inability to successfully challenge U.S. economic power has been a consistent theme in the history of U.S.-Canada trade relations. Despite some efforts to use retaliatory tariffs, Canada's economic policy often had to align with U.S. interests because of the overwhelming leverage the U.S. held, particularly through its large and dominant market. This dynamic of economic interdependence ultimately culminated in NAFTA and the Canada-U.S. Free Trade Agreement, where Canada, despite its resistance, ultimately accepted a deeper economic integration with the United States.

Chapter 6: NAFTA, USMCA

NAFTA, USMCA, and the Controlled Collapse of Canadian Sovereignty

How "Free Trade" Became a Tool for Economic Annexation

NAFTA (North American Free Trade Agreement), while presented as a free trade agreement, was far more than just a trade deal—it was structured in a way that integrated Canada into a U.S.-dominated economic system. While NAFTA technically aimed to eliminate tariffs and trade barriers between the U.S., Canada, and Mexico, its deeper implications were about solidifying economic interdependence and increasing the dominance of multinational corporations over national governments.

The elimination of tariffs under NAFTA was an important component of the agreement, as it allowed goods to move more freely between the three countries. On the surface, this was touted as a win for free trade, where the barriers to entry for Canadian and Mexican products in the U.S. market were reduced. However, the reality was that the deal gave U.S. corporations preferential access to Canadian and Mexican markets, making it easier for American companies to expand their operations and control sectors of the Canadian and Mexican economies. Over time, this shifted power away from Canadian governments and placed it in the hands of U.S. multinational corporations that could now operate more freely across borders.

NAFTA effectively bound Canada's economy even more tightly to the United States, making it increasingly difficult for Canada to pursue independent economic policies. While the agreement did allow for greater market access and opportunities for Canadian exports, the structure of NAFTA favored U.S. economic interests in a way that Canada had limited power to contest. For example, investor-state dispute settlement (ISDS) provisions gave U.S. corporations the ability to sue Canadian governments over policies they felt could negatively affect their profits, regardless of whether those policies were democratically enacted or in the public interest. This gave corporations a kind of sovereignty, allowing them to challenge national policies and legislation, further eroding the ability of Canadian governments to enact laws that could prioritize public welfare over corporate interests.

The agreement also incentivized companies to outsource jobs and relocate manufacturing to Mexico, where labor was cheaper, which benefited U.S. corporations but often at the expense of Canadian and Mexican workers. The power shift was particularly evident in industries like automotive manufacturing, agriculture, and energy, where U.S. corporations gained significant control over Canadian resources and markets. Canada, despite its vocal participation in the negotiation process, had little say in the structural implications of the deal, which heavily favored U.S. economic and corporate interests.

In practice, NAFTA was never just about removing tariffs or creating a more competitive market. It was designed to integrate the economies of the U.S., Canada, and Mexico into a single, cohesive trading block, but with the U.S. at the center of that integration. The agreement allowed U.S. businesses to use Mexico as a low-wage manufacturing base while also providing them unfettered access to Canadian resources—often with little regard for environmental protections or labor rights. This arrangement increasingly made Canada reliant on U.S. demand for its natural resources and agricultural products, while simultaneously undermining Canadian efforts to diversify its trade relationships.

In essence, NAFTA was less about free trade and more about economic integration, with the United States at the core of a system that benefited multinational corporations and increasingly limited the autonomy of national governments. The U.S., with its larger economy and greater corporate influence, was able to dictate terms that favored U.S.-based companies at the expense of Canadian sovereignty and the well-being of the Canadian population. The removal of tariffs only shifted the power dynamics further in favor of corporations, making it harder for governments to assert control over their own economic policies or to pursue laws that protected national interests over the interests of multinational corporations.

The consequences of this shift were far-reaching. Canada found itself more interdependent on the U.S. economy, and even though it retained formal political independence, its economic policies and decisions were increasingly shaped by U.S. corporate interests. For Canada, the decision to join NAFTA was largely driven by economic necessity—the U.S. was its largest trading partner, and access to the U.S. market was critical for Canadian industries. However, by entering into the agreement, Canada effectively agreed to a system that reduced its power in trade negotiations and handed significant influence to corporate interests, further integrating it into the U.S. economic orbit.

In conclusion, NAFTA was never truly about free trade in the classical sense of promoting unrestricted competition or fostering mutual economic benefit. Instead, it served as a tool for the economic integration of Canada into a U.S.-dominated system, where multinational corporations had far more influence than national governments. The removal of tariffs and trade barriers facilitated this integration, but it also shifted the power balance, making it harder for Canada to maintain independent economic policies in the face of U.S. corporate interests. This set the stage for further economic dependency and political challenges for Canada as it navigated the complexities of a globalized trade environment dominated by U.S. economic power.

Under NAFTA, several key industries saw increased American control and influence, leading to a shift in Canada's economic structure. While the agreement was billed as a way to reduce trade barriers and enhance economic cooperation between the U.S., Canada, and Mexico, it inadvertently facilitated the dominance of U.S. corporations in critical sectors of the Canadian economy. Two of the most impacted industries were energy and manufacturing, both of which underwent significant changes as a result of NAFTA's provisions.

In the energy sector, the agreement opened the door for increased U.S. control over Canadian resources, especially in oil, gas, and electricity. Prior to NAFTA, Canada had largely retained control over its energy resources, with the Canadian government able to set domestic policies and exert significant control over the development of its vast natural resources. However, NAFTA's provisions on energy were structured in such a way that U.S. companies were granted expanded access to Canadian energy markets, creating an increasingly interdependent relationship between the two countries.

A key component of NAFTA was its commitment to the free flow of energy between the member countries, which included oil, natural gas, and electricity. Under NAFTA, Canada was bound by a "most-favored-nation" clause, which effectively meant that Canada could not discriminate against American energy companies or create policies that would hinder their ability to access Canadian resources. U.S. companies gained the right to invest in and control energy production in Canada, particularly in oil sands development in Alberta and natural gas extraction in British Columbia. These developments increased American ownership and investment in Canada's energy infrastructure, consolidating U.S. dominance over the flow of Canadian energy resources.

As a result, Canada became more reliant on U.S. demand for its oil and gas, with American companies controlling much of the extraction, transportation, and distribution processes. This made it more difficult for Canada to exercise independent control over its own energy policies, as any move to restrict energy exports or impose higher prices would risk upsetting its trade relationship with the U.S., which had become a key market for Canadian energy exports. This energy dependency would only deepen over time, culminating in high-profile pipeline projects such as the Keystone XL pipeline, which was ultimately focused on ensuring the steady flow of Canadian oil to U.S. refineries.

In the manufacturing sector, NAFTA played a key role in facilitating the movement of production to low-cost areas, particularly in Mexico. While the agreement eliminated tariffs and trade barriers, it also created incentives for U.S. corporations to relocate manufacturing operations to Mexico, where wages were lower and environmental and labor standards were less stringent. This had a direct impact on Canada's industrial base, particularly in automotive manufacturing, textiles, and electronics.

For example, the automotive industry—once a significant part of Canada's manufacturing base—saw a significant shift in production to Mexico, where labor costs were considerably lower. U.S. manufacturers, including companies like General Motors, Ford, and Chrysler, began to establish more production plants in Mexico, allowing them to take advantage of the lower wages while still maintaining tariff-free access to both Canadian and U.S. markets. As a result, Canada's auto manufacturing sector faced intense competition and lost a considerable number of jobs to Mexico. Over time, this relocation of manufacturing jobs not only weakened Canada's industrial sector but also increased the pressure on Canadian workers, who faced higher unemployment rates and stagnating wages.

Similarly, other industries such as textiles and electronics saw production moved to Mexico, where lower labor costs and fewer regulatory restrictions made it more attractive to American manufacturers. This trend eroded Canada's manufacturing base and undermined its ability to compete with the U.S. for jobs and production capacity. While Canada did gain access to the U.S. and Mexican markets, the loss of manufacturing jobs and the shift in industrial production to Mexico created a structural imbalance in Canada's economy. This left Canada more dependent on resource extraction and low-cost assembly work, as opposed to a more diversified, value-added manufacturing base that would have allowed it to better compete with the U.S. in the global market.

In essence, NAFTA inadvertently reinforced U.S. economic dominance over Canada by giving U.S. companies greater control over key sectors, particularly energy and manufacturing. By ensuring the free flow of energy resources and encouraging offshoring of manufacturing jobs to low-wage regions, the agreement deepened Canada's economic dependence on the U.S., undermining its ability to assert independent control over its own resources and industries. This economic integration with the U.S. was presented as a path to greater prosperity, but in reality, it left Canada vulnerable to external economic pressures and further solidified American dominance in key areas of the Canadian economy.

NAFTA significantly reshaped Canada's agricultural sector, forcing Canadian farmers into direct competition with heavily subsidized U.S. agribusinesses. Before NAFTA, Canada's agricultural industry had already been struggling with the growing dominance of U.S. agricultural exports. However, the agreement eliminated tariffs on U.S. agricultural products, including grains, meats, and dairy, and this opened Canadian farmers to direct competition from U.S. agribusinesses, which benefited from heavily subsidized production. U.S. farmers could produce goods at a lower cost due to government subsidies, giving them a competitive edge in the market.

As a result, Canadian farmers found themselves in a situation where their prices were driven down by the influx of cheap U.S. agricultural goods, which had artificially lower production costs due to U.S. subsidies. This made it harder for Canadian farmers, particularly those in sectors like dairy and grains, to compete without their own government subsidies, which were less generous compared to the massive support provided by the U.S. government. The NAFTA terms placed Canadian farmers in a vulnerable position, often forcing them to accept lower prices for their products and leaving them less able to maintain their businesses and livelihoods.

One of the most controversial aspects of NAFTA was its Investor-State Dispute Settlement (ISDS) mechanism, which gave corporations the power to sue national governments if they felt that new laws or regulations interfered with their profits. This system was designed to provide investors with a way to seek compensation for government actions that were seen as discriminatory or detrimental to their investments. However, it also had significant consequences for Canadian sovereignty, particularly when it came to environmental protection and labor laws.

The ISDS system undermined Canadian sovereignty by granting U.S. corporations the ability to challenge Canadian laws and regulations, especially when these laws interfered with corporate profits. The ISDS provisions allowed corporations to bypass domestic courts and take their cases to international arbitration tribunals, where decisions often favored investors over national policies. This effectively limited Canada's ability to enact laws in the public interest if these laws were seen as potential barriers to corporate profit, even if they were aimed at improving environmental standards or protecting workers' rights.

One high-profile example of U.S. businesses using ISDS to override Canadian laws involved the case of Ethyl Corporation, a U.S. chemical company. In the late 1990s, Canada banned the use of MMT (Methylcyclopentadienyl Manganese Tricarbonyl), a gasoline additive produced by Ethyl, due to concerns about its health and environmental impacts. Ethyl sued Canada under the NAFTA ISDS mechanism for $251 million in damages, arguing that the ban violated their right to free trade under NAFTA. In response, the Canadian government settled the case and reversed the ban on MMT, paying a $13 million settlement to Ethyl. This case is often cited as a stark example of how ISDS allowed a U.S. corporation to override Canadian environmental protection laws for the sake of corporate profit.

Another case involved Vivek and Doreen Sangha, who owned a business producing packaged foods in Canada. They sued the Canadian government after environmental laws were introduced in their region that would affect their operations. The tribunal ruled in favor of the Sanghas, ordering compensation for the losses that were said to arise from the implementation of the environmental regulations. These cases illustrated how ISDS effectively subordinated Canadian sovereignty to the interests of multinational corporations, allowing them to overrule national legislation if it interfered with profits.

Additionally, NAFTA restricted Canada's ability to pursue independent trade agreements outside of North America. The agreement's "most-favored-nation" clause essentially meant that any trade agreement Canada entered into with countries outside the U.S. and Mexico would have to provide the same favorable terms as those offered within NAFTA. This limited Canada's ability to negotiate independently with other global markets on favorable terms. For example, if Canada signed a trade agreement with a country that offered more favorable terms than the ones dictated by NAFTA, the U.S. and Mexico would be entitled to the same terms under the "most-favored-nation" provision.

This restrictive clause not only hampered Canada's flexibility in global trade but also tied its trade negotiations to the economic priorities of the United States, which, as the dominant economic force in NAFTA, had a large influence on Canada's ability to make independent trade decisions. Canada's economic policy became constrained by NAFTA for the duration of the agreement, making it difficult to explore alternative trade routes or expand into emerging markets without giving up preferential treatment for the U.S. and Mexico.

In summary, NAFTA's influence over Canada's agricultural sector, sovereignty, and ability to make independent trade agreements was far-reaching. Canadian farmers were forced into competition with subsidized U.S. agribusiness, and NAFTA's ISDS mechanism made it easier for U.S. corporations to override Canadian environmental protections and labor laws. Furthermore, NAFTA's restrictions on trade agreements limited Canada's ability to chart an independent trade course, binding it to the economic strategies of the U.S. and Mexico. As a result, while NAFTA provided some benefits in terms of market access, it also imposed significant economic limitations on Canada's sovereignty and economic independence.

The Shift from NAFTA to USMCA—A New Deal or a Tighter Leash?

The renegotiation of NAFTA into the United States-Mexico-Canada Agreement (USMCA) in 2018 marked a significant shift in the balance of power within North America, further entrenching U.S. dominance over Canada's economy and policies. While the agreement kept many elements of NAFTA, it also introduced key changes that increased U.S. influence and compromised Canadian sovereignty in various ways.

One of the primary ways in which Canada's bargaining position was weakened during the USMCA negotiations was the timing and context of the renegotiation process. Under President Trump's administration, the U.S. had adopted a more aggressive and unilateral approach to trade negotiations, using tactics such as tariff threats and trade wars to exert pressure on its trading partners, including Canada. The U.S. had already imposed tariffs on Canadian steel and aluminum before the USMCA negotiations, and the threat of additional tariffs on automobiles was used as leverage throughout the process. The trade war tactics undermined Canada's position by putting it at a disadvantage, as the U.S. could afford to escalate economic pressure on Canada, while Canada had little ability to retaliate due to its economic dependence on U.S. markets. This diplomatic pressure essentially forced Canada to accept a deal that was more favorable to U.S. interests than it would have been under more equal bargaining conditions.

The USMCA negotiations also took place in a climate of rising protectionism and American first policies, where President Trump's administration made it clear that the U.S. was looking for deals that would shift the balance of economic power in its favor. As a result, Canada had little leverage in these negotiations, as its own economic interests were heavily tied to U.S. markets and its dependence on American trade meant it couldn't afford to walk away from the table or hold out for a more favorable deal. This economic dependence made Canada's negotiating position weak, and ultimately Canada had to accept terms that were less advantageous than what NAFTA had originally offered.

Several key changes in USMCA further compromised Canadian sovereignty. These changes not only restricted Canada's ability to make independent trade decisions but also gave U.S. corporations and political interests more power over Canadian economic policies.

Dairy and Agricultural Market Access: One of the significant compromises for Canada was the expanded U.S. access to Canada's dairy, poultry, and egg markets, which was a major concession in agricultural trade. Under the USMCA, Canada agreed to open up a larger portion of its dairy market to U.S. producers, reducing the protections that Canadian farmers previously had under the supply management system. This concession not only undermined the Canadian government's ability to support its own agricultural sector but also left Canadian farmers vulnerable to U.S. pricing and competition, further entrenching U.S. dominance in Canadian agriculture.

Investor-State Dispute Settlement (ISDS) Provisions: The ISDS mechanism in NAFTA allowed U.S. corporations to sue the Canadian government over policies that threatened their profits. While the USMCA made some changes to the ISDS system, it retained many of its core provisions, effectively continuing the ability of U.S. companies to challenge Canadian laws and regulations that were seen as a threat to their investments. This allowed corporations to override Canadian sovereignty on issues such as environmental regulations and labor laws, making it difficult for Canada to regulate industries in the public interest without facing potential lawsuits from multinational companies.

Auto Industry and Content Requirements: Another key change in USMCA was the requirement that 75% of the content of vehicles produced in North America be made in the region to avoid tariffs. This change favored U.S. automakers and meant that Canadian auto manufacturers would have to meet stricter content requirements to maintain tariff-free access to U.S. markets. It also made it more difficult for Canada to maintain a diversified manufacturing sector, as American companies had greater leverage over Canada's industrial production. This provision shifted the balance of power further in favor of U.S. corporate interests, undermining Canada's ability to maintain independent control over its manufacturing base.

Chapter 19 Dispute Resolution Mechanism: Under NAFTA, Chapter 19 allowed Canada and Mexico to challenge U.S. anti-dumping and countervailing duties in an independent binational panel. This system was largely preserved in the USMCA, but the U.S. retained significant influence over the process, which limited Canada's ability to defend its own industries from what it perceived as unfair U.S. trade practices. While the panel system offered a form of recourse, it was not as robust as a more independent trade dispute mechanism, and U.S. interests had significant leverage over the process.

Digital Trade and Data Flows: One of the most significant shifts in USMCA was the protection of U.S. tech companies' ability to operate freely in Canada, particularly in the realm of digital trade. The agreement included provisions that made it more difficult for Canada to regulate cross-border data flows and impose privacy regulations on U.S. tech giants like Google, Facebook, and Amazon. This shift in policy undermined Canada's sovereign ability to regulate its digital economy and created a situation where Canadian laws on privacy, data protection, and tech regulation were aligned with U.S. interests, potentially to the detriment of Canadian consumers and data security.

The Sunset Clause in the USMCA is one of the most significant pro-visions that ensures Canada remains economically tethered to the U.S.. The clause stipulates that the agreement will expire every 16 years, and a renegotiation of the deal is required to extend it. This provision places Canada in a position where its trade relationship with the U.S. is con-tinually subject to renewal and renegotiation, giving the U.S. leverage over Canada's economic policies and perpetuating the dependence of Canada on the American market.

The Sunset Clause creates ongoing uncertainty for Canadian busi-nesses and the government. Every 16 years, Canada must engage in re-newal negotiations with the U.S. and Mexico to keep the agreement in place. During these negotiations, the U.S. will have the upper hand, as it holds a larger, more powerful economy and has the ability to leverage its market dominance. Canada, on the other hand, has a much smaller economy and relies heavily on the U.S. as its largest trading partner, making it more vulnerable to any changes that could be imposed during these renegotiations.

The clause forces Canada into a constant cycle of renegotiation, en-suring that the country is continually locked into trade terms that are heavily influenced by U.S. priorities. With each renegotiation, the U.S. has an opportunity to push for changes that align with American eco-nomic goals—whether that involves further opening Canadian markets to U.S. companies, tightening regulations on Canadian industries, or re-vising trade terms in favor of American interests. This dynamic means that Canada has less freedom to independently pursue trade policies that may benefit its own economy without the looming pressure of a potential unfavorable renegotiation.

For Canada, the Sunset Clause creates a situation where the country cannot ever truly secure permanent, independent economic relations with its neighbors. Instead, it is always at risk of being forced into new concessions every 16 years. This perpetual cycle of renegotiation effec-tively ties Canada's future trade relations to U.S. policies and interests, maintaining the economic status quo where Canada's trade policies are heavily influenced by its much larger, more powerful southern neighbor.

In essence, the Sunset Clause in the USMCA ensures that Canada's economic relationship with the U.S. is never truly stable or independent, reinforcing the idea that Canada is always dependent on the U.S. for its economic future. Every 16 years, Canada must once again face the prospect of renegotiating its trade terms, which prevents Canada from developing fully independent trade policies and continues to consolidate its economic ties with the U.S.

The China Clause in the USMCA is a provision that further entrenches U.S. dominance in Canadian trade relations by requiring Canada to seek U.S. approval before entering into trade deals with China or other non-U.S. economic powers. This clause reflects the U.S. government's growing concerns about China's rising global influence and its desire to ensure that Canada does not strengthen its economic ties with China in a way that could undermine U.S. interests. By restricting Canada's ability to make independent trade agreements with other global powers, this clause reinforces Canada's economic alignment with the U.S. and limits its autonomy in pursuing its own trade relationships.

The clause essentially gives the U.S. the ability to veto Canadian trade deals with China or other major economic powers, especially those that might compete with or challenge U.S. global influence. It reflects U.S. geopolitical priorities, particularly in the context of the ongoing U.S.-China rivalry, and places Canada in a position where it must align its foreign economic policy with U.S. strategic interests. This means that Canada can no longer freely negotiate trade agreements with countries like China, Russia, or the European Union without first consulting the U.S. and receiving its approval, a constraint that undermines Canada's sovereignty in global trade decisions.

From Canada's perspective, the China Clause represents a clear limitation on its ability to expand trade ties with some of the world's most powerful and rapidly growing economies. China, for example, has emerged as one of the world's largest and most dynamic economies, and many countries, including Canada, have been eager to deepen economic ties with China, particularly in sectors such as technology, infrastructure, and natural resources. The clause prevents Canada from capitalizing on such opportunities without first securing approval from the U.S., a country that has historically viewed China as a strategic rival.

This provision effectively hinders Canada's ability to pursue independent foreign policy and economic opportunities that might diverge from U.S. interests, especially in Asia. With the U.S. exerting control over Canada's trade options, this clause further deepens Canada's economic dependency on the U.S. and limits its ability to establish alternative trading partnerships that could reduce its reliance on the U.S. market. This dependence on U.S. approval also disempowers Canada in the context of global negotiations, as it must always weigh its need for U.S. approval against the potential benefits of new trade agreements with other countries.

Ultimately, the China Clause highlights the unequal nature of the USMCA and the continued subordination of Canadian economic policy to U.S. priorities. It reinforces the notion that Canada's trade policy—and, by extension, its economic and geopolitical strategy—must always be aligned with American interests, rather than allowing Canada to develop its own economic relationships that might not always coincide with those of the U.S. This clause is an example of how the USMCA solidifies U.S. dominance in North American trade and geopolitics, while restricting Canadian sovereignty in its global economic dealings.

U.S. negotiators used tariffs and economic pressure as powerful tools to ensure that Canada complied with U.S. demands during the USMCA negotiations. This approach built upon tactics used by the U.S. in previous trade deals, where the U.S. leveraged its dominant economic position to extract favorable terms from Canada. Prior to the

USMCA talks, the U.S. had imposed tariffs on Canadian steel and aluminum, escalating trade tensions and creating a climate of economic vulnerability. These tariffs, combined with the threat of additional duties on other products like automobiles, effectively put Canada in a position where it had little choice but to negotiate under duress.

The U.S. used these tariffs as a bargaining chip, knowing that Canada's economic reliance on the U.S. meant that the Canadian economy would suffer significantly from the imposition of tariffs on key exports. The U.S. effectively weaponized its trade policies, threatening to impose further tariffs or maintain existing ones unless Canada agreed to terms that favored U.S. economic and strategic interests. This tactic limited Canada's ability to pursue independent trade policies and further reinforced its dependence on the U.S. market. The U.S. also made it clear that Canada's access to the U.S. market, which is crucial for many Canadian industries, would be compromised if Canada did not comply with U.S. terms.

The USMCA made this economic vulnerability even more pronounced by restricting Canada's ability to make independent policy decisions. One of the most detrimental aspects of the agreement was its provision on tariffs and trade policy. While the agreement eliminated some trade barriers, it also ensured that Canada would not be able to unilaterally alter trade policies without U.S. approval. Provisions such as the Sunset Clause and the China Clause effectively tethered Canadian trade policy to U.S. priorities, preventing Canada from engaging in trade deals with non-U.S. economic powers, particularly China, without first obtaining U.S. consent. These clauses significantly restricted Canadian sovereignty over its trade decisions, forcing the country to align its economic and geopolitical strategies with those of the U.S.

By making it increasingly difficult for Canada to independently pursue economic policies, the USMCA effectively deprived Canada of the ability to exert full control over its own trade. Canada's options were now bound by U.S. demands, ensuring that any future trade agreements or regulatory changes would be influenced by U.S. interests. This situation made Canada more vulnerable to future economic coercion by the U.S. and further cemented the unequal nature of the trade relationship. The tariffs imposed before the agreement's renegotiation and the restricted flexibility in the USMCA reinforced Canada's dependence on the U.S., making it difficult for Canada to escape the influence of U.S. policies.

The USMCA also raised questions about the possibility of a future North American economic union, in which Canada could increasingly function as a de facto U.S. economic colony. The agreement effectively locked Canada into an economic system where the U.S. has significant control over trade and investment policies. This economic integration, while framed as a benefit in terms of access to the U.S. market, also limited Canada's autonomy, especially when it came to policies that could be seen as interfering with U.S. interests. Provisions such as the China Clause (which restricts Canada's ability to negotiate trade agreements with countries like China) and the ISDS system (which allows U.S. companies to challenge Canadian laws) suggest that Canada's policy space is increasingly constrained by the needs of U.S. multinational corporations.

As Canada is increasingly integrated into the U.S. economic orbit, the potential for a North American economic union becomes more plausible. In such a scenario, Canada's sovereignty would continue to erode, as it would be bound by U.S. economic priorities with limited flexibility to pursue independent economic or foreign policies. This scenario could eventually lead to economic integration on the level of a single economic zone with minimal political control for Canada, effectively turning the country into a satellite economy that operates within the broader framework of U.S. dominance.

In conclusion, USMCA increased Canada's economic vulnerability by locking it into a trade system dominated by the U.S., where policymaking is increasingly influenced by U.S. priorities. The agreement curtailed Canada's ability to make independent trade agreements, especially with economic powers like China, and introduced provisions that made it difficult for Canada to assert its own economic sovereignty. While NAFTA had already created significant economic ties between the U.S. and Canada, USMCA deepened these ties and created an environment where future Canadian economic independence is continually challenged by the overwhelming influence of U.S. corporations and government policy.

How American Corporations Control Key Canadian Industries

The influence of Wall Street and American financial institutions over Canadian monetary policy has become a defining feature of the economic relationship between the U.S. and Canada. Canadian banks, while independent in name, are heavily influenced by the global financial system, which is dominated by American institutions. U.S. financial power plays a critical role in shaping Canadian economic decisions, as Canadian banks are intertwined with major U.S. financial players, and the larger U.S. economy directly impacts Canada's monetary policies.

Canadian financial institutions often align with U.S. practices and interests, given their heavy dependence on American capital markets. Many of Canada's largest banks have significant operations in the U.S. or are subsidiaries of American financial firms. For example, Royal Bank of Canada (RBC) and Toronto-Dominion Bank (TD) operate substantial branches in the U.S., and are deeply embedded in the American financial ecosystem. This relationship means that U.S. financial policies and market fluctuations often dictate or influence Canadian banking decisions, including interest rates, investment practices, and regulatory policies. The ties between U.S. and Canadian financial sectors create a scenario where Canadian monetary policy is often more aligned with the interests of Wall Street than with independent Canadian economic goals.

Additionally, U.S. financial institutions often have significant influence over Canadian investment practices. Major American players like Goldman Sachs, JPMorgan Chase, and Morgan Stanley often direct investment flows into Canadian markets, particularly in areas like real estate and resource extraction. These institutions also play a key role in shaping the Canadian debt market, as many of Canada's government bonds and corporate debts are purchased by American financial entities. As a result, Canada's economic stability is often contingent on U.S. investor confidence and decisions made in American financial centers, making Canada increasingly vulnerable to economic decisions made by institutions that do not prioritize Canadian interests.

In the energy sector, U.S. firms have long dominated Canada's vast natural resources, and their control over pipelines and refineries has given them substantial economic leverage. U.S. corporations such as ExxonMobil, Chevron, and ConocoPhillips are major players in the Canadian oil sands industry, owning vast shares of the extraction and refining process. U.S. investment in Canada's energy sector has not only allowed these companies to control significant portions of Canadian resources but also to dictate the terms of extraction and exportation. This dominance means that the U.S. has a strong say in the development and exportation of Canadian oil, particularly with regard to pipelines that transport oil and gas across the country.

The control of pipelines and refineries by American corporations has major implications for Canada's economic sovereignty. For example, TransCanada (now TC Energy), a major Canadian pipeline company, is heavily intertwined with American capital and interests. The Keystone XL pipeline, which would carry oil from Alberta to Texas, is a symbol of U.S. control over Canadian oil resources, as it is largely funded and operated by U.S. investors. This project, alongside others, demonstrates how U.S. companies dictate the flow of Canadian natural resources, often prioritizing U.S. refineries over Canadian ones.

Moreover, the reliance on U.S. companies to operate Canadian energy infrastructure means that Canada has limited ability to regulate its own energy policies without facing the risk of capital withdrawal or interference from U.S. companies. U.S. firms can exert economic pressure by either restricting investments in Canadian energy projects or by lobbying for policies that favor their own interests. This limits Canada's ability to establish an energy strategy that is independent from U.S. influence or that prioritizes Canadian environmental standards or resource control.

Wall Street and American financial institutions have significant influence over Canada's monetary policy and banking practices, largely due to the interconnected nature of the two countries' economies. Canadian banks are deeply involved in U.S. financial markets, and American financial institutions dictate investment practices within Canada. Similarly, U.S. control over Canadian energy resources, through ownership of pipelines, refineries, and oil sands, has given American firms substantial influence over Canadian natural resources, with major implications for Canada's ability to exercise sovereignty in its economic and environmental policies. These two dynamics exemplify the economic dependency Canada faces in a system where U.S. economic power dominates key sectors of its economy.

Media and Big Tech play a crucial role in shaping the cultural landscape of any nation, and Canada is no exception. However, the pervasive dominance of U.S. media, social platforms, and tech giants has eroded Canada's national identity, making it difficult for Canadian culture to thrive independently. U.S. corporations like Netflix, Amazon, Facebook, Google, and Disney dominate the Canadian media and entertainment space, pushing Canadian content to the margins.

In the entertainment industry, U.S. media giants control the distribution channels that define popular culture in Canada. Streaming platforms like Netflix, which offer an overwhelming amount of U.S.-produced content, leave Canadian-made shows and films struggling for visibility. Hollywood continues to hold a near monopoly on the entertainment that shapes Canadian culture, while Canadian media companies are relegated to niche markets. The sheer volume of U.S. content consumed daily by Canadians has made it difficult to preserve and promote distinctively Canadian cultural products, thus undermining the Canadian cultural identity in favor of a more Americanized narrative.

Similarly, Big Tech companies such as Facebook, Google, and Twitter control vast swaths of the digital landscape, making it increasingly difficult for Canadian voices to be heard. These platforms do not only dominate the advertising sector but also shape public discourse, dictate trends, and set the agenda for news and information. The cultural influence of U.S. tech giants undermines Canadian journalism, often pushing Canadian issues out of focus in favor of U.S. interests. In addition, the growing reliance on U.S.-controlled social platforms for advertising and consumer engagement has weakened local businesses and Canadian media outlets, making them more susceptible to external influence and less competitive on the global stage.

In the retail and food supply chains, U.S. corporate dominance is just as pervasive, reinforcing Canada's dependence on American supply chains. Major American retail giants like Walmart, Costco, Target, and Home Depot have a massive presence in Canada, dictating much of what Canadian consumers buy and how it is sold. These U.S.-based companies control supply chains, and as a result, Canadian retailers are forced to comply with the policies and practices set by their American counterparts. In terms of food production and distribution, the U.S. has considerable influence over Canadian agriculture. American agribusinesses, like Cargill and Monsanto, not only control significant portions of the Canadian food industry but also dictate farming practices, the use of pesticides, and genetically modified crops. This level of control places Canada at the mercy of U.S. agricultural policies, and Canadian farmers face increasing difficulty competing against the massive scale and subsidized practices of U.S. agribusinesses.

The food supply chains are also deeply intertwined with U.S. logistics and distribution networks, meaning that Canada relies on American infrastructure to move goods across its own borders. The free flow of goods between the U.S. and Canada under agreements like NAFTA and USMCA has further reinforced the dominance of U.S. corporations in the Canadian retail sector. As Canadian retailers are pushed to rely on U.S. suppliers and distribution centers, they become more vulnerable to disruptions in American supply chains, which further undermines Canada's economic sovereignty in retail and food production.

The defense and aerospace sector is perhaps one of the most striking examples of how Canada's military-industrial complex has become deeply integrated with the U.S. military. Canada is a major partner in NORAD (North American Aerospace Defense Command), an institution designed to defend the continent from external threats. Through NORAD, Canadian military policy is heavily influenced by the U.S. defense agenda, and Canada's defense spending is often shaped by the needs of the U.S. military. As part of the U.S. defense umbrella, Canada's military procurement often aligns with U.S. priorities, particularly in sectors like aerospace, fighter jets, and military technology.

In terms of aerospace, companies like Lockheed Martin, Boeing, and Raytheon, which are dominant players in the U.S. defense industry, have a substantial presence in Canada. Canada's defense contracts frequently rely on U.S. companies for military technology, weapons systems, and aircraft. This dependence on U.S. defense contractors means that Canada's defense policies are often influenced by American military and technological requirements. The joint development of military technology between the two countries further ties Canadian defense strategies to U.S. priorities. Additionally, U.S. military spending and defense budgets dictate much of the direction of Canada's own defense strategy, leaving little room for Canada to pursue independent defense policies that do not align with the U.S. military-industrial complex.

Regaining true economic independence for Canada is a complex and challenging endeavor, particularly given the deep interdependencies that have been built over decades with the United States. However, while it is not necessarily too late, it would require significant structural changes in Canada's economic policies, a reorientation of trade relations, and the assertion of sovereignty over its natural resources, industries, and financial systems. The path to independence would be long and difficult, but not impossible if Canada were to prioritize its long-term interests over short-term economic gains or reliance on U.S. markets.

One of the most critical steps would be redefining Canada's trade relationships. NAFTA and its successor, USMCA, have tied Canada's economic future too closely to the U.S., making it increasingly difficult to negotiate independent trade deals and diversify its market access. **Canada would need to pursue a more diverse portfolio of trade relationships, prioritizing markets in Asia, the European Union, and other growing economies. Strengthening ties with emerging economic powers like China, India, and regional partners in the Pacific Rim would provide an alternative to the reliance on U.S. trade and reduce the economic leverage the U.S. has over Canada.

Reevaluating trade agreements, particularly those that restrict Canada's ability to independently negotiate deals (like the China Clause in USMCA), would be key to ensuring economic flexibility. This could involve renegotiating or even seeking alternatives to current trade agreements that are overly restrictive, allowing Canada to explore new avenues for growth without constantly being bound to U.S. demands and interests. Canada would have to make hard decisions about the tradeoffs involved in securing better agreements, but a more balanced approach to trade could help restore a degree of sovereignty.

Another major area where Canada could regain economic independence is in its energy sector. U.S. corporations dominate Canadian energy extraction, and Canadian oil and gas, especially from the oil sands, are heavily integrated into U.S. supply chains. For Canada to truly regain control over its energy resources, it would need to take significant steps to nationalize certain aspects of the energy sector, increase domestic ownership, and diversify its energy exports beyond the U.S. markets. Investing in alternative energy sources, such as renewable energy technologies and clean tech industries, could help reduce Canada's reliance on fossil fuels, shift toward a more sustainable energy future, and create new economic opportunities.

At the same time, Canada would need to assert more control over its financial sector. Currently, major U.S. financial institutions have significant influence over Canada's banking system, and many Canadian banks are intertwined with American financial entities. To reduce this reliance, Canada would need to strengthen its domestic financial institutions, possibly by restricting foreign ownership and focusing on policies that encourage domestic investment. This could include reforming the banking system to ensure that Canadian banks serve Canadian interests, rather than prioritizing global investors. Additionally, increasing control over capital markets, allowing for greater Canadian involvement in financial decision-making, would help insulate the country from external shocks or pressures from American financial interests.

Cultural sovereignty is another area where Canada could work toward economic independence. U.S. media dominance continues to undermine Canadian identity, and the sheer scale of American entertainment and social platforms makes it challenging for Canadian culture to thrive independently. Canada would need to strengthen its domestic media and support local creative industries with increased funding and protectionist policies designed to keep Canadian content in the forefront. By protecting the cultural industries through regulation and promoting Canadian talent, Canada could rebuild its cultural independence, ensuring that its national identity is no longer shaped primarily by U.S. content and influence.

Moreover, Canada must address its overreliance on U.S. corporations in critical sectors like retail, agriculture, and defense. The U.S. dominance in retail supply chains and the agriculture sector has made it difficult for Canada to pursue its own policy goals. Supporting local agriculture, moving away from industrial farming models, and promoting sustainable food systems would provide more economic resilience. Similarly, a more independent defense policy would ensure that Canada is not simply an extension of the U.S. military-industrial complex. This could involve investing in homegrown defense technologies and military infrastructure, while also seeking stronger defense partnerships with other nations, such as European powers, rather than relying solely on the U.S. for security.

Finally, achieving true economic independence would require a fundamental shift in political will and public perception. Canadians would need to recognize that economic sovereignty is vital for the country's future and prioritize policies that support long-term independence over short-term trade or political conveniences. This might involve reforming political structures, such as reducing the influence of external lobbying from U.S. corporations or tech giants, and putting Canadian interests first when making decisions in areas such as foreign trade, defense, and resource management.

Chapter 7: Tariffs, Trade Wars

T ariffs, Trade Wars, and Economic Coercion – Trump's Playbook

Trump's 25% Tariffs on Canadian Aluminum and Steel—Was This Economic Warfare?

Trump's 2018 tariffs on Canadian aluminum and steel marked a significant shift in the U.S.-Canada trade relationship, transforming what had traditionally been an economic partnership into a relationship dominated by coercive tactics. Prior to these tariffs, Canada and the U.S. enjoyed relatively favorable trade relations under NAFTA, with tariffs largely eliminated between the two nations. However, Trump's decision to impose tariffs on Canadian steel and aluminum disrupted this long-standing trade framework and signaled a fundamental change in how the U.S. approached its economic relationship with Canada.

Trump justified the imposition of 25% tariffs on steel and 10% tariffs on aluminum by invoking national security concerns, claiming that foreign steel and aluminum posed a threat to the U.S. military and infrastructure. His administration argued that the U.S. needed to protect its domestic production of these metals to ensure that it could meet military and infrastructure needs during times of crisis. Specifically, the justification rested on the idea that U.S. military capabilities could be compromised if the country was overly reliant on foreign supplies of critical materials, particularly in the context of a potential military conflict or geopolitical instability.

While national security concerns are often used as justification for tariffs in the U.S., the legitimacy of this argument was highly contested. Canada—as a U.S. ally and member of NATO—was hardly a national security threat. In fact, Canada is one of the U.S.'s closest trading partners and is intimately involved in joint defense projects through NORAD and other military agreements. The aluminum and steel that Canada exports to the U.S. is primarily used for civilian purposes and does not directly impact U.S. defense infrastructure. Many critics of the tariffs argued that the national security justification was a thinly veiled pretext for more protectionist policies, aimed at benefiting U.S. producers rather than addressing any real security threats.

Additionally, Trump's imposition of these tariffs was part of a broader strategy to protect American manufacturing and reduce the U.S. trade deficit. While the national security argument may have been convenient, the real underlying motive seemed to be the desire to create a more favorable trade balance for the U.S., particularly in industries like steel and aluminum, where U.S. producers had been struggling to compete with foreign suppliers who offered cheaper products. By imposing tariffs on Canadian exports, Trump aimed to shield U.S. producers from competition, raising the cost of foreign aluminum and steel and making domestic products more competitive.

The tariffs were a stark departure from previous U.S.-Canada trade relations, which were historically marked by a mutual respect for free trade and a shared commitment to open markets. The move symbolized a shift from partnership to coercion, as Trump used the tariffs to pressure Canada into complying with U.S. demands in the renegotiation of NAFTA and later the USMCA. This tactic reflected a broader "America First" policy, which aimed to reduce reliance on global supply chains and revitalize U.S. industries, but it came at the expense of established relationships with trading partners like Canada.

In response, Canada strongly rejected the tariffs, calling them unjust and unjustified, and imposed retaliatory tariffs on a range of U.S. goods, including steel, aluminum, and agricultural products. These retaliatory measures were intended to signal Canada's resistance to U.S. coercion and to defend Canadian industries that were being negatively impacted by the U.S. tariffs. Ultimately, Canada viewed the tariffs as an unprovoked attack on its economy, especially given that it was already operating within a long-standing, mutually beneficial trade relationship with the U.S.

Trump's 2018 tariffs on Canadian aluminum and steel were justified on the grounds of national security, but this justification was widely regarded as weak and largely disingenuous, considering Canada's status as a close ally and trusted trading partner. The tariffs marked a significant departure from the cooperative U.S.-Canada economic relationship, turning what was once an economic partnership into a coercive arrangement, where the U.S. leveraged its economic power to force Canada into compliance with U.S. priorities. The imposition of these tariffs reflected a broader trend under the Trump administration toward protectionism and economic unilateralism, which often sought to benefit U.S. industries at the expense of its trading partners.

The "national security" argument used by the U.S. to justify the 2018 tariffs on Canadian steel and aluminum was widely regarded as a weak pretext for what appeared to be a coercive economic strategy aimed at exerting pressure on Canada. Canada, as a close ally of the U.S. and a member of NATO, was hardly a security threat. In fact, the two countries have a long history of shared defense and military cooperation, notably through NORAD (North American Aerospace Defense Command) and various other military and security agreements. It is difficult to reconcile Canada's role as a trusted military partner with the notion that its steel and aluminum exports posed any real national security threat to the U.S.

Instead, the national security justification was seen by many as a convenient excuse to apply economic pressure on Canada. The U.S. had, by that point, already implemented tariffs on Canadian aluminum and steel under the Section 232 provision of the Trade Expansion Act, which allows for tariffs to be imposed for national security reasons. However, the real motive behind these tariffs seemed more related to broader trade war tactics than any legitimate concern over security.

Trump's tariffs on Canadian metals fit into the broader trade war strategies the U.S. had begun to employ against a range of other countries, including China, Mexico, and the European Union (EU). The U.S. applied similar tariffs to Chinese goods, citing issues like intellectual property theft and unfair trade practices. With Mexico and the EU, Trump's administration sought to address trade imbalances, particularly with respect to auto manufacturing and agriculture. The U.S. aimed to pressure its trade partners into restructuring agreements that would shift the terms more in favor of American producers.

These tariffs on Canada were part of the same strategy—to use economic leverage to force trade partners into more favorable agreements for the U.S., often using tariffs as bargaining chips in negotiations. Trump believed that tariffs could be an effective tool for restructuring trade relationships and leveraging U.S. economic power over global partners. In the case of Canada, the imposition of steel and aluminum tariffs seemed aimed at not only disrupting the Canadian economy but also bringing Canada to the negotiating table during the renegotiation of NAFTA (which would later become the USMCA).

The impact of the tariffs on Canadian industries was significant. Canadian steel and aluminum producers faced increased production costs due to the imposition of U.S. tariffs, which ultimately made it harder to sell their goods in the U.S. market, where many of them traditionally sold a large portion of their production. For Canadian manufacturers that relied on steel and aluminum for production, the tariffs meant higher input costs and price increases, which in turn made their products less competitive in both the Canadian and international markets. Industries like automobile manufacturing, construction, and aerospace were hit particularly hard, leading to job losses, financial strain, and a slowdown in production across several sectors.

These tariffs disrupted supply chains, especially in industries that are deeply integrated with U.S. producers. Canadian businesses had to adjust to the sudden increase in material costs and deal with disruptions in export markets. For instance, steel producers in Canada were forced to find alternative markets for their goods, and many had to absorb the increased costs rather than pass them on to customers, which reduced their profitability. The broader economic consequences were felt across the country, as the tariff dispute led to uncertainty in Canada's business environment, causing investors to hesitate and slow growth in key sectors.

As for the intention behind these tariffs, it was widely believed that the U.S. never fully intended to permanently maintain them on Canadian products. Instead, the tariffs were likely part of a broader strategy to gain leverage in the USMCA negotiations. By imposing tariffs on a vital trading partner like Canada, Trump likely hoped to force Canada to make concessions in the renegotiation of trade terms. Once the new agreement was reached—one that favored U.S. economic interests—it was expected that the U.S. would lift the tariffs or at least reduce their severity as a goodwill gesture, or as a reward for Canada agreeing to U.S. terms in the trade deal.

However, this tactic also revealed a longer-term approach by the U.S., where tariffs could be seen as tools of economic coercion rather than just temporary measures. In many ways, the imposition of tariffs on Canadian steel and aluminum was likely an opening move, meant to weaken Canada's negotiating position and extract future concessions in areas like agriculture, automobile manufacturing, and intellectual property in the USMCA. By placing Canada in a vulnerable economic position, Trump was able to force Canada to the table and accept terms that might have otherwise been unacceptable in a more balanced negotiation.

In conclusion, the 2018 tariffs on Canadian aluminum and steel under the guise of national security were largely seen as a coercive tactic rather than a legitimate response to any real threat. They aligned with broader trade war strategies aimed at forcing global trading partners to make concessions. The tariffs caused significant disruptions to Canadian industries, leading to job losses and financial strain in affected sectors. While the U.S. eventually removed these tariffs as part of the USMCA deal, they were never truly intended as a permanent fixture but rather as a bargaining chip in a broader strategy to reshape trade relationships in favor of U.S. interests. The tariffs were an opening move, meant to apply pressure and extract future concessions, rather than a permanent policy shift based on national security concerns.

Trudeau's retaliatory tariffs in response to the 2018 U.S. tariffs on Canadian steel and aluminum were an important show of resistance, but ultimately, they failed to make a significant impact on the U.S. economy. The decision to impose $16.6 billion worth of retaliatory tariffs on U.S. products, including steel, aluminum, and agricultural goods, was a direct response to the U.S. tariffs, meant to signal that Canada would not accept the U.S.'s protectionist approach. However, Canada's limited economic leverage became glaringly obvious as the tariff war unfolded.

The primary reason these retaliatory tariffs failed to make a significant impact on the U.S. was the disparity in economic power between the two countries. Canada's economy is highly dependent on the U.S. market, which absorbs a significant portion of Canada's exports. In contrast, the U.S. economy is far more diversified and self-sufficient, meaning that the tariffs imposed by Canada on U.S. goods had a much smaller impact on the U.S. economy than the U.S. tariffs had on Canadian industries. For example, U.S. steel producers might have been impacted by the tariffs on Canadian steel, but U.S. consumers could easily find alternative suppliers, and industries like automobiles, which rely heavily on cheap steel, could simply adjust to the tariffs by sourcing from other countries. Canadian industries, on the other hand, were far more vulnerable, especially given the lack of alternative markets to absorb the losses from the U.S. tariffs.

This imbalance in economic power underscored Canada's limited leverage in the tariff war. While the retaliatory tariffs were politically important, particularly as a demonstration of Canada's willingness to defend its interests, they ultimately had limited economic efficacy because Canada's dependence on the U.S. market left it unable to significantly harm U.S. industries in return. Even when Canada targeted high-profile U.S. exports such as whiskey, jeans, and motorcycles, the effects were much more limited than the economic disruption caused by the U.S. tariffs on Canadian industries.

This tariff war wasn't just about specific industries or sectors; it was a broader test of Canada's resilience and an attempt to determine how far Canada could be economically squeezed without having a major political or economic breakdown. The U.S. tariff strategy appeared to be a way to force Canada into submission, testing whether the economic pressure of the tariffs would force Canada to make concessions in the renegotiation of NAFTA or in future trade relations. Trump's administration was likely hoping that by economic coercion, they could extract concessions from Canada, such as more favorable terms in the USMCA (formerly NAFTA) or in future trade deals, while at the same time, diverting attention from the broader trade war with China.

The U.S. recognized that Canada's economic vulnerabilities made it more difficult for Canada to escalate the dispute in a way that would be painful enough to force a major change in U.S. trade policy. The tariffs on Canadian goods were not about protecting specific U.S. industries, but rather about exercising economic pressure on Canada, potentially making it more willing to yield in trade negotiations. This approach was a way for the U.S. to test the limits of Canada's willingness to resist U.S. policies and to find out just how much economic strain Canada could tolerate before it was forced to make trade concessions or even accept less favorable agreements in the context of the USMCA negotiations.

In conclusion, Trudeau's retaliatory tariffs were important as a symbol of resistance, but their economic impact was limited due to the power imbalance between the U.S. and Canada. The tariff war was not simply about protecting specific industries but about testing Canada's resilience and determining how far the U.S. could economically squeeze Canada. The U.S. used these tariffs as a coercive tool to extract concessions and further integrate Canada into the U.S.-dominated economic system, making it clear that Canada's economic leverage in this relationship was relatively weak.

"51st State"

Throughout his presidency, Donald Trump made several notable statements regarding Canada's status as a "quasi-state" of the U.S., reflecting his view of the economic relationship between the two nations as one in which Canada was dependent on the U.S. for its economic prosperity and security. Trump often framed Canada as being in a subordinate position, reliant on the U.S., and incapable of asserting true independence in its economic and trade policies.

One of his more explicit comments came in the context of NAFTA renegotiations, where he made remarks about Canada's economic vulnerability. Trump referred to Canada's reliance on U.S. trade as being so deep that it made Canada more of a quasi-state of the U.S., implying that Canada's autonomy in global economic affairs was largely an illusion. In Trump's view, Canada was too economically tied to the U.S. to make independent decisions, and this interdependency placed Canada in a position where it had little choice but to align its policies with U.S. interests. This framing painted Canada as more of a satellite state than a fully sovereign nation, suggesting that it would eventually have to give in to American demands because of its economic reliance on the U.S. market.

The Trump administration made frequent use of economic pressure to bring Canada into compliance with U.S. interests, especially in the context of the trade war with China and the renegotiation of NAFTA. Through the imposition of tariffs on Canadian steel and aluminum under the Section 232 provision (a national security justification), the Trump administration essentially used economic coercion to gain leverage over Canada. Trump's strategy involved using tariffs as tools of intimidation, knowing that Canada's economy was highly reliant on access to U.S. markets, and that Canadian businesses and industries would be severely impacted by restrictions on exports to the U.S. This created a situation in which Canada had to bend to U.S. demands in order to maintain its economic stability and access to the lucrative U.S. market.

Trump's mockery of Trudeau's economic vulnerability was a frequent part of his rhetoric. Trump would often publicly diminish Canada's capacity for independent economic decision-making, highlighting that Canada's economic survival was so dependent on U.S. trade that it had little leverage in negotiations. He mocked Prime Minister Justin Trudeau, suggesting that Canada had little room to maneuver, and implying that Canada's prosperity and security were inextricably tied to the U.S. As an example, Trump openly criticized Canada's trade surplus with the U.S. and often portrayed the relationship as one in which the U.S. was acting as a benevolent protector, while Canada was seen as a vulnerable economic partner that lacked the autonomy to assert its own economic interests.

Trump also often made comments suggesting that Canada's economic vulnerability meant that it had no real independence in trade negotiations, framing Canada as a country that was too reliant on the U.S. to oppose American economic demands. This was especially evident during his trade war with China, where Canada's position in global trade was seen as secondary to the U.S.-China conflict. For Trump, Canada was not an equal partner in the economic relationship but rather a nation that had to align its policies with U.S. priorities, particularly in regard to issues like trade imbalances, agriculture, and manufacturing.

Regarding Trump's threats of tariffs, they were likely both a negotiating tactic and a real push toward a more dominant relationship with Canada. On one hand, Trump used tariffs as a bargaining chip in trade negotiations, hoping to force Canada into agreeing to more favorable terms in the renegotiation of NAFTA (which became USMCA). These threats were meant to show that the U.S. could inflict significant economic pain on Canada, using its economic leverage to extract concessions. On the other hand, Trump's rhetoric often suggested that the tariffs were not just a negotiating tool, but part of a broader economic strategy aimed at restructuring trade relationships to benefit U.S. interests—even if it meant imposing long-term pressure on Canada.

In the broader context of economic annexation, Trump's tariff strategy did hint at a desire to reshape Canada's economic relationship with the U.S. into something more coercive and asymmetrical, rather than simply a partnership. By using economic pressure in the form of tariffs, Trump was signaling that Canada's economic autonomy was, in his view, secondary to U.S. demands, and that Canada's dependence on U.S. trade made it susceptible to future economic coercion. This wasn't necessarily about outright annexation, but rather about ensuring that Canada remained within the U.S. economic orbit, unable to chart its own path or pursue trade agreements that were not aligned with U.S. interests.

Trump's comments about Canada's status as a "quasi-state" of the U.S. were a reflection of his broader view that Canada's economic sovereignty was subordinated to U.S. interests. His administration framed economic pressure as a tool to force Canada into compliance with U.S. trade priorities, mocking Canada's vulnerability and highlighting its dependence on the U.S. for its economic well-being. Trump's tariffs were both a negotiating tactic and part of a broader strategy to reshape the economic relationship between the U.S. and Canada, pushing Canada toward a more subordinate role in the North

American economic framework. While not necessarily a direct push for economic annexation, it was clear that Trump aimed to reinforce U.S. dominance over Canada by exerting significant economic pressure.

How Modern Tariffs Mirror Past Economic Pressure Campaigns Against Weaker Nations

The United States has a long history of using tariffs and economic embargoes as tools to exert pressure on foreign governments and weaken their economies in order to achieve political or strategic goals. These economic tactics have been used in a variety of contexts, from punishing adversaries and forcing trade concessions to suppressing foreign competition and enforcing foreign policy objectives. Here are some notable historical precedents:

1.   **The Embargo Act of 1807**
     One of the earliest examples of the U.S. using economic measures to exert political pressure was the Embargo Act of 1807, signed by President Thomas Jefferson. In response to the impressment of American sailors by the British navy and the British blockade of France during the Napoleonic Wars, Jefferson implemented a comprehensive embargo that prohibited American ships from engaging in trade with foreign nations. The goal was to pressure Britain and France into respecting U.S. sovereignty and trade rights. While the embargo was a failure economically, devastating American merchants and the economy, it represented an early use of economic coercion to achieve political aims. The embargo was eventually repealed in 1809 after it proved to be ineffective in changing British or French behavior, but it set a precedent for the U.S. using trade restrictions as a form of diplomatic leverage.

2. The Civil War Blockade of the Confederacy (1861-1865)

During the American Civil War, the Union imposed an extensive naval blockade on the Confederate States to cripple their economy and prevent them from trading with foreign countries, particularly Great Britain and France, which had sympathies toward the Confederacy. This blockade was part of the Union's Anaconda Plan, aimed at strangling the Southern economy by cutting off access to foreign markets for goods like cotton and tobacco. The blockade was highly effective, significantly weakening the Confederacy's ability to sustain its war effort by restricting its imports and exports, and it remains one of the most notable examples of the U.S. using economic warfare to achieve a military and political objective.

3. Tariffs Against China in the Late 19th Century

In the late 19th century, the U.S. used economic pressure in the form of tariffs to exert influence on China. The Chinese Exclusion Act of 1882 was a direct attempt to limit the influx of Chinese immigrants into the United States. Additionally, tariff policies were part of broader efforts to gain greater control over Chinese trade during the period of "Open Door" policy in the early 20th century. The Boxer Rebellion in 1900 saw the U.S. use its economic leverage as a tool of foreign policy by pressuring the Chinese government to accept the foreign powers' demands for reparations. While these efforts were largely diplomatic and strategic, the U.S. utilized its market dominance and trade policies to push China into accepting unequal treaties that favored American interests.

4. The Cuban Embargo (1960-Present)

One of the most famous and ongoing examples of economic embargoes is the U.S. trade embargo against Cuba, which began in 1960 after the Cuban Revolution and the rise to power of Fidel Castro. In response to Cuba's nationalization of American-owned properties and its alignment with the Soviet Union during the Cold War, the U.S. imposed a comprehensive economic embargo that restricted trade, travel, and financial transactions between the two countries. The goal was to economically isolate Cuba, weaken its government, and force regime change. Despite the continuation of the embargo for over six decades, Cuba's government has remained in power, but the embargo has significantly harmed the Cuban economy, limiting access to foreign goods, capital, and investment. The embargo remains a powerful tool of U.S. foreign policy, though it has been relaxed at times (such as during the Obama administration) and remains a contentious issue in U.S.-Cuba relations.

5. Sanctions Against Iraq (1990s)

In the aftermath of Iraq's invasion of Kuwait in 1990, the United Nations imposed economic sanctions against Iraq, heavily backed by the United States. These sanctions, which included restrictions on oil exports, were intended to pressure Saddam Hussein's regime into withdrawing from Kuwait and complying with UN resolutions. The sanctions were part of the broader strategy to weaken Iraq economically and force it to adhere to international law. The sanctions had a devastating impact on the Iraqi economy and caused significant humanitarian consequences for its population. While they were intended to bring about political change, they were ultimately criticized for harming civilians without achieving their primary goal of regime change.

6. Tariffs in Trade Wars with European Powers

The U.S. has also used tariffs as a tool of economic coercion during various trade disputes, notably with European powers. For example, during the early 20th century, the U.S. imposed tariffs on European goods in an attempt to protect its own industries and assert economic dominance. The Smoot-Hawley Tariff Act of 1930, which significantly raised tariffs on imports, is one of the most infamous examples. The tariff was intended to protect American agriculture and manufacturing from foreign competition, but it triggered retaliatory tariffs from other countries and worsened the Great Depression. The Smoot-Hawley tariffs, although primarily aimed at bolstering domestic industries, also reflected the use of economic power to influence foreign markets and trade policies.

7. Tariffs Against Japan in the 1980s

In the 1980s, the U.S. imposed a series of tariffs against Japan, especially in the automobile industry, as part of a broader strategy to address trade imbalances and market access issues. Japan, at the time, was seen as a rising economic rival, particularly in automotive manufacturing and technology. U.S. manufacturers felt that Japan's high tariffs and non-tariff barriers were preventing American products from competing fairly in Japanese markets. In response, the U.S. sought to force Japan into compliance by imposing tariffs and pushing for trade concessions that would allow American companies greater market access in Japan. These efforts were seen as economic coercion and were aimed at ensuring that Japan would open its markets to U.S. goods.

Throughout its history, the U.S. has used tariffs, sanctions, and embargoes as tools of economic pressure to achieve political goals, weaken adversaries, and assert its economic dominance on the global stage. From the Embargo Act of 1807 to the ongoing Cuban embargo, U.S. trade policy has frequently been used as a strategic weapon to challenge foreign governments that were seen as threats to U.S. interests. Whether used to punish enemies, reshape trade relationships, or enforce geopolitical dominance, these economic measures have played a central role in the U.S.'s ability to exert influence over global affairs and push other nations to comply with American policies.

Part III: Military, Political

Part III: Military, Political, and Strategic Integration

Chapter 8: NORAD

N ORAD and the Merging of U.S.-Canadian Defense

The North American Aerospace Defense Command—How Canada Surrendered Strategic Control

NORAD, established in 1958, was initially framed as a mutual defense pact between Canada and the United States to defend the continent from potential threats, especially the Soviet Union's expanding missile capabilities during the Cold War. The agreement was intended to provide a unified defense system where both nations would cooperate on early warning systems, surveillance, and defense strategies to protect North American airspace. This cooperative defense system was meant to be a joint venture where both countries participated equally, sharing responsibilities for monitoring aerospace threats and coordinating military strategies.

When Canada entered into NORAD, it had several sovereignty concerns. Canada's strategic location, especially near the Arctic, made it a critical player in defending North American airspace from the threat of long-range Soviet bombers and missile strikes. Canada also had a primary interest in maintaining sovereignty over its airspace while cooperating with the U.S. to counter the Soviet threat. One of the key concerns for Canada was ensuring that, while it would cooperate with the U.S. military, it would not lose control over its own defense policy and military decisions. The Canadian government was careful to maintain autonomy in foreign policy and wanted to ensure that participating in NORAD wouldn't make Canada merely a subordinate partner to U.S. military interests.

Over time, however, control of NORAD began to shift toward the U.S. military, especially as the U.S. maintained technological and strategic superiority over Canada. Initially, both countries had equal participation in decision-making, but as the years passed and the Cold War tensions eased, the U.S. began to assume a more dominant role in NORAD. The U.S. military took the lead in operations, particularly in military technology and surveillance systems, and Canada's role became more supportive. As the U.S. became the dominant military force, particularly after the end of the Cold War, Canadian involvement became more restricted, and the U.S. essentially drove the direction of defense operations in NORAD.

Canada's sovereignty concerns have been partly validated over the years. Initially, Canada wanted to ensure that it could participate in continental defense without giving up its independent military policies. Over time, however, Canada's involvement in NORAD has meant that it has often had to align with U.S. defense priorities. Key decisions in NORAD, particularly those related to nuclear defense or military installations, were largely shaped by U.S. strategic interests rather than equally negotiated terms. For Canada, this meant that its ability to set its own defense agenda was increasingly compromised as the U.S. military began to lead the operations and strategies within NORAD.

In terms of decision-making authority, Canada retains a significant, yet secondary role in NORAD. The commander of NORAD has always been a U.S. general, and the U.S. holds operational control. Although Canada contributes key personnel and is involved in strategic discussions, the U.S. retains ultimate decision-making authority. The technological and operational decisions—particularly those related to missile defense or airspace defense strategies—are typically dictated by U.S. priorities. While Canada does have input in certain aspects of NO-

RAD operations, it remains a supporting partner rather than an equal participant in strategic military decisions.

NORAD began as a mutual defense pact between Canada and the U.S. to protect the continent from external threats. However, over time, the U.S. has assumed more control within the organization, particularly in military strategy, technology, and operational decision-making. While Canada retains a significant role, especially in surveillance and defense coordination, its military sovereignty has been compromised by its increasing subordination to U.S. priorities in the context of NORAD. Canada's initial desire to protect its sovereignty within NORAD has become more challenging as the U.S. military increasingly shapes defense decisions on the continent.

Canada's role in NORAD is far from purely symbolic, but it is certainly limited compared to the U.S. dominance in the decision-making processes. Canada's involvement in NORAD is critical for continental defense, especially given Canada's geographic location and its role in monitoring airspace in the Arctic region. Canada's military personnel serve in key positions within the NORAD command structure, contributing to the surveillance of North American airspace, early-warning systems, and defensive strategies. However, real influence in NORAD's decision-making is weighted heavily in favor of the U.S., especially when it comes to strategic decisions and military operations.

The structure of decision-making within NORAD is joint, but it is designed in such a way that the U.S. has the final say in a crisis. While both nations contribute to defense strategy and planning, the U.S. military holds the lead, with U.S. personnel occupying the highest positions in command. The commander of NORAD is always a U.S. general, and the U.S. has operational control over aerospace defense and military strategy. Canada's role, while essential in terms of participation and support, often aligns with U.S. military decisions, particularly in matters involving missile defense, nuclear strategy, and continental air defense.

In a crisis scenario, the U.S. holds the final authority within NO-RAD. In a military emergency, while Canadian personnel would certainly be involved in tactical discussions and operational decisions, U.S. command would take the lead. This reflects the hierarchical nature of NORAD, where Canada's sovereignty in defense matters is somewhat subordinate to the U.S. military establishment. Despite its contributions to defense policy, Canada's independent defense decisions are frequently shaped by the broader goals of U.S. defense priorities, particularly as NORAD operates within the framework of U.S. military supremacy.

Historically, the U.S. military doctrines such as the Monroe Doctrine and Manifest Destiny set the stage for viewing North America as America's exclusive domain, thus influencing the U.S.'s approach to defense and territorial claims.

The Monroe Doctrine (1823), which asserted that any European intervention in the Americas would be seen as a direct threat to U.S. interests, placed North America under the U.S. sphere of influence. While this doctrine focused primarily on preventing European powers from interfering in Latin America, it also suggested that the U.S. would act to maintain exclusive control over the hemisphere. Over time, this notion developed into a broader understanding that the U.S. had the right to dominate the political and military affairs of North America, including Canada. While the Monroe Doctrine did not directly call for U.S. control over Canada, it laid the groundwork for viewing the Western Hemisphere as the U.S.'s special responsibility—reinforcing the idea that North America was, in many ways, America's domain.

Manifest Destiny, a later doctrine in the 19th century, built on this foundation, with the belief that it was the U.S.'s divine mission to expand across the continent. This belief led to territorial expansion and shaped U.S. attitudes toward Canada. Even though Canada was never fully annexed by the U.S., the notion of Manifest Destiny suggested that the U.S. viewed itself as the inevitable leader of the North American continent. The U.S. had ambitions to bring all of North America under its control, and in many ways, Canada's sovereignty was seen as a barrier to be overcome, whether through military conquest or economic dominance.

These historical doctrines framed the U.S. approach to Canada as a relationship of dominance and control—a theme that resonates even in the context of NORAD. While Canada retains formal sovereignty as an independent state, the strategic and military relationship between the U.S. and Canada, particularly in the NORAD context, reflects a power imbalance in favor of U.S. interests. Canada's participation in NORAD, while critical to the defense of North America, is part of a broader context in which U.S. military priorities are dominant, and Canada's role—though vital—is primarily supportive rather than independent. This echoes the long-standing historical narrative where U.S. doctrines positioned North America as America's exclusive domain, shaping the way the U.S. perceives its relationship with Canada today.

NORAD's integration of Canadian and U.S. airspace control has, in many ways, placed Canada's national security under U.S. oversight. The very nature of NORAD's joint defense structure means that both countries share responsibility for monitoring and defending North American airspace. However, the balance of this shared responsibility is tilted heavily toward U.S. dominance. U.S. military technology, operational control, and decision-making processes play a central role in how airspace is managed and how defense responses are carried out in the event of a threat.

Canada's geographic proximity to the Arctic and its vital role in monitoring airspace over the northern part of the continent has made it an integral partner in the early-warning systems and surveillance that NORAD oversees. However, while Canada's contributions are crucial, U.S. forces typically hold command over military operations within NORAD, particularly in times of crisis. The U.S. operates the most advanced radar systems, missile defense technologies, and aerospace defense strategies, making it the lead nation when responding to threats.

This means that, even though Canada is a full partner, the U.S. holds the operational control, particularly in situations where the response to a threat requires military action or nuclear strategy.

In a missile defense scenario, Canada's autonomy is even more limited. NORAD's primary function is to protect the continent from aerospace threats, including missiles. The decision-making process, particularly concerning how to intercept or respond to a missile attack, is governed by a shared framework, but with the U.S. in control of much of the military technology and defense systems. Canada does not have a veto over major defense decisions within NORAD, particularly those that involve the use of U.S.-led missile defense systems, such as interceptors or radar networks. Canada can certainly contribute to the discussion, but the U.S. military would ultimately have the final say in terms of engagement strategies. If a missile defense response is necessary, the U.S. would lead the charge, with Canada's role generally more focused on coordinating and supporting actions rather than making final decisions on whether or how to defend the continent from missile attacks.

In this context, the idea of Canadian sovereignty in terms of national defense is somewhat diluted. While Canada's participation in NORAD ensures that the country is a part of a shared defense strategy, it does not retain full independent control over military decisions that are central to national security. The integration of U.S. and Canadian defense systems means that Canada's national security is, in many ways, subordinated to U.S. defense priorities, particularly when dealing with threats of a global scale, such as missile attacks or air defense crises. Canada's military has the ability to contribute and coordinate but is increasingly dependent on U.S. military assets to execute complex defense operations, especially those related to missile defense and nuclear strategy.

The question of whether Canada's involvement in NORAD has made it more secure or more dependent on U.S. defense capabilities is complex. On the one hand, NORAD has made Canada more secure by providing a unified continental defense system that allows both countries to share intelligence, surveillance, and defensive technologies. The early-warning systems and aerospace defense capabilities provided by NORAD make it more likely that Canada would be protected in the event of a missile or airstrike.

However, this increased security comes at the cost of dependence on the U.S. military and its technological and operational capabilities. The more that Canada's military and defense systems are integrated with the U.S., the less autonomy Canada has in terms of making independent defense decisions. Canada's security is now fundamentally tied to the U.S. defense infrastructure, making it difficult to pursue independent defense strategies or control over its airspace and military operations without U.S. support. This has been particularly true since U.S. technological advancements in missile defense and satellite surveillance have made Canada increasingly reliant on U.S. assets for comprehensive defense.

Furthermore, Canada's role in NORAD increasingly aligns it with U.S. geopolitical priorities. While Canada benefits from shared defense resources, it also becomes more aligned with U.S. military strategies that may not always reflect Canada's foreign policy interests. This is particularly evident when Canada has to contribute to U.S.-led operations, such as those related to missile defense or global security efforts, which can place Canada in situations where it may have to support U.S. military operations that might not be in its national interest.

In conclusion, NORAD's integration of Canadian and U.S. airspace control places Canada's national security under U.S. oversight in practical terms, as the U.S. plays a dominant role in decision-making, particularly when it comes to missile defense and aerospace defense. Canada's authority in NORAD is more about supporting U.S. strategy rather than exercising independent control over defense decisions. While NORAD has contributed to Canada's security, it has simultaneously made Canada more dependent on U.S. defense capabilities, diminishing Canada's ability to make decisions independently in global defense matters. This dynamic reflects a broader geopolitical relationship where Canada's sovereignty in military matters is increasingly tied to U.S. military priorities.

U.S. Bases in Canada and Joint Military Operations—Who's Really in Charge?

The presence of U.S. military personnel and facilities on Canadian soil is a significant feature of the military relationship between the two countries. While the U.S. does not have extensive military bases in Canada compared to other nations, there are several key facilities and operations that are part of bilateral defense agreements, especially through frameworks like NORAD. These operations are primarily focused on air defense, surveillance, and missile defense. One of the most important areas of cooperation involves early-warning systems and radar facilities located in Canada to support North American defense efforts.

These U.S. military sites are integrated into Canadian defense systems, often under shared command structures and operations. For example, the U.S. Air Force has personnel stationed at Canadian military bases such as Canadian Forces Base Bagotville and CFB Cold Lake, where they work alongside Canadian forces to monitor and defend North American airspace. The U.S. also operates radar stations and early-warning systems in remote areas of Canada's Arctic to ensure comprehensive defense coverage. While these facilities and personnel are technically stationed in Canada, the cooperative nature of the operations often means that decisions about their use and deployment are heavily influenced by U.S. military priorities.

The legal authority these U.S. military facilities hold is grounded in a series of mutual defense agreements between Canada and the U.S., primarily through frameworks like NORAD and the Canada-United States Defense Agreement. Under these agreements, Canada provides the land and allows U.S. military personnel to operate on Canadian soil, but this is done under the terms of shared defense and with the understanding that Canadian sovereignty is still respected. That being said, the U.S. military has operational control over some aspects of defense activities, particularly those related to missile defense and air defense. Canadian forces often work in partnership with U.S. personnel, but in practice, much of the military decision-making is guided by U.S. priorities, especially when the operations are under the NORAD umbrella.

The presence of U.S. military personnel in Canada has had the effect of blurring the lines of sovereignty. While Canada retains formal control over its territory, the integration of U.S. military operations within its borders means that military decisions regarding continental defense are often made with U.S. influence and direction. The fact that Canada allows U.S. personnel to operate on its soil, particularly in high-security areas like the Arctic and northern airspace, has raised concerns about Canada's ability to act independently in defense matters. The presence of these foreign military personnel—who often operate under U.S. command—raises the question of how much control Canada truly has over its own defense policies and its military sovereignty.

While Canada's involvement in NORAD and other defense agreements ensures a level of protection and military cooperation, it also places Canada's defense priorities at the mercy of U.S. military strategy. In the event of a military crisis or defensive action, Canada's sovereignty in making independent defense decisions could be limited by its reliance on U.S. military assets and control structures. The joint nature of NORAD operations and the significant U.S. military presence on Canadian soil has made Canada's military policy increasingly intertwined with U.S. geostrategic interests, especially as the U.S. leads in military technology, aerospace defense, and missile defense systems. Therefore, while Canada technically retains control over its sovereignty, the practical influence of U.S. military operations in Canada means that true autonomy in military decision-making has become increasingly limited.

Canada has been involved in several major military operations where it acted as a junior partner in U.S.-led missions. These include both NATO operations and coalition missions where the U.S. played the lead role in military strategy, command, and decision-making.

One of the most notable examples is Canada's involvement in the Iraq War (2003), which, despite the controversial nature of the invasion, saw Canada contribute non-combat support forces to the U.S.-led coalition. While Canada did not participate directly in the combat phase, it supported the mission by providing logistical support, intelligence, and humanitarian assistance. Similarly, during the Afghanistan War, Canada was a key member of the NATO-led International Security Assistance Force (ISAF), operating in the southern provinces of Afghanistan, but often under the strategic direction of the U.S. military. Canadian troops were engaged in combat operations, but their overall strategy and objectives were aligned with U.S. goals and NATO directives. In these cases, Canada was involved in U.S.-led operations, but in a supportive role, often with Canadian forces operating under U.S. military command.

Canada's role as a junior partner in these operations is part of a broader trend where its military doctrine has increasingly been shaped by U.S. strategic goals. Canada's independent military doctrine, particularly during the Cold War, emphasized self-reliance, peacekeeping, and limited engagement in conflicts unless directly tied to Canadian interests. However, over time, Canada's participation in NATO, its role in NORAD, and its commitment to U.S.-led coalitions have led to a gradual subsuming of Canada's independent military doctrine under U.S. military strategies.

Canada's military doctrine has been increasingly aligned with U.S. objectives, especially after the end of the Cold War and the U.S. emerged as the world's sole superpower. This shift occurred because of the close integration between Canadian and U.S. forces in joint military operations, such as those within NORAD and NATO missions. In many of these operations, Canada's military strategy has often been adapted to support the global security goals of the U.S. and its NATO allies, meaning that Canada's military priorities are often shaped by the U.S. lead in global conflicts. For instance, Canada's military involvement in the War on Terror in the early 2000s highlighted how Canada's military policies increasingly aligned with U.S. counterterrorism objectives, rather than maintaining an independent strategic stance.

The War on Terror and NATO obligations have entrenched Canadian military alignment with U.S. objectives in several ways. The War on Terror, which began after the 9/11 attacks, saw Canada become a staunch ally in the U.S.-led effort to dismantle terrorist organizations, most notably al-Qaeda and the Taliban. Canada participated in combat operations in Afghanistan under the auspices of NATO, but the overall mission was U.S.-led, with Canada's military supporting U.S. counterinsurgency strategies. This involvement reinforced the alignment of Canadian military policy with U.S. objectives, as Canada's role in these conflicts was primarily to support U.S. military strategy rather than pursue an independent course of action.

Moreover, Canada's NATO obligations further tied its military doctrine to U.S. strategic priorities. As a member of NATO, Canada has been obligated to participate in NATO-led missions, which are often shaped by U.S. military priorities. This alignment was particularly evident during the NATO interventions in the Balkans and Afghanistan, where Canadian forces operated under NATO command but were effectively part of the broader U.S.-led coalition efforts. While Canada's participation in NATO was intended to demonstrate commitment to collective defense, it has also led to Canadian military forces being used to support U.S. objectives in regions like the Middle East and Central Asia.

In conclusion, the War on Terror and NATO obligations have not only deepened Canada's involvement in U.S.-led military operations, but they have also led to a situation where Canada's military doctrine is increasingly shaped by U.S. strategic priorities. Canada's role as a junior partner in U.S.-led missions, its growing dependence on U.S. military assets, and its participation in NATO operations have blurred the lines of Canada's independent military decision-making, leaving Canada's defense strategy more aligned with U.S. global objectives than with its own national priorities. This shift reflects the increasing integration of Canada's military with U.S. forces and the subordination of Canada's sovereignty in military affairs to the broader geopolitical goals of the United States.

The integration of intelligence-sharing within the Five Eyes alliance—which includes the U.S., U.K., Canada, Australia, and New Zealand—has significantly influenced Canada's military and intelligence operations. The alliance facilitates the sharing of classified information and coordinated intelligence gathering, ensuring that the countries involved can respond quickly to security threats. However, this cooperation also limits Canada's ability to operate independently in several ways, particularly in matters of foreign policy and military strategy.

Being part of the Five Eyes network means that Canada's intelligence services (like the Canadian Security Intelligence Service and the Communications Security Establishment) are deeply integrated with their U.S. counterparts. Intelligence-sharing within the Five Eyes framework is not only about sharing raw data but also about coordination in global intelligence operations, including counterterrorism, counterintelligence, and military surveillance. This close relationship means that Canada's intelligence agencies are often aligned with U.S. interests in terms of monitoring global threats and responding to security challenges. As a result, Canada is frequently bound by U.S. intelligence priorities, making it difficult for Canada to pursue an independent intelligence strategy or make decisions that conflict with U.S. priorities.

In a practical sense, Canada's participation in Five Eyes limits its ability to withhold certain intelligence from the U.S. and other allies. If a situation arises where Canada wants to make a diplomatic or military decision that contradicts U.S. interests, the intelligence-sharing relationship might force Canada to compromise or align with U.S. objectives, especially if the information shared directly affects national security. This dynamic has made Canada's foreign policy increasingly subordinated to U.S. priorities, as intelligence cooperation becomes an effective tool of political influence and military alignment.

In the context of a future global conflict, Canada's ability to remain neutral is increasingly questionable. The deep integration of Canadian forces and intelligence agencies with the U.S. military through frameworks like NORAD, Five Eyes, and NATO means that Canada is already effectively locked into U.S. military plans. In the event of a major conflict, especially one involving the U.S., it is unlikely that Canada could maintain a neutral stance without compromising its relationship with the U.S. or facing severe economic and military consequences. Given that Canada's military and intelligence structures are so closely tied to U.S. operations, particularly in North American defense and global military strategy, Canada would be compelled to participate in any military response that the U.S. initiated in defense of shared interests.

In practical terms, Canada's military neutrality is constrained by its commitments to collective defense agreements. NATO's Article 5, which obligates member states to defend any member under attack, would likely pull Canada into a conflict, especially if the U.S. were involved. Moreover, Canada's close involvement with the U.S. military through NORAD, which manages North American defense, would make it exceedingly difficult for Canada to remain neutral in a conflict that directly threatens North American security.

Furthermore, Canada's strategic geography—especially in the Arctic and along the U.S.-Canada border—means that any global conflict involving the U.S. military would likely require Canadian participation in defense operations. In many scenarios, Canada's sovereignty in military matters would be increasingly undermined by its military integration with the U.S. This means that Canada is already effectively bound to U.S. defense policies, making neutrality in a future global conflict a challenging and highly unlikely position.

The Five Eyes intelligence-sharing network, along with Canada's deep integration into U.S. military strategies, limits Canada's ability to operate independently, particularly in matters of foreign policy and military operations. Canada's participation in intelligence-sharing binds it to U.S. priorities and reduces its autonomy in global security matters. In the event of a future global conflict, Canada would likely be forced to align with U.S. military objectives due to its strategic obligations and the deep integration of its military and intelligence capabilities with the U.S. Therefore, neutrality is no longer a viable option, and Canada's military role is already deeply intertwined with U.S. defense goals.

Chapter 9: The Role of Mexico

The Role of Mexico – Will It Join the Fold?

U.S. Military Intervention in Mexico Under the Guise of "Cartel Wars"

U.S. foreign policy has historically framed Mexican instability as a justification for intervention, citing national security concerns, economic interests, and the desire to maintain regional stability. The Monroe Doctrine, established in 1823, laid the groundwork for U.S. intervention in the Western Hemisphere by declaring that European powers should not interfere in the Americas. Mexico's internal instability, whether from political turmoil, revolutions, or external threats, was often seen as a potential vulnerability that could be exploited by European or other foreign powers, thus justifying U.S. intervention to protect its interests in North America.

One of the most significant U.S.-led operations in Mexico was the Mexican-American War (1846-1848). The war was partly a result of the U.S. desire to expand westward under the doctrine of Manifest Destiny. Following the annexation of Texas, which Mexico still considered its territory, tensions led to armed conflict. The war resulted in the U.S. gaining vast territories, including California, Arizona, and New Mexico, effectively weakening Mexico's sovereignty and territorial integrity. The Treaty of Guadalupe Hidalgo, which ended the war, forced Mexico to cede a significant portion of its land to the U.S. This intervention not only solidified U.S. territorial expansion but also diminished Mexico's influence over its own borders.

In the early 20th century, U.S. interventions continued, particularly during the Mexican Revolution. In 1914, the U.S. occupied the port of Veracruz in response to the arrest of American sailors by Mexican forces. The U.S. justified this action as necessary to protect American citizens and property. While the U.S. claimed to be acting in the interest of restoring order, the occupation further undermined Mexico's sovereignty by enforcing U.S. military and economic priorities. The intervention was a direct assertion of U.S. power in the region, and while it temporarily stabilized U.S. interests, it left Mexico with a sense of diminished autonomy.

U.S. interventions continued through the 1920s and 1930s, particularly in the realm of economic interests. The nationalization of Mexico's oil industry in 1938, a move by President Lázaro Cárdenas to assert national control over the country's resources, led to significant tensions with U.S. corporations, which had extensive investments in Mexican oil. The U.S. imposed economic pressure in response, using its influence over international markets and diplomacy to try to reverse the nationalization. This economic intervention showed that while direct military action may not always have been taken, U.S. leverage still played a crucial role in influencing Mexico's economic sovereignty.

In all these cases, U.S. interventions in Mexico were framed as efforts to protect U.S. citizens, economic interests, or regional stability. However, these actions often had the side effect of weakening Mexico's sovereignty, as the U.S. imposed its own political and economic agendas. Whether through territorial conquest, military occupation, or economic pressure, U.S. interventions in Mexico repeatedly demonstrated how Mexican instability was used as a justification for U.S. domination. These operations not only shaped Mexico's political landscape but also entrenched a long-standing pattern of U.S. involvement in Mexican affairs, making it difficult for Mexico to assert its full independence in the face of American power.

Operation Fast and Furious (2009-2011) was a controversial operation conducted by the Bureau of Alcohol, Tobacco, Firearms, and Explosives (ATF) under the U.S. Department of Justice. The operation's goal was to track firearms being sold to suspected straw purchasers—individuals who buy firearms legally and then sell them to criminals or cartel members in Mexico. The operation aimed to dismantle gun-running networks and trace weapons used by Mexican drug cartels. However, it became infamous for the flawed execution and the unintended consequences that resulted from allowing firearms to be sold to criminal organizations rather than stopping the sales and tracking them immediately.

In Fast and Furious, U.S. agents allowed approximately 7100 firearms to be sold to suspected straw purchasers with the intent of tracing those weapons to Mexican drug cartels. The idea was that by allowing these guns to enter the hands of cartels, authorities could track their movements and use the weapons to eventually capture cartel leaders or disrupt their operations. However, the operation was poorly managed, and the firearms were lost in the process, with few being recovered or traced effectively.

One of the most damaging outcomes of Fast and Furious was that many of the firearms ended up in the hands of Mexican cartels, fueling the violence associated with drug trafficking and contributing to the deaths of hundreds of Mexican civilians, law enforcement officers, and U.S. border agents. The operation gained infamy after two U.S. law enforcement agents, including Border Patrol Agent Brian Terry, were killed in 2010 by suspects using guns that were part of the operation.

The operation was intended to gather intelligence and disrupt cartel activity, but instead, it ended up inadvertently arming criminal organizations. The decision to allow firearms to flow to Mexican cartels under the guise of tracking them became a serious scandal when it became clear that the ATF's handling of the operation was flawed and that it failed to accomplish its stated objectives. The operation sparked an outcry in both Mexico and the U.S. for its recklessness and raised serious questions about the ethics of government agencies arming cartels in an effort to combat criminal organizations.

The fallout from Operation Fast and Furious included numerous congressional investigations, criticism of the Obama administration, and calls for greater oversight of U.S. law enforcement agencies. In 2012, Attorney General Eric Holder was held in contempt of Congress for failing to provide documents related to the operation, further fueling the controversy. Despite the original intent of the operation being to trace weapons and disrupt cartel operations, the consequences of arming cartels ended up undermining U.S. law enforcement's credibility and exacerbating the violence in Mexico and beyond.

Plan Mérida (2008-Present) was a U.S.-Mexico initiative aimed at combating drug cartels, organized crime, and drug trafficking in Mexico. The plan was born out of growing concerns in the U.S. about the increasing violence associated with Mexican drug cartels, particularly as drug violence began to spill over into U.S. border states. The U.S. provided financial and logistical support to strengthen Mexico's military and police forces in the fight against cartels and organized crime. The plan was framed as a cooperative partnership, intended to enhance Mexico's security infrastructure and improve its ability to combat drug trafficking organizations (DTOs) and transnational criminal groups.

From the outset, Plan Mérida focused on three main pillars: counternarcotics cooperation, institutional reform, and capacity-building for Mexico's security forces. The U.S. provided significant financial support through aid packages, including funding for training programs, intelligence-sharing, and the provision of military hardware and logistical support for Mexico's military and law enforcement agencies. This included everything from helicopters, surveillance equipment, and specialized training for police and military personnel.

One of the most significant aspects of the plan was its focus on enhancing Mexico's security forces. U.S. assistance helped bolster Mexico's military capacity, particularly in intelligence-gathering and counter-narcotics operations. U.S. agencies like the Drug Enforcement Administration (DEA), FBI, and Department of Homeland Security (DHS) collaborated with Mexican authorities, providing intelligence and supporting operations against drug cartels and organized crime. This military and law enforcement cooperation was framed as critical for dismantling criminal organizations that had grown increasingly violent and entrenched across the country.

However, while U.S. support was aimed at strengthening Mexico's ability to deal with organized crime, Plan Mérida also contributed to the increasing militarization of Mexico's security apparatus. By providing military equipment and training, the U.S. helped bolster the Mexican military's role in combating cartels, leading to a situation where the military took on increasingly prominent roles in policing operations. The Mexican military was deployed in counter-narcotics operations and patrols, often working in tandem with local law enforcement, but also stepping into law enforcement roles traditionally held by police forces. This expansion of military influence in domestic security raised concerns about the erosion of civilian control over law enforcement and the increased militarization of policing in Mexico.

Moreover, U.S. assistance provided logistical support, such as the construction of counter-narcotics infrastructure and border security improvements, but it also meant that Mexico's security apparatus became more dependent on U.S. support, which led to questions about Mexico's sovereignty and autonomy in its security policies. While Mexico's government welcomed U.S. help in confronting powerful criminal organizations, there were concerns that U.S. influence in military and law enforcement operations might undermine Mexico's political and judicial independence.

The plan also led to the deepening of U.S.-Mexico cooperation in areas of intelligence-sharing and coordinated operations against drug trafficking organizations. However, this relationship has not been without controversy. While U.S. assistance improved Mexico's military and police capabilities, it has also contributed to serious human rights concerns, particularly when Mexican military units and police forces, equipped and trained by the U.S., have been linked to human rights abuses. There have been reports of extrajudicial killings, torture, and abductions by military and police forces, which have sometimes been facilitated or overlooked due to the strong U.S.-Mexico security partnership.

Furthermore, the U.S. support through Plan Mérida created a vicious cycle of militarization, where military forces became central in tackling cartel violence, but in doing so, they increasingly replaced local law enforcement, which was often plagued by corruption and inefficiency. This led to greater reliance on military solutions and a reduced emphasis on the necessary reform of police institutions in Mexico, which remained weak and susceptible to cartel infiltration.

The involvement of the U.S. military in Mexico has grown over the years, particularly through drone surveillance and special forces operations. While the U.S. does not have official military bases in Mexico, American military presence is increasingly felt through intelligence operations and joint actions with Mexican forces. One key area of involvement is drone surveillance, where the U.S. has used drones for aerial reconnaissance over Mexico's northern border and areas impacted by cartel violence. These drones are employed to gather intelligence on drug trafficking routes, monitor cartel activity, and track the movements of drug convoys and cartel leaders. The drones provide real-time surveillance, which can then be shared with Mexican authorities to assist in operations targeting the cartels.

Special forces operations also play a critical role in the U.S. presence in Mexico, particularly in counter-narcotics efforts. While the U.S. military does not engage in direct combat within Mexican territory, U.S. special forces, including those from Delta Force and Navy SEALs, have been reported to work in close coordination with Mexican law enforcement and military forces to dismantle cartel operations. These special forces are involved in training Mexican forces, providing intelligence for joint operations, and sometimes directly supporting high-stakes missions to capture or neutralize key cartel figures. The U.S. military has also been involved in the training of Mexican counter-narcotics forces, providing specialized training in intelligence gathering, counterinsurgency, and advanced technology such as surveillance systems and weaponry.

While American military presence in Mexico has largely been conducted under the umbrella of cooperation with the Mexican government, it is often invisible to the public, with limited acknowledgment of the scale of involvement. U.S. intelligence agencies, such as the DEA and CIA, often work in close coordination with the Mexican military and police, providing logistical support, surveillance assistance, and intelligence-sharing to help combat the cartels. This collaboration has led to growing concerns about Mexican sovereignty, as U.S. military actions and surveillance activities in Mexico are often conducted without significant oversight by the Mexican public or government.

In terms of the political framing of cartel violence, both Trump and Biden have portrayed Mexican drug cartels as a national security threat to the United States. Under Trump, the narrative focused heavily on the violence and drug trafficking emanating from Mexico as immediate threats to U.S. safety. Trump frequently used cartel violence as a justification for military action and enhanced border security. He often suggested that cartels were undermining U.S. law enforcement by flooding U.S. communities with illegal drugs like fentanyl and methamphetamines. The rhetoric of Trump's administration positioned cartels as existential threats to U.S. public health and safety, laying the groundwork for expanding U.S. intervention in Mexico through enhanced military collaboration, intelligence-sharing, and surveillance efforts.

In contrast, Biden's administration has continued a similar framing of cartel violence as a national security threat, but with a somewhat different emphasis. Under Biden, the focus has been more on collaboration and cooperation with Mexico, as well as addressing the root causes of cartel violence, such as poverty and social instability. Biden's rhetoric still highlights the need to combat drug trafficking, but with an emphasis on joint efforts to enhance security and law enforcement capacity in Mexico, while also addressing broader economic conditions that fuel cartel activity. Biden's framing suggests that while cartel violence remains a serious threat to the U.S., there is also a focus on diplomacy and working with the Mexican government to combat the cartels and reduce the violence that spills across the border.

Both administrations have justified U.S. intervention in Mexico through the lens of national security, but the approach to addressing cartel violence has shifted from Trump's focus on aggressive action and military support to Biden's more cooperative approach, which includes the use of diplomatic channels and collaboration with Mexico. Nonetheless, both have treated cartels as a significant threat to U.S. interests, continuing a policy of increasing U.S. military presence and intervention in Mexican territory. This framing has allowed the U.S. to justify the expansion of its military operations and intelligence-sharing agreements in Mexico, effectively creating a scenario where Mexico's sovereignty is increasingly compromised by U.S. actions aimed at combating cartel violence.

The framing of cartel violence as a national security threat by both U.S. administrations and certain segments of the American political establishment can indeed be seen as a pretext for furthering U.S. military and law enforcement influence over Mexico and broader Latin America. While cartel violence is undeniably a serious problem that requires attention, the military and law enforcement measures being implemented often serve not only to combat drugs and organized crime but also to expand U.S. power and influence in the region. By portraying drug cartels as direct threats to U.S. national security, the U.S. has been able to justify the expansion of its military footprint and intelligence-sharing operations in Mexico and across Latin America.

In the case of Mexico, the U.S. has increasingly provided financial support, military equipment, and training to Mexican forces, particularly in the fight against drug cartels. The Plan Mérida initiative and the U.S. presence in intelligence-sharing, drone surveillance, and special forces operations have allowed U.S. agencies to extend their reach in Mexico, often without the same level of public scrutiny or oversight that would accompany direct military intervention. This type of intervention is difficult to challenge under the pretext of a shared fight against transnational criminal organizations (TCOs), which the U.S. frames as a regional threat that undermines not just Mexican sovereignty but also U.S. security.

This approach is not new, and there are strong historical parallels between the U.S. War on Drugs and earlier American interventions in Latin America. For example, the War on Drugs mirrors the rhetoric and strategies used by the U.S. during its interventions in countries like Panama, Nicaragua, and Colombia, where drug trafficking was used as a justification for military involvement and political intervention. Just as the U.S. framed the fight against drug cartels as necessary for national security, earlier interventions often involved similar justifications, including combating communism, protecting democracy, or securing economic interests.

In Panama, for example, the U.S. used the invasion in 1989—ostensibly to protect American citizens, fight drug trafficking, and combat the Panamanian military—as a means of asserting economic control over the region. Similarly, in Nicaragua, the U.S. supported the Contras (a rebel group) in their fight against the Sandinista government in the 1980s, using drug trafficking as a justification for their intervention, though the real goal was often tied to containing communism and ensuring that U.S. interests in the region remained protected.

These interventions were part of a broader strategy of economic and geopolitical dominance over Latin America. The U.S. frequently justified its actions as efforts to maintain stability and security in the region, while, in practice, the interventions served to ensure that U.S. influence over Latin American economies and politics remained strong. Military aid and support for puppet governments often helped to protect U.S.

economic interests, particularly in terms of resources, trade routes, and investments.

In the case of Colombia, U.S. intervention in the 1990s through Plan Colombia involved military aid and training to combat drug cartels, but it also had significant implications for U.S. economic dominance. The U.S. military and economic aid package helped maintain Colombia as a key U.S. ally in the region and opened up opportunities for American corporations to benefit from access to Colombian resources and markets. These examples illustrate that U.S. military and law enforcement interventions in Latin America have often been tied to broader geopolitical goals and economic interests, rather than simply responding to the immediate threat of crime or drug trafficking.

The pattern of military aid, support for authoritarian regimes, and economic dominance is a core feature of U.S. foreign policy in Latin America, which has consistently used national security concerns—such as drug trafficking, communism, or instability—as justifications for interventions. In many cases, these interventions have undermined local sovereignty and often replaced governments that were not aligned with U.S. interests with more U.S.-friendly regimes. The military aid provided to these countries, while ostensibly aimed at addressing local issues like drug violence or political instability, also helped to secure U.S. economic dominance by ensuring that economic and political structures in Latin America were friendly to U.S. business interests.

How Economic and Security Pressures Are Pushing Mexico Closer to Integration

Mexico's economic dependency on the United States serves as a powerful informal method of control, making it difficult for Mexico to act fully independently, especially when it comes to economic policy, trade decisions, and political sovereignty. This dependency has grown significantly over the last several decades, primarily driven by trade agreements, foreign investment, and remittances that bind Mexico's

economic interests tightly to those of the U.S. The U.S. plays an outsized role in shaping Mexico's economic trajectory, and this relationship
has been leveraged in ways that limit Mexico's ability to fully assert its
autonomy.

A significant portion of Mexico's GDP is directly tied to its trade
relationship with the U.S. Approximately 80% of Mexico's exports are
to the United States, making it the country's largest trading partner.
This economic interdependence is a key factor in the informal control
the U.S. exercises over Mexico. When a country is so heavily reliant
on another for its economic growth, it becomes vulnerable to policy
shifts in the larger partner. The U.S. market is critical for Mexico's manufacturing and agriculture sectors, and any disruption in this trade,
such as tariffs or trade disputes, can have devastating consequences for
Mexico's economy. The NAFTA agreement, which came into force in
1994 and was later replaced by the USMCA (United States-Mexico-
Canada Agreement), further solidified this relationship by eliminating
trade barriers and creating a framework that aligns Mexico's economy
more closely with that of the U.S.

U.S. corporate dominance in Mexican industries is another major
factor limiting Mexico's ability to act independently. U.S. corporations
have significant control over key sectors of the Mexican economy, particularly in manufacturing, energy, and agriculture. For instance, U.S.
companies control large portions of the Mexican oil sector, automobile
production, and agriculture. The free trade environment facilitated by
NAFTA allowed American firms to set up factories and operations in
Mexico, taking advantage of lower labor costs and offering limited benefits to Mexican workers. This dependence on foreign-owned enterprises
has left Mexico vulnerable to U.S. economic fluctuations. American
influence in these industries can influence Mexican economic policies,
pushing the country to adopt policies that favor U.S. business interests
over Mexico's domestic priorities. Furthermore, when U.S. firms dominate key sectors, it reduces Mexico's control over its own economy and
forces it to compete on terms set by its more powerful neighbor.

Remittances from Mexican workers in the U.S. are another crucial aspect of Mexico's economic dependency. Mexican workers who have migrated to the U.S. send significant amounts of money back to their families in Mexico, making remittances a critical source of income for many Mexican households. In 2020, remittances to Mexico exceeded $40 billion, accounting for approximately 4% of Mexico's GDP. This constant influx of financial support from the U.S. creates a financial leash that keeps Mexico dependent on the economic relationship between the two countries. With such a significant portion of the population relying on income from the U.S., Mexico is often reluctant to pursue policies that might jeopardize the flow of remittances or alienate the U.S. in any way. This dependence on remittances also underscores the lack of economic diversification in Mexico and its reliance on U.S. labor markets.

Finally, NAFTA, and its successor the USMCA, played a major role in hollowing out Mexico's domestic agricultural and manufacturing sectors, making the country more economically reliant on the U.S. NAFTA led to the opening up of Mexico's agriculture sector to U.S. imports, which had devastating effects on Mexican farmers. With the flood of cheap American agricultural goods, many small-scale Mexican farmers were unable to compete, leading to massive job losses and the displacement of millions of rural workers. The U.S. also gained greater access to Mexico's manufacturing sector, particularly in automobiles and electronics, shifting production away from Mexican domestic industries and making Mexico's industrial base more dependent on U.S. supply chains. As a result, Mexico became a labor hub for U.S. companies, rather than building its own robust domestic economy. This shift weakened Mexico's economic independence and made it even more vulnerable to U.S. economic cycles and decisions, such as tariffs and trade policies.

In conclusion, Mexico's economic dependency on the U.S. has effectively created a system of informal control, where U.S. trade policies, corporate influence, remittances, and economic integration shape Mexico's economic decisions and limit its ability to act independently. With such a large portion of its GDP tied to trade with the U.S., Mexico finds itself in a precarious position, unable to pursue truly autonomous economic policies without risking major economic repercussions. The hollowing out of key domestic sectors, such as agriculture and manufacturing, further entrenches Mexico's reliance on the U.S., ensuring that the country remains within the sphere of U.S. economic influence.

Mexico's economic dependency on the United States serves as a powerful informal method of control, with economic, political, and social pressures that limit Mexico's autonomy. Over decades, the interwoven economic ties between the two nations have made it difficult for Mexico to operate independently without risking significant economic repercussions. This dependency has created a situation where the U.S. can exert influence over Mexico's decisions by leveraging economic pressure, trade negotiations, and border policies.

Approximately 80% of Mexico's exports go to the U.S., which ties a significant portion of Mexico's GDP to trade with its northern neighbor. This dependency on the U.S. market leaves Mexico vulnerable to economic shifts in the U.S., especially in terms of trade tariffs and market access. Any disruption to this relationship—such as changes in trade agreements or the imposition of tariffs—could have devastating consequences for Mexico's economy. This high level of dependence gives the U.S. leverage to shape Mexico's economic policies and priorities, often pushing Mexico to align its policies with U.S. interests to avoid economic harm.

U.S. corporate dominance in Mexican industries further limits the country's ability to act independently. Many key sectors of the Mexican economy, including automobile manufacturing, energy, and agriculture, are heavily influenced by American corporations. Foreign direct investment from U.S. companies has integrated Mexico's economy into the U.S.-dominated global supply chain, which often leaves Mexico reliant on U.S. capital and technology. This limits the country's economic sovereignty by tying its development and growth to U.S. business interests rather than fostering a truly independent and diverse industrial base.

Remittances from Mexican workers in the U.S. further entrench Mexico's economic dependency. Mexican immigrants in the U.S. send billions of dollars back home each year—accounting for approximately 4% of Mexico's GDP. These remittances act as a financial leash, keeping Mexico dependent on the economic relationship with the U.S. While they provide vital support for many Mexican families, they also reinforce Mexico's reliance on the U.S. for economic stability. Because a large portion of Mexico's economic lifeblood depends on its citizens working in the U.S., the country is often reluctant to challenge U.S. policies that could jeopardize this flow of money, even when those policies may undermine Mexico's sovereignty or internal politics.

The North American Free Trade Agreement (NAFTA), signed in 1994, further solidified Mexico's economic dependency on the U.S. by creating a trade environment that primarily benefited U.S. interests. NAFTA eliminated most tariffs between the U.S., Mexico, and Canada, but it also led to the hollowing out of Mexico's domestic agricultural and manufacturing sectors. Small farmers in Mexico, particularly those involved in corn production, were unable to compete with the influx of subsidized U.S. crops, leading to widespread job losses in rural areas. The agreement also led to the relocation of manufacturing jobs to Mexico from the U.S., but many of these jobs were in assembly plants that offered low-wage labor with little opportunity for Mexico to diversify its economy beyond being a low-cost manufacturing hub for U.S. corporations. This shift forced Mexico to remain reliant on U.S. supply chains and market access.

U.S. border security policies have also had a significant impact on Mexico's internal politics. The militarization of the U.S.-Mexico border and policies like the "Remain in Mexico" program, which requires asylum seekers to wait in Mexico for U.S. court hearings, have forced Mexico to police its own population to meet U.S. border control demands.

These policies have led to Mexico acting as a barrier between Central America and the U.S., pushing Mexico to adopt more restrictive immigration policies and to enforce U.S.-directed migration control. The U.S. has used aid packages and the threat of border restrictions as tools to push Mexico into this role, often without full regard for the humanitarian consequences for migrants or Mexico's sovereignty in determining its own immigration policies.

Mexico's role as a buffer state between Central America and the U.S. reflects the U.S. vision of Mexico as a strategic partner in managing regional migration. While this arrangement may benefit the U.S. in controlling illegal immigration and drug trafficking, it has placed a heavy burden on Mexico, forcing the country to intercept migrants and deal with the humanitarian crisis on behalf of the U.S. This has further entrenched Mexico's role in regional U.S. geopolitical strategies, often at the expense of Mexico's own internal priorities and the well-being of migrants traveling north.

U.S. threats of economic sanctions and border restrictions have been used as blackmail to ensure Mexico's compliance with U.S. policy demands, particularly on issues like immigration control and drug trafficking. These tactics exploit Mexico's economic reliance on the U.S. by threatening to disrupt trade relations or cut off access to the U.S. market if Mexico does not comply with specific U.S. demands. This economic pressure has forced Mexico to align its policies with U.S. objectives, limiting its ability to pursue more independent foreign policies or domestic reforms that are not in line with U.S. interests.

Finally, the militarization of the U.S.-Mexico border echoes past U.S. interventions and occupations in Latin America, where the U.S. sought to maintain influence over the region through military presence and control over borderlands. Just as the U.S. has used military interventions in countries like Honduras, Nicaragua, and Panama to protect U.S. interests, the U.S. has now used border militarization to influence Mexico's internal security policies. This increased presence has led to greater U.S. control over Mexico's border enforcement and immigration management, limiting Mexico's ability to assert its own control over its territorial integrity.

Mexico's economic dependency on the U.S. serves as a powerful tool of informal control, limiting Mexico's sovereignty and ability to act independently. The country's reliance on trade, remittances, and foreign investment from the U.S. creates a financial leash that can be easily used to exert economic pressure. The militarization of the U.S.-Mexico border and the enforcement of U.S. immigration policies have further entrenched Mexico's position as a buffer state and a partner in U.S. geopolitical strategies, often to the detriment of Mexico's autonomy in determining its own domestic policies. This arrangement demonstrates the informal but powerful influence that the U.S. wields over Mexico, dictating many aspects of the country's political and economic landscape.

Part IV: The Path to Annexation

Part IV: The Path to Annexation – Consent, Coercion, or Collapse

Chapter 10: The Weakening

Chapter 10: The Weakening of Canadian National Identity

The Decline of Canadian Nationalism and Increasing American Cultural Dominance

Canada's national identity has always been shaped by the influence of larger empires, first Britain and now the United States, which has posed challenges to the development of a uniquely Canadian identity. While Canada has made efforts to carve out a distinctive sense of national self-awareness, its history has often been one of dependency and subordination to foreign powers. From its founding as a British colony to its current status as a close neighbor to the U.S., Canada's identity has frequently been subjugated to external forces.

Historically, Canada's national identity was closely tied to its status as part of the British Commonwealth. The British imperial influence was paramount in shaping early Canadian institutions, culture, and political systems. The country's Monarchy, legal system, and education were largely British in structure, reinforcing Canada's colonial identity. Even after achieving dominion status in 1867, Canada remained tied to Britain in a way that kept it firmly in the shadow of a larger empire. During this period, Canadian identity was more a reflection of loyalty to the British Crown than any specific national consciousness rooted in Canadian soil. This connection to Britain created an identity that was still heavily influenced by European colonialism and not fully autonomous or self-determined.

The shift from British Commonwealth nationalism to a more North American continentalism has further eroded what could have been a distinct Canadian identity. After the Second World War, Canada's sense of independence was tested by economic ties to the United States, and the country's increasing reliance on U.S. trade and political influence began to change its cultural and political landscape. The Americanization of Canadian society began in earnest, as U.S. culture, media, and consumer goods flooded the Canadian market. The emergence of continentalism has made Canada's relationship with the U.S. more central to its identity, leaving Canada's unique national traits increasingly blended with U.S. influence. As U.S. cultural exports dominated the Canadian media, the distinct Canadian narrative began to lose ground, and Canadians began to feel less defined by their unique heritage and more by their proximity to the U.S.

The shift away from British Commonwealth ties and toward a more continental identity was solidified with post-WWII globalism. After the war, Canada sought to integrate more into the international community, becoming a member of key institutions like the United Nations and NATO. However, this globalist shift also meant that Canada became more enmeshed in the broader economic, political, and military systems dominated by the United States and other global powers. In this environment, Canada's self-sufficiency and ability to craft independent policies were undermined by the economic and political pressures of global capitalism, often directed by American interests. The rise of free market ideology and the push for economic liberalization in the 1980s and 1990s further connected Canada to global markets in ways that often subordinated national sovereignty to global and U.S.-led priorities. This was particularly evident in the cultural sphere, as Canada began to adopt policies that made it easier for foreign media—particularly from the U.S.—to dominate Canadian consumption, weakening the cultural distinction that had existed.

The era of free trade agreements, beginning with NAFTA in 1994 and continuing with the USMCA (the new trade agreement between the U.S., Canada, and Mexico), has only accelerated Canada's economic and cultural assimilation into the U.S. sphere of influence. NAFTA eliminated barriers to trade and investment, which has led to greater economic integration between the two countries. However, it has also blurred the lines between Canadian and American economies, making it increasingly difficult for Canada to pursue independent economic policies. The trade deals helped solidify a continent-wide economic bloc in which Canada became more dependent on the U.S. market for its economic well-being, pushing Canada's identity further into the orbit of its southern neighbor.

The cultural impact of these trade agreements has been just as profound. As the U.S. economy and media dominated the region, Canada's own culture began to erode under the weight of American popular culture. From Hollywood films to American television networks, the constant influx of American culture has led to a shared cultural space across the continent, often at the expense of Canada's unique linguistic, cultural, and historical narratives. This has further entrenched the idea that Canada is less a distinct nation with its own identity and more an extension of the North American continent, defined by its proximity to the U.S. rather than its own cultural heritage.

Canada has made efforts to forge a distinct national identity, its history has been shaped by external forces—first British imperialism and now the overwhelming influence of the United States. The shift from British Commonwealth nationalism to North American continentalism has increasingly eroded the Canadian identity, as economic integration, military alliances, and cultural assimilation have tied Canada to U.S. interests. The era of globalism and free trade has only deepened this relationship, making it harder for Canada to act independently and reinforcing the perception of Canada as an integral part of the broader North American system, often at the expense of its own distinct national identity.

Generational trends have increasingly reflected a decline in attachment to Canadian national identity, particularly among Millennials and Gen Z. These younger generations, having grown up in a world of globalization and intensified cultural exchange with the United States, show signs of being less attached to Canada as a distinct nation than previous generations. This shift is driven by various social, cultural, and economic factors, most notably the overwhelming influence of American culture, political discourse, and media.

Millennials and Gen Z have been raised in a time when the U.S. is seen as the dominant cultural, economic, and political force in North America. The proximity and omnipresence of U.S. media—through television, movies, music, and especially the internet—have made American culture a central part of young Canadians' lives. The globalization of media has blurred the lines between national identities, with the influence of American entertainment, political debates, and lifestyle trends often taking precedence over Canadian-centric content. As a result, many younger Canadians find it more natural to identify with U.S. political movements or cultural trends, given their shared media and social networks.

Social media, in particular, has played a significant role in this shift. Platforms like Twitter, Instagram, YouTube, and TikTok have connected young Canadians to global movements and American political discourse, with many consuming news and opinions from both sides of the border. As younger Canadians engage in political conversations, they are often exposed to the U.S. political climate and its polarized debates, making them more likely to align with movements or ideas that resonate with the broader North American or global zeitgeist. This stands in contrast to older generations, who were more likely to identify with Canadian traditions, values, and political institutions that were more independent from U.S. influence.

Younger Canadians also seem to show less interest in traditional Canadian institutions, such as the Monarchy or the Canadian military, and are more likely to engage with American political movements and ideas. The Americanization of Canadian youth culture—whether through their preference for U.S. entertainment, participation in American-led social movements, or their general exposure to American politics—has led to a generation that is less rooted in Canada's national narrative. For example, political movements like Black Lives Matter or social justice causes, which began in the U.S., have gained substantial traction among younger Canadians, who often feel more connected to them as global movements rather than issues tied to Canadian-specific struggles.

Moreover, many Millennials and Gen Z have come of age in a world where Canada's role on the world stage is increasingly framed in the context of its relationship with the U.S. rather than as a distinct international player. The NAFTA and USMCA agreements, along with shared military operations and border security cooperation, have made it difficult for younger generations to view Canada as an independent, stand-alone nation with its own political identity. Instead, they often perceive Canada as a part of the U.S. orbit, which weakens national pride and distinctiveness in comparison to older Canadians who were more likely to define themselves by their country's history, independence, and separate cultural identity from the U.S.

These trends reflect a larger shift in national identity in Canada, as Millennials and Gen Z seem to increasingly adopt a North American or global identity over a specifically Canadian one. The decline of traditional Canadian symbols, institutions, and political narratives in favor of U.S.-centric movements suggests a generation that views its cultural, political, and economic identity through the lens of global interconnectedness, with American influence continuing to grow stronger than Canada's own unique national identity.

Millennials and Gen Z are less attached to Canada as a nation than previous generations, influenced by factors such as globalization, the dominance of U.S. media, and a greater identification with American political movements. As Canada continues to integrate economically and culturally into the North American continent, younger generations are more likely to identify with the broader, globalized world than with Canada's national traditions or sovereignty. This generational shift reflects the erosion of a uniquely Canadian identity, with the U.S. increasingly seen as the dominant cultural and political force.

Canada's increasing focus on multiculturalism and a global identity has led to a diminished sense of a shared, cohesive national culture. While the country's embrace of diversity has been celebrated as a model for inclusivity, it has also contributed to a fragmented national identity where the idea of a unified, Canadian culture becomes increasingly difficult to define. As Canada continues to champion its image as a global player, with an emphasis on tolerance, immigration, and cultural exchange, the country's historical identity rooted in British colonialism, French-Canadian heritage, and Indigenous traditions becomes less of a unifying force.

Under the leadership of Prime Minister Justin Trudeau, the promotion of multiculturalism and a post-national model of governance has become more pronounced. Trudeau's rhetoric often emphasizes global citizenship and the importance of Canada being part of the world community, rather than focusing on a distinct Canadian identity. For example, his "post-national" country comments, where he suggested that Canada has no core identity but is instead a collection of diverse groups, resonated deeply with the idea of a country without a unifying cultural thread. This vision reflects a broader trend in Canadian politics, especially under Trudeau, where the notion of a national culture is less about shared traditions and more about inclusivity and global integration.

The embrace of multiculturalism—officially adopted by Canada in the 1970s—has been heralded as a progressive policy, but it has also created a lack of cohesion around a common national narrative. The celebration of diverse cultures has led to the rise of distinct communities within Canada, each with its own cultural markers, often at the expense of a cohesive, collective identity. While it is true that diversity can enrich a society, the challenge lies in balancing that diversity with a sense of shared values and national pride. For many, this emphasis on multiculturalism has made it harder to define what it means to be Canadian, as the country increasingly becomes an aggregation of identities rather than a unified whole.

Justin Trudeau's policies reflect a deliberate shift toward a more globalized and inclusive vision, in which nationalism is downplayed in favor of global unity. His leadership has often aligned with progressive global values, such as climate change activism, immigration, and diversity, but it has come at the expense of asserting Canadian values that might challenge global norms. Trudeau's approach is largely post-national, emphasizing the importance of Canada's role on the world stage rather than focusing on the preservation of a unique Canadian identity. By positioning Canada as a post-national country, Trudeau has distanced the nation from traditional forms of national pride, such as those rooted in history, culture, and heritage.

The decline of nationalism in Canada can be seen as both a sign of progress and a potentially dangerous trend. On one hand, multiculturalism has made Canada a model for inclusion, social tolerance, and diversity, and has allowed the country to stand out as an advocate for human rights and global cooperation. Canada has become an international beacon for how to manage cultural diversity and immigration, offering a vision of a world where people of different backgrounds can coexist peacefully. The rise of globalism, where nations are seen as part of a broader, interconnected international community, has made this vision appealing to many.

However, there are those who argue that the decline of Canadian nationalism signals a loss of sovereignty and a drifting away from Canadian traditions. Nationalism, in the traditional sense, often plays a key role in ensuring a country maintains its cultural distinctiveness, economic independence, and political autonomy. The increasing focus on multiculturalism and global identity could be seen as a way to undermine Canadian nationalism in favor of a more homogenized global culture. With a less defined national identity, some critics argue that Canada is more vulnerable to external influence, particularly from the United States, and could be primed for absorption into larger political or economic systems, such as the North American Union or the U.S. sphere of influence.

In this context, the embrace of multiculturalism and globalism may not only weaken the cohesion of Canada's national identity but also undermine its political sovereignty. As Canada's identity becomes more fluid and less rooted in historical traditions, it may lose the political will to assert its own interests in the face of powerful external forces. By focusing more on global citizenship and immigration, Canada may increasingly align itself with external priorities that are more reflective of global consensus than of its own national aspirations.

The Role of Media, Tech, and Entertainment in Erasing Borders

The cultural influence of Hollywood, American social media, and U.S.-based digital platforms has profoundly impacted Canada's national identity, making it increasingly difficult to differentiate Canadian culture from that of the United States. The global dominance of American entertainment and media has overwhelmed Canada's own cultural outputs, resulting in a blurring of borders when it comes to popular culture, political discourse, and social values.

One of the most significant changes has been the decline of Canadian content regulations (CanCon), which were designed to ensure a strong presence of Canadian-made programming on television, radio, and in cinemas. These regulations, once a cornerstone of Canadian cultural policy, mandated that a certain percentage of broadcast content be created in Canada. However, as the digital era has taken hold, platforms like Netflix, YouTube, and TikTok have become the dominant forces in shaping cultural narratives. These platforms are overwhelmingly American-dominated, and they have made Canadian content less visible, especially for younger audiences who consume most of their media online. This shift has eroded the influence of traditional Canadian institutions like the Canadian Broadcasting Corporation (CBC) and the National Film Board of Canada, which once played key roles in fostering a distinct Canadian cultural identity. The sheer volume of American content—from Hollywood movies to U.S.-produced television shows and streaming services—has crowded out Canadian narratives and made it increasingly difficult for Canadians to engage with content that reflects their own cultural context.

The dominance of streaming services like Netflix and platforms like YouTube and TikTok has further exacerbated this issue. These platforms offer instant access to U.S.-based media and are not bound by CanCon regulations, meaning that American content floods the Canadian market without the same regulatory barriers that existed in traditional media. For many Canadians, their cultural consumption is increasingly shaped by Hollywood movies, American TV shows, and social media influencers. These media often set the cultural tone for the country, from the fashion people wear to the political issues they discuss. The CBC, once a central pillar of Canadian identity, has struggled to maintain its relevance in an era where digital platforms—many of them American—control the narrative. This has led to a cultural shift in which Canadian voices and Canadian stories are sidelined in favor of Americanized content.

As a result, Canada's cultural landscape has become increasingly indistinguishable from that of the United States, especially for younger generations who are more likely to consume media online than through traditional broadcast channels. The youth culture of Canada has become heavily influenced by American pop culture, political movements, and media narratives, leading to a generation of Canadians whose values and cultural references often align more closely with their American counterparts than with their own national heritage. This blending of cultures has weakened Canada's distinct national identity, making it harder for the country to assert its own cultural sovereignty in the face of overwhelming American influence.

The collapse of independent Canadian media outlets has also played a significant role in diminishing Canada's cultural distinctiveness. As Canadian media companies have faced financial struggles, particularly in the digital age, many have been absorbed by larger foreign conglomerates, reducing the availability of independent Canadian journalism. This consolidation of media power has led to near-total reliance on American news outlets, such as CNN, Fox News, and The New York Times, to set the political agenda in Canada. The dominance of U.S.-based media has shifted the political conversation in Canada toward issues that are shaped by American interests and priorities, often overshadowing Canadian political discourse. For example, U.S. political issues like the Trump administration's policies, immigration debates, and cultural controversies have come to dominate Canadian media coverage, leading many Canadians to engage more with American politics than with the issues affecting their own country. The lack of independent Canadian media means that Canadians are less likely to access news that reflects their own experiences or challenges the American-centric perspective that now dominates the Canadian media landscape.

In sum, the cultural and media landscape in Canada has been profoundly shaped by the dominance of American entertainment, social media, and news outlets. The decline of CanCon regulations, the rise of globalized streaming services, and the collapse of independent Canadian media have all contributed to a Canada increasingly indistinguishable from the U.S. in terms of cultural values, political discourse, and media consumption. The forces of American media dominance have made it harder for Canada to maintain a distinct national identity, and younger Canadians, in particular, are often more connected to American culture and politics than to Canadian traditions or institutions. This has created a situation where Canada's cultural sovereignty has been increasingly undermined by external forces, further embedding the country within the larger North American cultural and political sphere.

The increasing dominance of U.S.-style social justice movements such as Black Lives Matter (BLM), gender activism, and woke corporate culture has significantly shaped Canadian political discourse over the past decade. While Canada has its own history of social justice activism, these American-born movements have taken on a disproportionate influence in Canadian society, especially among younger generations, corporations, and media outlets. The rise of these movements, often rooted in American social and political struggles, has led to the adoption of similar political language, values, and agendas in Canada, further blurring the lines between Canadian and American political ideologies. This shift has fostered a convergence of political culture, with many Canadians embracing activist movements and progressive causes that were initially popularized in the U.S., such as anti-racism and gender inclusivity.

A significant factor in this process has been the role of Big Tech in ensuring that Canada operates under American-style digital governance. As platforms like Google, Meta (formerly Facebook), and Amazon have become dominant forces in shaping global discourse, they have also shaped the way Canadians engage with political and social issues. These companies wield extraordinary influence over digital spaces and social media platforms, which have become central to public dialogue. By dominating online discourse, these American tech giants have imposed American cultural values, such as political correctness, cancel culture, and corporate social justice, on the Canadian public. The reach of these platforms, combined with their algorithm-driven content curation, ensures that American political narratives and cultural movements dominate Canadian online conversations, creating a sense that Canadians are often more in tune with U.S. political trends than with their own national political traditions.

The power of U.S.-based tech companies also extends to digital infrastructure, advertising, and commerce, giving American firms control over the economic and political channels through which Canadians receive information and engage in commerce. Google and Meta dominate online advertising, which shapes not only public perception but also political messaging. Since these platforms operate primarily under U.S. governance, they control the flow of news, advertising, and content that Canadians encounter daily. These platforms, often prioritizing U.S.-based content, are deeply embedded in Canadian daily life, dictating which voices are amplified and which are silenced. For example, Google and Meta's content moderation policies, which are largely shaped by American corporate values and political leanings, have a profound influence on what can and cannot be discussed online in Canada.

This dominance of U.S.-based platforms has significant implications for freedom of speech and political discourse in Canada. The integration of Canadian online speech laws with U.S. content moderation policies means that Canadians may be subject to American political censorship. Big Tech companies have substantial control over what content is visible or censored based on their own political agendas, even though the majority of these platforms are regulated under American law. As Canada's regulatory approach to online content becomes more aligned with the U.S., it risks subjecting Canadians to the same standards of political censorship that American tech companies enforce. For instance, in recent years, there has been a significant push in Canada to regulate online speech, in part due to concerns over hate speech and disinformation, but these regulations often align with or defer to the content moderation practices of U.S. tech giants.

This convergence of Canadian speech laws with U.S. policies has raised concerns that Canadians may be subject to American-style censorship on social media, particularly as platforms like Facebook, Twitter, and YouTube increasingly enforce content bans related to political speech, disinformation, and hate speech—all policies largely influenced by U.S. political agendas. For example, the de-platforming of certain political figures and the moderation of controversial speech can have unintended consequences for freedom of expression in Canada, where such actions are shaped by American laws rather than those that are uniquely Canadian. This growing alignment of Canadian and American content moderation policies means that Canadians may be subject to U.S.-driven digital governance, where corporate decisions made in Silicon Valley have profound effects on Canadian political discourse.

The impact of U.S.-controlled algorithms on Canadian news and culture has been profound, leading to a blurring of the traditional cultural distinctions between Canada and the United States. Algorithms used by platforms like Google, Facebook, YouTube, and Twitter are heavily influenced by U.S.-based interests, and they prioritize global content that often reflects American cultural norms and political narratives. This has led to a situation where Canadians increasingly consume media that is not only American in origin but is also filtered through U.S.-based algorithms that prioritize content based on engagement rather than national origin. As a result, Canadians are more likely to encounter American news, entertainment, and political discourse, with Canadian content often relegated to the background or left out entirely.

U.S.-controlled digital platforms have replaced traditional media sources in many Canadian homes, making American cultural influence more pervasive than ever before. Whether through the dominance of Hollywood movies, U.S. television shows, or social media influencers, American culture now permeates Canadian society to an extent that Canadian news outlets and cultural institutions struggle to keep pace. Platforms like Netflix, YouTube, and TikTok curate content based on algorithms that cater to global audiences, meaning Canadian users are likely to encounter more content from the U.S. than from their own country. The globalization of media through digital platforms has made it easier for Canadians to access U.S.-based news, entertainment, and culture, but more difficult for them to find content that reflects their unique national identity.

Traditional barriers between Canadian and U.S. culture have certainly collapsed, especially as digital platforms and social media have made it more difficult to distinguish between national cultures. What was once a more distinct Canadian culture, shaped by the influences of British colonialism, French heritage, and Indigenous traditions, has increasingly been absorbed into a North American cultural sphere, driven by the American entertainment industry and media landscape. The cultural differences between the two countries have become less noticeable, especially for younger generations that are immersed in U.S.-dominated media from a young age. From language to values, Canadian identity has become increasingly difficult to pinpoint in the face of American cultural dominance, and many young Canadians now identify more with American trends than with their own national heritage.

The collapse of these traditional cultural barriers between Canada and the U.S. has left economic and political distinctions as some of the few remaining differentiators between the two countries. In the realm of politics, Canada's social policies, healthcare system, and immigration approach provide some contrast to the U.S. political system, but these differences have become less pronounced as globalization and social media have allowed U.S. political debates to spill over into Canadian discourse. Social movements like Black Lives Matter, gender activism, and climate change advocacy, which originated in the U.S., have become widespread in Canada, reflecting a shared North American political climate that often mirrors U.S. activism and political struggles.

Economic integration through trade agreements like NAFTA and USMCA has further intensified the similarities between the two nations, reinforcing the idea of Canada as a complementary part of the U.S. economy rather than as a distinct nation with its own separate economic structure. Many Canadian businesses are closely tied to U.S. markets, and the country's reliance on American capital and corporate presence has made it increasingly difficult for Canada to assert economic autonomy. Canadian industries are often shaped by U.S. corporate priorities, and Canadian consumers are frequently exposed to American products, advertisements, and cultural products, further integrating the two nations on an economic and cultural level.

Are Canadians Being Conditioned to Accept Integration?

Decades of American cultural dominance have undeniably softened Canadians' perspectives on the idea of deeper integration with the United States. The pervasiveness of American media, political discourse, and consumer culture has shifted Canadian attitudes in a way that makes integration seem less like a threat to sovereignty and more like a natural extension of the North American relationship. U.S.-dominated entertainment, news outlets, and social media platforms have made Canadian identity increasingly porous, especially for younger generations who consume most of their content from American sources. This cultural assimilation has diluted the distinction between Canada and the U.S., leading to increased acceptance of the idea that the two countries could merge economically and politically in the future.

Many Canadians are now more likely to view the U.S. as a partner and protector rather than as a foreign power with distinct interests. The longstanding defense relationship, particularly through frameworks like NORAD (North American Aerospace Defense Command) and NATO, has helped solidify the U.S. as a military ally and security partner. Additionally, economic ties have made the U.S. seem like an essential ally rather than a competing power. With trade agreements like NAFTA and USMCA, the U.S. has become deeply embedded in Canada's economic infrastructure. The intensifying reliance on American markets, investment, and corporations has fostered a sense of shared destiny between the two countries, and many Canadians increasingly see the U.S. as a necessary partner for economic prosperity and security.

However, this shift has also led to a gradual erosion of Canadian sovereignty, as U.S. influence becomes more pervasive in political, cultural, and economic spheres. The closeness of the relationship has made sovereignty seem less like a fundamental principle and more like a potentially burdensome constraint on economic growth and geopolitical alignment. In some circles, the idea of closer integration with the U.S. is no longer seen as a loss of autonomy but rather as a natural evolution of the North American continent becoming a more unified bloc in a globalized world.

The education system has also played a role in fostering this globalist outlook, often downplaying Canadian sovereignty in favor of teaching globalist ideals. While Canadian schools still emphasize the country's history and cultural heritage, the curriculum has increasingly emphasized global citizenship, multilateralism, and cooperation between nations over a distinct national identity. Global issues like climate change, immigration, and trade are often taught through the lens of international collaboration rather than focusing solely on Canadian priorities. The result is that young Canadians, particularly those in postsecondary education, are often more attuned to global trends than to the importance of protecting Canadian autonomy.

Furthermore, Canadian students are increasingly exposed to American political discourse and media, which shape their understanding of governance and social issues. With American universities influencing educational trends, and American media setting the cultural agenda, young Canadians are more likely to align with global values and American political movements than with the specific concerns of their own country. This globalist framing has subtly shifted the perspective of many Canadians toward the idea that the country's interests are best served by aligning with international norms—often set by the U.S.—rather than prioritizing Canadian-specific policies.

The mainstream Canadian media has also contributed to normalizing the idea of a North American Union. In Canada, media outlets, which are increasingly owned by large corporations with American ties, often frame North American economic integration as an inevitable reality rather than a controversial policy. The discussion around trade agreements like NAFTA/USMCA is frequently framed as a positive outcome for Canada, often glossing over the economic compromises and loss of sovereignty that come with such agreements. Political discourse in Canada often reflects the same globalist narrative that is dominant in the U.S., with a focus on cross-border collaboration in issues like environmental policy, immigration, and defense. The mainstream media tends to present the integration of Canada into the larger North American economic and political system as beneficial and progressive, emphasizing the advantages of collaboration and globalism over concerns about Canadian independence.

The portrayal of U.S.-Canada relations in Canadian media is often framed as a partnership rather than a subordination. The shared cultural and economic ties are emphasized, and resistance to deeper integration is sometimes portrayed as isolationist or outdated, which feeds into a broader narrative that Canada should embrace the economic union and political cooperation that have already taken shape over the last few decades. With American corporate dominance, cross-border trade, and shared military concerns, the mainstream media in Canada plays a significant role in normalizing the idea of a North American Union—one where Canada is closely linked to the U.S., not just economically but politically and culturally.

Political elites, particularly those aligned with international organizations like the World Economic Forum (WEF), often view Canadian nationalism as an obstacle to globalist objectives and regional integration. These elites typically advocate for greater global cooperation, multilateralism, and economic integration across borders. As such, Canadian nationalism, with its emphasis on sovereignty, self-determination, and independent political action, stands in stark contrast to their vision of a more globalized world where countries are seen as part of a larger system that prioritizes international agreements over national self-interest.

For these elites, Canadian nationalism represents a barrier to the type of economic integration and political cooperation they seek. Nationalist movements, which emphasize the importance of maintaining distinct national identities and controlling economic policy or military actions, are often viewed as retrogressive or parochial in a world that is increasingly interconnected and interdependent. The emphasis on Canadian sovereignty, especially in areas like trade and defense, complicates efforts to align Canadian policy with globalist agendas or to integrate Canada more fully into larger economic and political frameworks such as the North American Union, the WEF's globalist vision, or broader UN-based initiatives.

From the perspective of global elites, Canada's relatively independent identity and its longstanding history of asserting sovereignty in economic, military, and cultural matters can be seen as a hindrance to the globalized systems they aim to build. For example, economic sovereignty—which includes having control over natural resources, industrial policies, and trade practices—is viewed as counterproductive to the global supply chains and international trade systems that benefit multinational corporations and international powers. Similarly, military sovereignty, including Canada's independent defense policies, is increasingly subordinated to NATO and NORAD, with U.S. influence directing much of Canada's military and security policies.

In the realm of cultural sovereignty, the rise of multiculturalism and the embrace of a post-national identity by Canadian elites, particularly under Prime Minister Justin Trudeau, further aligns with globalist goals. The view that Canadian identity should be fluid and inclusive, rather than based on a historical or cultural core, fits into the larger narrative of global citizenship and multicultural harmony promoted by organizations like the WEF. In this context, Canadian nationalism, which may emphasize traditional symbols, heritage, and national pride, is often viewed as an impediment to the worldwide vision of cultural fusion and economic interdependence.

Given that Canada's economic, military, and cultural sovereignty are already compromised, many elites argue that full political integration is not only inevitable but also desirable. They believe that integration into broader continental or global systems is simply a natural progression, where national boundaries become less important as global governance structures increasingly shape policy decisions. For example, the deepening economic integration through trade deals like NAFTA and USMCA, combined with military cooperation through NORAD and NATO, has already blurred the lines between Canada and the U.S., making political integration seem like a logical extension of existing policies.

From this perspective, the idea of full political integration into a larger North American or global governance system may be viewed as merely a formality—an official recognition of the de facto political reality that Canada is already economically and culturally linked to the U.S. and the global system. Rather than resisting integration, political elites see it as an opportunity to further consolidate power and consolidate Canada's position within the global framework. Political integration, in this view, is less about losing sovereignty and more about aligning with global policies, where national borders are seen as artificial barriers to progress.

Therefore, for many global elites, the push for deeper political integration is viewed not as a loss of sovereignty but as an embrace of a global future. The belief is that, with Canada's economic, military, and cultural systems already in alignment with those of the U.S., further political integration will streamline policy-making and enhance the country's role in the global order. The sovereignty of the nation-state, in their view, has become outdated in an era where global issues, such as climate change, trade policy, and immigration, require collaborative governance rather than individual national actions.

Chapter 11: The Collapse of the Canadian Dollar

The Collapse of the Canadian Dollar – A Trigger for Merger?

The Weakening of the Canadian Economy and the Push for a North American Currency

Canada's economy has increasingly become fragile and dependent on U.S. markets, driven by decades of economic integration and reliance on American trade and investment. This dependency has left Canada vulnerable to external forces, particularly U.S. economic policies, and has limited Canada's economic sovereignty. Several key factors, including the decline of Canadian manufacturing, the housing bubble and debt crisis, and the impact of U.S. interest rate hikes, contribute to Canada's growing vulnerability.

One of the most significant signs of Canada's growing dependency on the U.S. is the decline of Canadian manufacturing and the reliance on American imports. Over the past few decades, Canada's once robust manufacturing sector has been outsourced or moved to cheaper labor markets, especially in the U.S. and Mexico, in the wake of free trade agreements like NAFTA and USMCA. Canada's manufacturing base has largely shifted toward resource extraction and commodity exports, with many value-added goods now being imported from the U.S. or produced by U.S. companies operating within Canada. This has made

Canada's economy heavily reliant on U.S. demand for its resources and commodities, leaving Canada vulnerable to shifts in American consumer trends or economic slowdowns. U.S. corporations dominate key sectors of the Canadian economy, particularly in energy, automobiles, and technology, further entwining Canada's economic future with that of the U.S.

Canada's housing bubble and debt crisis are additional indicators of an economy in crisis, with increasing reliance on debt and foreign capital to fuel growth. Over the past two decades, Canada has seen an explosive rise in housing prices, particularly in cities like Vancouver, Toronto, and Montreal, driven by low interest rates, foreign investment, and demand from U.S.-based investors. The Canadian housing market has become a speculative investment vehicle, often out of reach for the average Canadian homebuyer. As housing prices have soared, Canadians have increasingly turned to debt to finance home purchases, leading to skyrocketing levels of household debt. As of recent years, Canadian household debt has been among the highest in the world, with many Canadians relying on credit and mortgages to fuel their consumption. This reliance on debt has created an unsustainable economic model that leaves Canadians vulnerable to interest rate increases and a slowdown in economic growth. With the housing market now overvalued, any correction could have devastating consequences for the broader economy, as many Canadians' wealth is tied to the value of their homes.

The U.S. interest rate hikes have only exacerbated Canada's inflationary pressures and borrowing costs. As the Federal Reserve has raised interest rates to combat U.S. inflation, the ripple effects have been felt across the border in Canada. Higher interest rates in the U.S. have pushed up borrowing costs in Canada, as Canadian banks typically follow the U.S. Federal Reserve's lead to maintain a stable exchange rate and manage inflationary pressures. As borrowing costs increase, Canadians are facing higher mortgage rates, consumer loan rates, and credit card interest, putting further strain on their already overleveraged households. The impact on inflation has been particularly severe, as the cost of living rises for Canadians, who are already struggling with high levels of household debt and an overvalued housing market. This interdependence with U.S. monetary policy means that Canada's economic health is increasingly subject to the decisions of the U.S. Federal Reserve, leaving Canadian policymakers with limited room to maneuver in terms of domestic economic control.

In sum, Canada's economic fragility is a direct result of its increasing reliance on U.S. markets and policies. The decline of Canadian manufacturing and the outsourcing of production have left Canada dependent on American imports and demand for its natural resources. The housing bubble and debt crisis have created an unsustainable economy fueled by debt and foreign investment, with the potential for a catastrophic economic correction. Finally, U.S. interest rate hikes have compounded inflationary pressures and borrowing costs, further squeezing Canadian households and businesses. As Canada's economic dependence on the U.S. deepens, its vulnerability to American economic policies grows, making it more difficult for the country to pursue independent economic strategies or assert its sovereignty in global markets.

The rise of government spending and the welfare-state expansion in Canada over the past few decades has led to a growing reliance on public sector programs and services to support the economic well-being of the population. This expansion has been driven by increased demand for healthcare, social services, and public programs designed to support vulnerable populations. While these programs have provided much-needed support to Canadians, they have also stretched the fiscal capacity of the government, raising serious questions about their long-term sustainability.

Government spending in Canada has grown significantly, particularly in areas like healthcare, education, and pensions, fueled by an aging population and rising costs of living. The COVID-19 pandemic further accelerated government expenditures, with billions of dollars allocated for stimulus packages, economic relief, and pandemic-related support programs. While these efforts have provided short-term relief, the question remains whether such spending levels can be maintained in the face of mounting national debt and fiscal deficits. The Canadian government has relied on borrowing to fund many of its programs, and as interest rates rise, the cost of servicing this debt will become increasingly burdensome. Without significant reforms, Canada could face a future where the welfare state becomes unsustainable, potentially leading to higher taxes or cuts to services in the future.

One of the key challenges to sustaining government spending is the rise of policies that prioritize environmental concerns and decarbonization over domestic energy production, particularly in the oil and gas sectors. The war on domestic energy production, particularly in oil-rich regions like Alberta, has been driven by policies designed to reduce carbon emissions and transition Canada toward a greener economy. While these policies have been supported by environmental advocates, they have significant economic implications, particularly for the energy-dependent provinces that rely on resource extraction for their economic health.

The decisions to limit oil production and shut down pipelines in the name of decarbonization have caused job losses in the energy sector and made it more difficult for Canada to generate revenue from its natural resources. As global demand for energy continues to rise, especially in emerging economies, Canada's energy policies have increasingly left the country dependent on foreign imports to meet its own energy needs. This reliance on foreign energy sources makes Canada vulnerable to global price fluctuations and disrupts its ability to maintain energy security. The impact of these policies is particularly evident in oil-producing regions like Alberta, where the government has restricted oil production in an effort to reduce carbon emissions, contributing to unemployment, economic stagnation, and a loss of investment in the region.

Additionally, the rise of decarbonization policies has led to the increased cost of energy for Canadian households and businesses, as the push for clean energy has often been accompanied by higher energy prices. This is particularly problematic for those living in rural and northern regions of Canada, where heating costs and energy access are critical to daily life. As traditional energy sources become more expensive or less accessible, the impact on low-income Canadians and small businesses could be devastating. In the longer term, the shift away from domestic energy production could further undermine Canada's economic self-sufficiency, as it becomes more reliant on external energy imports and less able to generate revenue from its own resources.

If the Canadian dollar were to collapse, the consequences would be profound, affecting every facet of Canada's economy, from consumer purchasing power to international trade. A collapse in the value of the loonie could trigger inflationary pressures, destabilize the housing market, and severely disrupt Canada's economic relationship with the United States and the global economy. The loonie's vulnerability to global currency fluctuations and inflationary pressures is shaped by several factors, including Canada's dependence on natural resources, global commodity prices, and the broader economic environment.

The Canadian dollar is particularly vulnerable to global currency fluctuations due to its close correlation with oil and commodity prices. Canada is a major exporter of natural resources, and its currency often moves in tandem with the prices of oil, natural gas, and other commodities. When commodity prices drop, the value of the loonie typically falls as well, making Canada more vulnerable to external economic shocks. Global inflationary pressures, such as those caused by supply chain disruptions, pandemics, or rising global demand, can also exacerbate domestic inflation, which would further devalue the Canadian dollar.

The Canadian dollar's vulnerability is compounded by the U.S. dollar's dominance in global markets. As Canada's largest trading partner, economic fluctuations in the U.S. have a direct impact on the loonie's stability. The Federal Reserve's interest rate decisions or U.S. inflation trends can spill over into Canada's economy, influencing the Canadian dollar's value and leading to volatility in exchange rates. In times of global financial uncertainty, such as during an economic downturn, investors often flock to the U.S. dollar as a safe haven currency, which can lead to a weakened loonie as demand for the Canadian dollar wanes.

If the Canadian dollar were to collapse or face a severe devaluation, it could prompt Canadian policymakers to consider drastic measures, such as pegging the currency to the U.S. dollar. This would essentially tie the loonie's value to that of the U.S. dollar, stabilizing the Canadian economy by aligning it more closely with U.S. monetary policy. However, such a move would come with significant risks, as it would mean Canada's monetary policy would be subordinated to U.S. decisions, leaving the Bank of Canada with limited control over interest rates and inflation. While pegging the Canadian dollar to the U.S. dollar could provide short-term stability, it would likely undermine Canada's sovereignty over its own economic policy and make the country more susceptible to U.S. economic fluctuations.

There are also speculations that some Canadian policymakers might be considering the idea of a shared North American currency, either formally or informally, in the context of deeper economic integration with the United States. Although such discussions are largely speculative and not officially endorsed, the concept of a single North American currency has occasionally surfaced, especially in the context of global economic shifts and the desire to strengthen ties between Canada, the U.S., and Mexico. A shared currency could eliminate currency risk in cross-border trade and reduce transaction costs, but it would also reduce Canada's economic sovereignty significantly. Canada would lose control over monetary policy, including interest rates, and would be subject to the economic policies of a unified North American bloc.

While there is no official movement toward a shared currency, the idea of deeper integration between the U.S., Canada, and Mexico has been gaining momentum, particularly in the context of trade and global economic shifts. The North American Free Trade Agreement (NAFTA) and its successor, USMCA, have already integrated Canada more closely with the U.S. and Mexico on trade and economic policy, creating a framework for potential future integration. Discussions around currency integration could become more pressing if Canada's economy becomes increasingly vulnerable to global economic crises or if the U.S. dollar becomes even more entrenched as the dominant global currency.

The idea of a North American monetary union, including the creation of a common currency, often referred to as the "amero", has been a topic of speculation and debate for years. While no formal proposals have been made, U.S. and international banking elites—along with organizations that advocate for deeper regional integration—may be laying the groundwork for such a union, particularly in light of growing economic interdependence between the U.S., Canada, and Mexico. Proponents of the idea argue that a North American dollar could streamline trade, reduce transaction costs, and provide economic stability in the face of global economic pressures. However, the implications for Canada's sovereignty and economic independence are profound and complex.

A North American dollar would function similarly to the euro in the European Union—a single currency that replaces the individual national currencies of its member countries. In this case, the amero would replace the Canadian dollar, the U.S. dollar, and the Mexican peso, creating a unified currency zone across the continent. A shared currency would allow for the elimination of exchange rate risk between Canada, the U.S., and Mexico, simplifying cross-border trade and financial transactions. It would also potentially strengthen the economic ties between these countries, fostering greater economic integration by aligning monetary policy, interest rates, and fiscal policy across the region.

The amero would likely be controlled by a central monetary authority—similar to the European Central Bank (ECB) in Europe—responsible for managing interest rates, money supply, and overall monetary policy. This authority would likely be made up of representatives from all three countries, though the U.S. would likely have the largest influence, given its dominance in the North American economy. Countries involved would need to surrender some degree of monetary sovereignty to this central body, as national governments would no longer have full control over their individual currencies or the ability to implement independent monetary policy.

The most significant question regarding the amero is whether Canada would have any real choice in adopting such a currency, or whether economic realities would force its adoption. The growing economic integration of Canada, the U.S., and Mexico—especially through trade agreements like NAFTA and USMCA—has already made the economies of these countries intertwined to an extent that undermines their economic independence. Canada's economic relationship with the U.S. is particularly critical: over 80% of Canada's exports go to the U.S., and U.S. corporations dominate several key sectors of the Canadian economy. Any move to a shared currency would not be an isolated decision, but rather a logical step driven by the need for increased economic cohesion and the elimination of trade barriers between the three countries.

However, the adoption of a North American currency would come at the expense of Canadian sovereignty. As Canada's monetary policy would be governed by a centralized body, the country would lose control over its own interest rates, inflation, and fiscal policy. For example, the Bank of Canada, which currently sets interest rates to suit Canada's specific economic conditions, would have limited influence over a shared currency system. This could lead to economic policies that are more suited to the U.S. economy than to Canada's unique needs, particularly in areas like regional economic disparity or inflation control.

The political and economic realities of Canada's situation suggest that the country may be increasingly vulnerable to the pressures of integration with the U.S. The collapse of Canadian manufacturing and resource industries, combined with the growth of U.S. corporate control in Canada, makes it harder for Canada to pursue an independent monetary policy. The Canadian economy is already deeply dependent on U.S. markets for its trade, investment, and employment, and the value of the Canadian dollar is often influenced by U.S. economic policies. This economic interconnectedness could make it difficult for Canada to resist joining a common currency zone, particularly if such a union is framed as an economic necessity to ensure stability and economic growth across the continent.

The possibility of a shared North American currency is not purely speculative, as certain global and regional trends—such as the rise of economic interdependence, the dominance of the U.S. dollar, and trade agreements that align the economic interests of Canada, the U.S., and Mexico—suggest that the amero could become a reality. While there is no current formal push for the amero, international banking elites and economic organizations are undoubtedly supportive of deeper integration in North America. The U.S. dollar's dominance, the pressure to simplify cross-border transactions, and the push for regional economic cohesion all point toward the eventual consideration of a shared currency.

What Happens If the U.S. Offers Financial Stability in Exchange for Political Control?

If Canada were to experience a currency collapse, hyperinflation, or a debt crisis, the prospect of U.S. intervention as a "savior" could be framed in a way that aligns with both economic necessity and political pragmatism. Washington could capitalize on the crisis to push for deeper economic integration and ultimately a U.S.-Canadian monetary merger. This type of intervention would not necessarily be portrayed as a power grab, but rather as a solution to stabilize a fragile Canadian economy that is deeply tied to the U.S. market. The narrative around this potential merger could easily be spun to present the common currency as the logical and inevitable answer to Canada's economic woes.

In such a scenario, Washington would likely frame a U.S.-Canadian monetary merger as a rescue plan designed to stabilize the Canadian economy, especially in the wake of a currency collapse or hyperinflation. By presenting this as a financial intervention to restore confidence in Canada's economic future, the U.S. could position itself as a benevolent power offering a lifeline to its neighbor. Washington would emphasize the benefits of monetary stability, suggesting that Canada's weakened financial system would be better equipped to recover under a common currency. This could be framed as crucial to restoring investor confidence, particularly if Canada's currency is plummeting or facing hyperinflation, which could make trade and investment untenable.

The argument could be made that currency unification is necessary for "stabilizing the economy" and avoiding further economic decline. A common currency, pegged to the U.S. dollar, would theoretically offer Canada monetary stability, especially if inflation is spiraling out of control. With Canada's debt levels rising and its currency value collapsing, Washington could present the amero or U.S. dollar as the only viable alternative to preventing further economic chaos. By linking Canada's financial woes to the stability of U.S. economic policy, the merger could be portrayed as a way to secure Canada's future, with the U.S. offering expertise in managing monetary policy and financial institutions.

From the perspective of trade, the merging of the Canadian dollar with the U.S. dollar or the introduction of a common currency could be framed as a way to "eliminate trade barriers" and "boost competitiveness". A shared currency would remove the risks associated with exchange rate fluctuations between the U.S. and Canada, making trade between the two countries even more seamless and predictable. Given that the U.S. is Canada's largest trading partner, a unified currency would allow for smoother transactions, greater integration of the two economies, and more efficient capital flows. Washington could present the currency merger as the key to maximizing North American competitiveness on the global stage, arguing that Canada's economic survival depends on its increased alignment with U.S. economic policy and the elimination of remaining barriers to trade and investment.

Another key narrative that would likely emerge in such a scenario is the financial inevitability of currency unification. As Canada's financial crisis deepens, U.S. officials, economists, and political leaders could frame the adoption of a shared currency as inevitable. With the economic integration of Canada and the U.S. already being so deep—through NAFTA/USMCA, military cooperation, and cross-border trade—the argument would be that resistance to a common currency would be futile. The message could be couched in economic rationality: "Why fight it? A common currency just makes sense." This approach would emphasize the mutual economic benefits of integration, suggesting that Canada's economic recovery could only be fully realized if it aligned with the U.S. under a common monetary system. The emphasis would be placed on the logical efficiency of eliminating currency volatility and aligning Canadian economic policy with U.S. priorities.

As part of this narrative, Washington could draw upon its historical influence over Canadian economic policies to highlight the long-term benefits of such a union. U.S. leaders could assert that Canada has already benefitted immensely from its economic relationship with the U.S., and therefore, adopting a common currency would be the natural next step to solidify that relationship. This rhetoric would likely be aimed at both Canadian elites and the Canadian public, framing the merger as a pragmatic response to the pressing financial challenges facing the country, rather than an attempt at subjugation.

The question of whether Canadian elites would be willing to sell out sovereignty for economic security is one of great significance, especially in the context of growing economic integration between Canada and the United States. In times of economic crisis or extreme financial instability, Canadian elites, including banking institutions, corporations, and political leaders, may see economic security—especially the stability of the Canadian economy—as a higher priority than maintaining full national sovereignty. The pressure to align more closely with U.S. economic policies or even to cede control of Canada's monetary system could be seen as a pragmatic solution to the challenges posed by currency instability, debt crises, or economic stagnation.

Canadian banking institutions and corporations would stand to benefit from U.S. control in several significant ways. Canadian banks, many of which already have close ties to U.S. financial institutions, would likely be integrated into a shared North American currency system, giving them more access to U.S. capital and the stability that comes with being tied to the U.S. dollar. The benefits for Canadian financial institutions would include increased liquidity, lower borrowing costs, and greater access to U.S. markets. Canadian corporations, especially those with extensive dealings in the U.S., would also benefit from a shared currency, which would eliminate exchange rate risk and make cross-border transactions smoother and more predictable. The integration of Canada's economy with U.S. corporations is already advanced, so the potential to align Canadian financial institutions even more closely with U.S. standards could be seen as a way to bolster corporate profits and create a stronger North American economic bloc.

However, the benefits for elites would come at the cost of Canadian sovereignty. A shared North American currency would require Canada to cede control over its own monetary policy, effectively limiting the ability of Ottawa to adjust interest rates or engage in independent financial strategies to address domestic concerns. By losing control of monetary policy, Canada would be deeply tied to the U.S. Federal Reserve's decisions, which may not always align with Canadian economic needs. In this context, economic sovereignty would be largely subordinated to U.S. interests, particularly as the U.S. economy would inevitably set the tone for North American economic policy.

The question remains whether the Canadian public would resist such a shift or whether desperation could lead to acceptance of a shared currency. There would likely be mass public resistance, particularly among those who value Canada's political independence, national identity, and cultural uniqueness. Political sovereignty is deeply ingrained in the Canadian ethos, and any move to merge with the U.S. under a common currency would likely spark intense debate. However, if economic conditions worsened—such as through a currency collapse, hyperinflation, or a financial crisis—the public might be more willing to accept such measures for the sake of economic survival. If Canada's economy were left vulnerable to U.S. economic fluctuations or global economic shocks, some may see the North American dollar as a necessary solution to prevent further decline, making acceptance a practical choice.

A North American currency would undoubtedly raise questions about the future of Canada as a separate nation. Political leaders and economic elites would likely argue that economic integration is a natural evolution for a continent with close economic ties. However, the creation of a shared currency would fundamentally undermine Canada's independence, particularly in matters of monetary policy. While Canada would still be politically separate, the loss of control over economic policy and currency would make it increasingly difficult for Canada to act in its own best interests without considering U.S. priorities. In the long term, the integration of Canada's economy into a North American framework could lead to greater political pressures for further alignment with the U.S., raising questions about whether Canada would retain its identity as a fully independent nation or move toward becoming an economic and political satellite of the U.S.

If Ottawa loses control of monetary policy, it would indeed lose much of its economic sovereignty. Monetary policy is a critical tool for any government to address domestic economic challenges, including inflation, unemployment, and economic growth. By ceding control over the currency and interest rates to a centralized authority, Canada would no longer have the flexibility to make decisions based on its own economic needs. Interest rate hikes or monetary easing would be dictated by a broader North American agenda, which may not always align with Canadian priorities. This loss of policy autonomy would make it difficult for Canada to independently navigate economic crises or pursue strategies tailored to its own economy.

A shared North American dollar would likely require the creation of a centralized North American economic authority, much like the European Central Bank in the Eurozone, which would manage monetary policy, interest rates, and the overall economic framework for the continent. This would essentially create a continental government that could have significant control over Canada's economic future, including decisions on trade, investment, and economic regulation. While Canada would likely retain its political institutions and national government, the growing influence of a North American economic authority could steadily undermine Canada's sovereignty over its domestic affairs.

Past Examples of Economic Collapse Leading to Forced Integration

Past financial crises have often been used as justifications for the surrender of national sovereignty, with governments and international organizations framing such measures as necessary for economic stability and recovery. The logic is typically that in times of economic upheaval, countries must sacrifice some degree of control over their own economic policy to facilitate a broader union that can manage systemic risks, stabilize financial markets, and ensure long-term prosperity. A key example of this phenomenon is the creation of the Euro and the subsequent European Union (EU), which were largely driven by the economic instability in Europe following major financial crises.

In the case of the Eurozone, the financial crises of the late 20th century, particularly the European debt crisis in the early 2000s, led to a significant loss of national sovereignty by individual European countries. The Euro was introduced in 1999 as a shared currency for member states of the EU, aiming to foster economic integration, reduce transaction costs, and boost competitiveness within the continent. However, the onset of the Eurozone crisis in the 2000s exposed the vulnerabilities of the common currency system, especially for countries like Greece, Portugal, and Italy, which struggled to meet the monetary union's fiscal requirements.

The Euro crisis was triggered by a combination of factors, including over-leveraged national economies, unsustainable debt levels, and global economic shocks. As some countries in the Eurozone found themselves unable to maintain budgetary discipline due to high levels of debt and deficits, they were forced to seek bailouts from international lenders, such as the International Monetary Fund (IMF) and the European Central Bank (ECB). In exchange for these bailouts, countries had to accept a series of austerity measures and structural reforms that imposed severe limits on their economic sovereignty.

The economic instability of the Eurozone during the crisis served as a compelling argument for increasing economic integration. To stabilize the currency, the EU expanded its powers and further centralized decision-making within Brussels. The European Central Bank (ECB) took on a more dominant role in regulating the monetary policy of member states, sidelining national central banks and essentially making the Eurozone's monetary policy a centralized function. This meant that individual countries could no longer control their own interest rates, inflation targets, or currency supply. The loss of fiscal independence was seen as a necessary compromise for the greater good of maintaining the Euro and ensuring financial stability across Europe.

As part of the broader EU framework, countries also surrendered some sovereignty over their economic policies to institutions like the European Commission and the ECB, which were tasked with enforcing fiscal discipline and ensuring that member states adhered to the stability pact. This pact imposed strict limits on deficit spending and public debt, further centralizing control over national economic decisions. This approach was often justified as the price for economic recovery and long-term stability in a unified European economy.

The monetary union and shared currency in the Eurozone were not only seen as solutions to the immediate financial instability of the time but were also framed as necessary steps for the future integration of Europe. Supporters of the Euro and the EU argued that, without further economic and political integration, Europe would remain vulnerable to global financial crises and market instability. By surrendering national control over fiscal and monetary policy, European countries could theoretically become part of a larger economic bloc that would be better equipped to handle global challenges, such as trade imbalances, currency fluctuations, and financial volatility.

However, the surrender of sovereignty in the European case has been contentious, with many critics arguing that the loss of national control over economic policy has led to unnecessary austerity measures, rising unemployment, and economic inequality in many countries. While Germany and other stronger economies in the Eurozone have benefitted from shared currency stability, the less robust economies have often struggled under the constraints of the union, leading to tensions within the EU. This ongoing debate reflects the trade-off between economic integration and national sovereignty, with countries having to balance the benefits of financial stability with the costs of lost political control.

The Greece debt crisis (2008-2015) stands as one of the most striking examples of how financial collapse can lead to the surrender of national sovereignty to international organizations like the European Union (EU) and the International Monetary Fund (IMF). Greece's financial turmoil—sparked by unsustainable debt levels, economic mismanagement, and global financial market shocks—forced the country into a position where it had to seek financial bailouts, ultimately ceding significant control over its economic and fiscal policies.

The crisis began in the wake of the global financial meltdown of 2008, which exposed deep flaws in Greece's fiscal health. Over the preceding years, Greece had accumulated a massive national debt, exacerbated by the government's public sector spending, generous welfare programs, and insufficient tax collection. By 2009, Greece's budget deficit was revealed to be far larger than previously reported, with the country's debt levels approaching 120% of GDP. This triggered a loss of investor confidence, and the Greek government faced rising borrowing costs on international markets. Unable to finance its debts, Greece turned to the EU and the IMF for a bailout.

The first bailout agreement was reached in 2010, when Greece agreed to a €110 billion rescue package from the European Union and the International Monetary Fund, in exchange for a series of austerity measures and structural reforms designed to reduce the country's budget deficit. These austerity measures included cutting pensions, raising taxes, and reducing public sector wages, which resulted in widespread economic hardship for Greek citizens. The bailouts were framed as necessary for Greece's survival in the Eurozone, but they came with severe consequences for its economic sovereignty.

The bailout conditions dictated by the EU and IMF essentially put Greece's economic policy in the hands of external bodies. The Troika—the trio of the European Commission, the European Central Bank (ECB), and the IMF—took control of Greece's fiscal policy, with the country's government required to implement the agreed reforms as a condition for continued funding. National sovereignty was significantly undermined as Greece's government was bound by external dictates regarding fiscal policy, tax increases, public spending cuts, and economic restructuring. For example, Greece had to implement structural reforms to make its labor market more flexible, privatize state assets, and liberalize its economy—policies that were often unpopular among the Greek public but were demanded by the creditors in exchange for continued financial support.

Despite multiple rounds of bailouts, Greece's debt continued to rise, and the country's economic conditions worsened. The austerity measures led to a severe recession, with unemployment skyrocketing and poverty levels climbing to historic highs. As Greece's economy shrank, tax revenues fell, making it even harder to meet its debt obligations. In response, the EU and IMF pushed for further austerity measures and insisted on more stringent fiscal discipline, effectively locking Greece into a vicious cycle of debt dependence and economic contraction. By the end of 2015, Greece's debt had ballooned to over 170% of its GDP, and the country had become essentially dependent on external financing and oversight.

The crisis and its aftermath raised important questions about the balance between economic sovereignty and global financial stability. In the context of Greece's EU membership, the crisis underscored how financial integration could lead to a loss of economic autonomy. By being part of the Eurozone, Greece had committed to following EU fiscal rules, but when those rules proved insufficient to prevent economic disaster, the country found itself subject to external control by organizations that prioritized Eurozone stability over national autonomy. The Troika's intervention was framed as a necessary response to prevent Greece from defaulting on its debt and potentially leaving the Eurozone. However, the conditions of the bailout created a scenario where Greece was trapped in an economic dependency on foreign powers, with limited control over its own economic policy.

The Great Depression of the 1930s marked one of the most profound economic crises in global history, and it fundamentally reshaped both national and global economic systems. The financial collapse led to widespread unemployment, mass poverty, and a dramatic decline in industrial output, with devastating effects on families and communities. In response to this turmoil, governments around the world, particularly in the United States and Canada, embraced centralized economic planning and government overreach as a means to stabilize their economies and restore public confidence.

The global economic turmoil of the Great Depression began with the Wall Street Crash in 1929, which triggered a financial panic and rapidly spread across international markets. The global nature of the Depression was exacerbated by trade protectionism, such as the Smoot-Hawley Tariff in the United States, which led to retaliatory tariffs and severely curtailed global trade. In the U.S., industrial production fell by almost 50%, and unemployment soared to nearly 25%. The Canadian economy, highly dependent on exports of natural resources, was equally devastated as demand for commodities plummeted, leading to a rapid decline in export revenues.

In the wake of the crisis, governments across the globe sought to address the economic collapse with increased intervention and the adoption of policies that would later be seen as key elements of centralized economic planning. The idea of hands-off laissez-faire capitalism, which had dominated in the decades leading up to the Great Depression, was increasingly viewed as inadequate for addressing the scale of the crisis. The role of government in economic affairs shifted dramatically, and the call for state intervention became more widespread.

In the United States, the New Deal, introduced by President Franklin D. Roosevelt in the 1930s, was a direct response to the economic chaos. Roosevelt's administration pushed through a series of reform programs aimed at reviving the economy and providing relief to those suffering. Central to these reforms was the expansion of the federal government's role in managing the economy, including banking reforms (e.g., the Glass-Steagall Act), the creation of social safety nets like Social Security, and the establishment of large-scale public works programs like the New Deal's Works Progress Administration (WPA). The government became deeply involved in regulating the banking sector, setting up labor laws, and overseeing financial markets, marking a dramatic shift from the previous policy of minimal government intervention.

In Canada, the Depression sparked similar responses, albeit with some differences in political context. Prime Minister R.B. Bennett, facing public unrest, implemented policies that included relief programs, wage controls, and attempts to stimulate the economy through government spending. Bennett's government was forced to act more centrally, introducing work relief programs and creating the Bank of Canada to stabilize currency and promote a unified monetary policy. While Bennett's approach was more conservative and less ambitious than Roosevelt's, the centralization of power in the federal government during the Depression years marked a turning point in Canadian economic governance.

Globally, the centralization of economic planning was a key response to the Depression. In countries like Germany, under Adolf Hitler, and in the Soviet Union under Joseph Stalin, the economic collapse provided the justification for the expansion of state control over all aspects of economic life. In Nazi Germany, the government initiated massive public works programs, such as the construction of the Autobahn, and exercised tight control over industry and labor. Similarly, in the Soviet Union, Stalin implemented a series of Five-Year Plans, which sought to rapidly industrialize the nation through state-directed planning, forced collectivization of agriculture, and heavy state investment in key industries.

The Depression also accelerated the rise of keynesian economics, which advocated for government intervention in the economy to manage demand, regulate employment, and maintain social welfare. The ideas of John Maynard Keynes, which argued that governments should stimulate the economy through public spending during times of economic downturn, gained widespread acceptance after the failure of free-market policies to address the Depression's consequences. Keynesian economics laid the foundation for a new era of economic planning, where governments would take an active role in managing the business cycle, moderating unemployment, and promoting public welfare.

The rise of centralized economic planning during the Great Depression fundamentally reshaped the relationship between the state and the economy. What was once seen as an intrusive or unnecessary role for government in economic affairs became a central pillar of economic policy. Governments, facing mass unemployment, collapsing industries, and public discontent, expanded their role in managing financial markets, labor markets, and public infrastructure. In countries around the world, the Depression acted as a catalyst for the development of social safety nets, public works projects, and the creation of regulatory bodies to control financial institutions, industries, and public services.

The crisis also laid the groundwork for the welfare state that would emerge in the post-World War II era, particularly in Western democracies. As governments took on new roles as economic planners and distributors of welfare, they also began to implement policies designed to reduce income inequality, provide health services, and ensure social security for workers. This growing dependence on government intervention in economic affairs continued to evolve throughout the 20th century, with centralized planning becoming a norm for economic governance.

Argentina's economic crises offer a striking example of how reliance on foreign loans and currency pegs can severely undermine national sovereignty, leaving a country vulnerable to economic collapse and forced integration into larger financial systems. Over the past few decades, Argentina has faced repeated economic crises marked by sovereign debt defaults, hyperinflation, and political instability, much of which can be traced back to the country's dependence on foreign borrowing and its decision to peg its currency to the U.S. dollar in the early 1990s. These decisions, meant to stabilize the economy, ultimately left Argentina at the mercy of international financial institutions and global market forces, leading to devastating consequences for its economic autonomy and national policy control.

Argentina's decision to peg its currency, the peso, to the U.S. dollar in the early 1990s was seen as a way to control hyperinflation and restore investor confidence after a period of significant economic instability. The fixed exchange rate system created an illusion of stability, and for a time, economic growth returned. However, by tying its currency to the U.S. dollar, Argentina essentially surrendered control over its own monetary policy. When global conditions shifted, particularly in the late 1990s and early 2000s, the fixed exchange rate became a significant burden. Argentina could no longer adjust interest rates or devalue its currency to respond to economic shocks, and when the global financial crisis hit, Argentina's ability to maintain its peg became untenable. This led to a massive devaluation of the peso, an economic collapse, and ultimately the defaulting on sovereign debt in 2001. The country's reliance on foreign loans and the global financial system made it difficult to navigate its own crises without external interference.

The financial strain from this debt crisis led Argentina into a cycle of dependency on international financial institutions like the International Monetary Fund (IMF) and the World Bank. These institutions imposed harsh conditions on the country, demanding austerity measures, cuts to public services, and structural reforms in exchange for bailout packages. While these measures were intended to stabilize Argentina's finances, they deepened the country's economic woes, leading to mass unemployment, social unrest, and growing disillusionment with the international financial system. The loss of sovereignty was profound, as Argentina's government was essentially forced to follow external dictates on economic policy, leaving it with little room for maneuver in terms of fiscal and monetary decisions.

Looking at Canada, there is a potential for a similar fate, particularly if the country faces severe economic hardship in the coming years. Canada's economy is increasingly intertwined with the U.S. through trade agreements like USMCA, and the country relies heavily on its natural resources, particularly oil and gas, for economic stability. However, global economic trends, such as rising inflation, commodity price volatility, and the challenges of decarbonization, could expose Canada to financial vulnerabilities that make it harder to maintain economic sovereignty. If Canada were to face a severe financial crisis—for example, from a collapse in resource prices, a real estate crash, or a sovereign debt crisis—there could be increasing pressure to deepen economic integration with the U.S. and other North American partners.

One possible scenario is that Canada could be absorbed into a larger North American financial system as a result of economic hardship. Similar to how Argentina's currency peg to the U.S. dollar made it difficult for the country to pursue independent monetary policy, Canada's economic integration with the U.S. could lead to a scenario where Canada's financial system becomes even more subordinated to U.S. economic policies. If Canada's debt were to become unsustainable, or if there were significant economic volatility, the U.S. might frame deeper financial integration as a necessary solution for stability. This could manifest in the form of a shared currency, a federal banking structure, or further alignment with U.S. economic and monetary policies.

Canada's already high reliance on U.S. markets, particularly through the energy sector, manufacturing, and trade ties, makes it vulnerable to U.S. economic shocks. If Canada's economic system becomes increasingly fragile, the push for integration into a North American economic bloc could gain traction. A shared currency or a common economic authority—similar to the systems set up in the Eurozone or under U.S. dominance—could be proposed as a way to stabilize Canada's fragile economy. The U.S. might present this as a way to eliminate trade barriers, boost competitiveness, and prevent further economic collapse, much like how the euro was justified in Europe during its financial crises.

As Canada faces increasing pressures from global financial forces, the loss of control over monetary policy could become a reality. Just as Argentina was forced into austerity measures under IMF pressure, Canada might face similar scenarios where it is forced to abandon its own economic policies to satisfy the demands of international financial institutions or U.S. economic priorities. This could lead to a situation where Canada's economic sovereignty is largely subordinated to the larger North American framework, leaving the country with little room to maneuver its own fiscal and monetary policies.

Chapter 12: Breaking the Cycle

Breaking the Cycle – Can Canada Avoid Absorption?

If Canada is on a slow march toward U.S. annexation—economically, militarily, and culturally—what would it take to reverse course? Is there a viable path to reclaiming true independence, or has the country already passed the point of no return? This chapter outlines what Canada must do to resist full integration and reestablish itself as a sovereign power.

Reclaiming Economic Independence – Breaking Free from U.S. Financial Control

Reducing Canada's economic dependency on the U.S. market, which currently accounts for around 75% of its exports, is a pressing challenge that requires a strategic shift toward diversifying trade and building new economic partnerships globally. With such a high reliance on a single market, any economic shock or policy shift in the U.S.—such as trade tariffs, protectionism, or economic downturns—can have a devastating impact on the Canadian economy. To reduce this dependency, Canada would need to take proactive steps to explore new trade avenues, strengthen relationships with other global markets, and develop a more balanced trade strategy.

One key way for Canada to decrease its reliance on the U.S. is by actively pursuing trade agreements with diverse regions that can provide access to new markets and reduce exposure to the U.S. economy. This would involve strengthening relationships with other major economic powers like China, Europe, and a potential revitalized Commonwealth trading bloc.

Pivoting to China could offer Canada an opportunity to tap into the world's second-largest economy, which is rapidly expanding and diversifying in areas like technology, manufacturing, and consumer goods. Over the last decade, China has become one of Canada's fastest-growing trading partners, particularly in the natural resources and agriculture sectors. However, a shift toward China would come with its own set of challenges, such as navigating geopolitical tensions, including Canada's relationship with the U.S. and the Chinese government's human rights record. The Canada-China trade relationship is complex, given the U.S.-China trade war and Canada's position as a U.S. ally. For this reason, any pivot toward China would require careful diplomacy and a commitment to securing favorable trade agreements that benefit Canadian businesses without provoking tensions with the U.S.

Europe presents another viable trading partner, especially with the Canada-European Union Comprehensive Economic and Trade Agreement (CETA) in place, which provides preferential market access to European markets. The EU is a large, stable economic bloc, and Canada's agricultural, technology, and manufacturing sectors could benefit from increased trade with Europe. Moreover, European nations are increasingly focused on sustainability and innovation, areas where Canada could leverage its natural resources and clean technology sectors to position itself as a critical partner in green trade and climate change initiatives. Europe is also a powerful political ally with a commitment to multilateralism, which could help Canada in navigating its future economic policies with more global influence.

Another strategic option is a revitalized Commonwealth trading bloc. Historically, the British Commonwealth was an important network of trading nations that included countries like Australia, India, New Zealand, and South Africa, many of which still maintain close ties

with Canada. As the U.K. exits the European Union, there is growing potential for the Commonwealth to serve as an economic counterweight to the U.S.. Canada could leverage its cultural ties, common legal
frameworks, and established trade relationships within the Commonwealth to create a more resilient trade network. Through this, Canada
could diversify trade and build mutually beneficial relationships with
emerging markets in Asia and Africa that are increasingly showing
promise in sectors such as technology, energy, and consumer goods.

Finally, an economic alliance with emerging global powers, such as
the BRICS nations (Brazil, Russia, India, China, South Africa),
ASEAN countries, and African states, could provide a counterweight to
U.S. pressure. BRICS, in particular, represents a group of large, growing economies that are increasingly focused on trade diversification and
shifting the global economic order away from U.S. dominance. China
and India, for example, are growing economic giants with expanding
middle classes and increasing consumption, which could create new
markets for Canadian exports. These alliances offer the potential for
long-term growth in infrastructure, energy, and technology sectors,
which could offer significant benefits to Canada's diversified trade strategy.

The ASEAN bloc (Association of Southeast Asian Nations) is also
a region worth exploring. With its rapidly growing consumer market
and strategic location in the Asia-Pacific, it presents an important opportunity for Canada to tap into emerging economies. Southeast Asia's
growth in areas like technology, manufacturing, and renewable energy
aligns well with Canadian export strengths, and expanding trade with
ASEAN could help Canada balance its trade dependency on the U.S.

Africa, with its growing populations and natural resource wealth,
also represents a strategic opportunity for Canada to expand trade relationships. Many African countries are undergoing rapid urbanization,
leading to increased demand for consumer goods, infrastructure, and
technology—sectors where Canada has much to offer. By diversifying

trade into Africa, Canada can tap into new markets, reduce reliance on the U.S., and play a larger role in global development.

Energy independence for Canada could be a critical step toward economic self-sufficiency and reducing dependence on the U.S. While Canada is blessed with vast reserves of oil, gas, and natural resources, much of this wealth is currently funneled southward, feeding the U.S. economy. The question of whether Canada can become truly self-sufficient in energy production and distribution is complex, but there are clear advantages to retaining and refining domestic resources, as well as redirecting exports to more diverse and profitable markets.

Retaining and refining Canadian oil, gas, and natural resources domestically would certainly make Canada more self-sufficient, but it would require significant investment in infrastructure and a shift in economic priorities. Currently, Canada exports a large percentage of its natural resources, especially oil and gas, to the U.S., often at a discounted price compared to global market rates. This export-driven model, while profitable, has left Canada vulnerable to fluctuations in the U.S. economy and to price controls imposed by American demand. Refining oil domestically would allow Canada to add value to its raw materials before selling them, creating jobs, boosting its manufacturing sector, and fostering technological innovation in the energy sector. Moreover, keeping the refining process within Canada would allow for greater control over the market and help secure long-term energy stability within the country.

Shifting focus toward domestic energy independence would also shield Canada from external pressures and energy vulnerabilities, particularly as global oil prices can be volatile, and market shifts in the U.S. can destabilize Canada's economy. By developing a more robust energy infrastructure, such as oil refineries, pipelining systems, and export facilities, Canada could reduce its reliance on U.S. buyers and be able to capitalize on global markets that may offer higher returns.

Redirecting oil and gas exports to other global markets, especially in Asia, Europe, and emerging economies, could be a critical component of this strategy. As countries in Asia, including China and India, experience rapid economic growth and increasing energy consumption, the demand for Canadian oil and gas is expected to rise. Establishing a broader, more diversified export strategy would reduce Canada's dependence on U.S. buyers and ensure more profitable trade agreements. To facilitate this, Canada would need to expand its energy infrastructure, such as pipelines and port facilities capable of exporting to Asia and other regions, or invest in liquefied natural gas (LNG) facilities to ship gas globally.

Currently, the U.S. remains Canada's dominant energy partner, but with significant growth in global demand and international competition for energy resources, Canada has a prime opportunity to tap into diverse markets and avoid being held hostage by U.S. policy changes or price manipulation. While it's critical for Canada to maintain strong economic relations with its neighbor, shifting a portion of its energy exports to non-U.S. markets would offer more economic leverage and greater resilience in the global energy sector. Additionally, this would allow Canada to diversify its energy customers, mitigate risk, and negotiate better terms in energy trade agreements.

In terms of monetary sovereignty, Canada faces significant risks tied to the strength of its currency. The Canadian dollar has historically been linked to commodity prices, and as a result, fluctuations in global commodity markets, especially energy prices, can lead to currency instability. If Canada continues to sell oil and gas at low prices to the U.S., this not only limits its potential profits but also puts the country at risk of undervaluing its currency. The dependence on U.S. markets leaves Canada vulnerable to U.S. dollar fluctuations, and any shift in U.S. economic policy—such as a trade war or currency devaluation—can have far-reaching impacts on Canada's monetary stability.

To protect the Canadian dollar from potential collapse, Canada must adopt a more independent approach to its energy policies and build a more resilient economy. This could involve investing in domestic production, new energy technology, and diversification of trade partners to stabilize its monetary system and make the Canadian dollar less susceptible to the economic whims of its southern neighbor. By retaining control of its energy exports, increasing domestic energy processing, and seeking more diversified global markets, Canada can ensure that its monetary system remains insulated from external forces and reduce the risk of financial instability.

A return to a gold-backed currency or a nationalized banking system could potentially insulate Canada from U.S. economic coercion, but such a move would involve significant economic restructuring and would not be without its risks. These measures are often considered by those advocating for economic sovereignty as a way to regain control over national monetary policy and reduce vulnerability to external pressures, particularly from a dominant economic power like the U.S.. However, whether these strategies could offer effective protection from U.S. financial influence depends on the broader context of global economic integration and Canada's existing financial interconnections.

A gold-backed currency would theoretically provide stability and resilience to Canada's monetary system. The gold standard limits the ability of governments to print money at will, which could prevent inflationary pressures caused by excessive currency creation. By tying its currency to gold, Canada could establish a more predictable monetary system, potentially reducing its reliance on the U.S. dollar. However, there are significant drawbacks to this approach, including the constraints it places on monetary policy. In times of economic crises or inflation, a country on the gold standard is restricted in its ability to adjust the money supply or engage in stimulus measures, as it must have the equivalent gold reserves to back its currency. Additionally, the global gold supply is limited, and relying on gold could hinder Canada's ability to grow its economy flexibly.

Alternatively, a nationalized banking system could provide Canada with more direct control over its financial institutions, limiting foreign influence and ensuring that banking policy aligns with national interests. By bringing the Bank of Canada back under full national control and possibly restricting foreign ownership of Canadian banks, Canada could have greater leverage in setting interest rates, managing inflation, and ensuring financial stability in a way that serves Canadian citizens rather than foreign investors. A nationalized banking system would also potentially reduce the influence of large, foreign-owned financial institutions, which may prioritize international profits over Canadian economic health. This would help insulate Canada from U.S.-led financial coercion, as the country would be less tied to the global financial system dominated by U.S.-based firms and institutions.

However, preparing for a worst-case scenario of U.S.-led financial destabilization—such as sanctions, currency devaluation, or economic warfare—would require more than just monetary or banking reforms. It would require comprehensive economic independence in sectors like manufacturing, agriculture, and resources, reducing Canada's reliance on U.S. supply chains. The U.S. has significant leverage over Canada in these areas, and in the event of economic coercion, Canada's vulnerability could be exposed. To prepare for such a scenario, Canada would need to pursue a policy of diversification in trade partners, resources, and domestic production capabilities to lessen its reliance on any one country.

Rebuilding domestic manufacturing and agriculture is critical in this context. If Canada can revitalize its industrial base and agricultural sectors, it would have greater economic autonomy and could better absorb the impacts of global economic shocks. By investing in modernizing industries and adopting new technologies, Canada could create a more self-sufficient economy that doesn't rely on U.S. imports for essential goods and services. Policies that encourage Canadian-made goods—through tax incentives, research and development subsidies, and trade protection measures—could support this transformation.

Supporting the domestic manufacturing of essential goods, from electronics to food products, would lessen the need for external imports and ensure that critical infrastructure is not beholden to U.S. supply chains. Rebuilding Canadian agriculture is equally important to provide food security and reduce Canada's dependence on global suppliers.

As for limiting foreign ownership of farmland and resources, this is a key aspect of economic sovereignty. A proactive strategy to prevent corporate takeovers by foreign firms, particularly American companies, would help Canada protect its land, water, and natural resources from being controlled by external interests. If foreign corporations own large swathes of Canada's agricultural land or mineral resources, they could prioritize profit extraction over Canadian national interests. Implementing measures that restrict foreign ownership of critical resources, while still allowing for foreign investment, could strike a balance between capital influx and resource control. By preserving Canadian control over its most valuable resources, Canada could ensure that its economic decisions align with national interests, rather than the demands of foreign powers. This could be an essential aspect of building a more resilient, self-sufficient economy that is less vulnerable to outside coercion.

Ending Military Dependence – Taking Back Canada's Defense

Exiting NORAD (North American Aerospace Defense Command) and building an independent Canadian defense strategy would mark a significant departure from decades of military cooperation with the U.S., but it raises fundamental questions about Canada's security needs, military independence, and national defense priorities. NORAD, established in 1958 as a joint U.S.-Canada military agreement, was originally designed to defend North America from external threats, particularly during the Cold War. However, as global threats have evolved, it's important to critically assess whether NORAD remains a genuine security benefit for Canada or whether it has instead become a backdoor for U.S. military control over Canadian defense decisions.

On one hand, NORAD's security benefit is clear: it provides a unified defense structure for North America, particularly in terms of early warning systems, airspace monitoring, and missile defense. Canada gains access to U.S. military technology and the broader American defense network, including the U.S. military's space capabilities and advanced missile defense systems. Canada also shares intelligence through NORAD, which helps enhance its national security. The arrangement is a significant force multiplier, providing Canada with defense infrastructure and strategic positioning that might otherwise be difficult to develop independently.

However, the downside of this military integration is that NORAD dilutes Canadian sovereignty over its own defense policy. The U.S. military has a dominant role in NORAD, with much of the command structure and decision-making aligned with U.S. military priorities. Canada's military posture is often constrained by the broader goals of U.S. defense policy, which could lead to mission creep or Canada being drawn into conflicts that don't directly serve Canadian interests. For example, Canadian forces stationed in NORAD's command structure could find themselves integrated into U.S. military operations that may not align with Canada's independent foreign policy. The U.S. dominance in NORAD often results in the U.S. having a larger say in decisions that impact Canadian national security. Moreover, Canada's military policy and capabilities are often shaped by the U.S. defense budget and priorities, making Canada's defense strategy highly dependent on U.S. military objectives.

If Canada were to exit NORAD and develop its own independent defense strategy, it would need to establish a comprehensive and self-sufficient military apparatus. This would involve not only developing advanced weapons systems, including the potential for a missile defense system, but also enhancing its intelligence capabilities to maintain a high level of security without the assistance of U.S. infrastructure.

A key element of this independent defense strategy would be the establishment of a missile defense system. Currently, Canada relies heavily on U.S.-led initiatives like the Ground-based Midcourse Defense (GMD) system and Aegis Ballistic Missile Defense, but leaving NORAD would mean Canada would no longer have access to these systems. Developing a national missile defense system would be both costly and technologically challenging but would ensure that Canada maintains the capability to defend against modern aerial and missile threats, including potential threats from hostile states or non-state actors. Canada could explore options like the National Missile Defense Program (NMD), though this would require substantial investment in space-based defense technologies and radar systems.

In addition to missile defense, Canada would need to build a more robust intelligence network. This includes developing satellite surveillance, cyber defense capabilities, and human intelligence networks, all of which would allow Canada to detect and respond to external threats independently. Canada currently shares much of its intelligence with the U.S. through Five Eyes (an intelligence alliance that includes the U.S., UK, Canada, Australia, and New Zealand), but to maintain an independent defense strategy, Canada would need to ensure that it has its own intelligence capabilities in areas like cybersecurity, global surveillance, and counterterrorism.

Canada would also need to upgrade its military infrastructure across air, land, and sea forces. The development of modern aircraft for interception, anti-missile defense ships, and land-based defense systems would be critical components of a strategy that positions Canada to defend its borders, including its arctic territories, coastal regions, and critical infrastructure without relying on U.S. military support. This might involve increased defense spending and potentially redirecting some of Canada's foreign aid budget to fund domestic military projects.

In considering whether Canada should exit NORAD and build an independent defense strategy, the most significant challenge is balancing military sovereignty with the costs and logistics of developing an independent defense system. Canada is geographically positioned in North America with U.S. borders on both sides, making it inherently vulnerable to attacks or threats that could also affect the U.S. This proximity to U.S. security infrastructure presents both an opportunity and a challenge—an opportunity for strategic alignment but also a challenge to Canada's autonomy in military matters.

Building a self-sufficient military that operates without U.S. dependence would be a significant shift for Canada, but it's a potential reality if the country invests in the necessary infrastructure, technology, and defense partnerships. Currently, Canada's military relies heavily on U.S. defense technology and infrastructure, from advanced aircraft like the F-35 to intelligence-sharing agreements within NORAD and NATO. While this integration has ensured mutual defense benefits, it also compromises Canada's ability to maintain full independence over its defense decisions and strategies.

Canada could certainly expand its military capabilities without dependence on U.S. technology. However, the transition would be costly and time-consuming. Developing indigenous defense technologies—such as fighter jets, air defense systems, and naval vessels—would require large-scale investment in research and development. Canada could tap into its existing military-industrial base to innovate and produce military technologies, but this would necessitate a shift in policy to prioritize self-sufficiency over reliance on U.S. manufacturers like Lockheed Martin or Boeing. As an example, while Canada currently operates the F-35 fighter jet, the country could explore the possibility of developing its own indigenous fighter aircraft, similar to Sweden's Saab Gripen or France's Dassault Rafale, which would allow it to better control its air defense capabilities. Canada would also need to build more domestic production capacity for naval vessels, submarines, and ground-based defense systems, which are currently procured from foreign suppliers.

The key to achieving military independence lies in Canada's ability to invest in domestic defense capabilities while maintaining global relationships. A potential strategy would involve forming stronger alliances with non-U.S. NATO members and European countries, such as Germany or France, which also have robust military systems and technological capabilities. For instance, Germany's military offers advanced tank and air defense systems, while France has the Airbus A400M military transport and Dassault Aviation systems. Partnering with these nations on joint defense programs, military exercises, and shared R&D could enable Canada to build a more diversified defense network that does not rely exclusively on the U.S. military-industrial complex.

Moreover, Canada could explore new alliances outside of NATO. While NATO provides security cooperation, it is also heavily influenced by U.S. military priorities, which sometimes conflict with Canada's independent defense interests. Partnering with BRICS countries, such as India or Brazil, could offer Canada access to new defense technologies and market opportunities. India has developed advanced missile defense systems, naval technologies, and aerial capabilities, which could serve as potential areas for military cooperation. Additionally, ASEAN countries and African nations are increasingly investing in their own defense capabilities, and Canada could form new defense partnerships with these emerging military powers to further diversify its security alliances.

If Canada were to leave NORAD and develop a national defense strategy, it would also need to establish its own missile defense systems and intelligence networks. Currently, Canada shares military intelligence with the U.S. through NORAD and other alliances, but an independent defense strategy would necessitate the development of advanced surveillance, missile detection, and cybersecurity systems. Building an indigenous missile defense system would be a critical step in ensuring that Canada's airspace and territorial borders remain secure without reliance on U.S. technology. The Canadian military's technological needs could be met by collaborating with non-U.S. defense contractors or through joint defense initiatives with European nations or global partners.

Rebuilding domestic manufacturing is crucial to supporting an independent defense strategy. By incentivizing Canadian-made goods—especially in the aerospace, shipbuilding, and defense industries—Canada could reduce its reliance on foreign imports for military equipment. This would require government-backed subsidies, tax incentives, and R&D grants to encourage investment in domestic manufacturing and innovation. Additionally, Canada would need to invest in workforce training to ensure that it has the skilled labor force required for these initiatives. By supporting Canadian-owned defense contractors and ensuring that key industries, such as steel, machinery, and electronics, are domestically sourced, Canada could build an independent and resilient military supply chain.

Limiting foreign ownership of farmland and natural resources is another key strategy to prevent external actors, particularly American corporations, from gaining control over essential sectors that could undermine Canada's economic and military independence. Foreign acquisitions of agricultural land, energy resources, and mining operations have been a concern, as they could potentially compromise Canada's food security, energy independence, and natural resource control. By enforcing stricter regulations on foreign ownership, Canada could ensure that its strategic assets remain under domestic control and are not vulnerable to foreign influence. This could be particularly important during times of global geopolitical tension, where countries like the U.S. could exert pressure through economic means, including controlling energy supplies or agricultural production.

The Arctic is increasingly becoming a focal point of global competition, particularly as climate change opens up new shipping lanes and increases access to the vast natural resources within the region. The U.S., along with other powers like Russia and China, has shown considerable interest in securing its stake in the Arctic, and there are growing concerns that it could lead to economic and military expansion into Canadian territory. The U.S., with its significant military presence and economic power, could seek to dominate the Arctic by using its proximity to the region as a strategic advantage, particularly given the Arctic's potential for new trade routes and natural resource exploitation. As climate change continues to melt the ice, new shipping lanes will become accessible, and resources like oil, gas, and minerals will become more economically viable to extract.

For Canada, the risk lies in losing control of its Arctic territories to the U.S. and other emerging powers. The region is strategically significant for both military defense and economic resources, and without a strong, independent stance, Canada could be overwhelmed by outside forces seeking to claim dominance over the region. Given the U.S.'s military presence and economic interests in the Arctic, there's a serious risk that the U.S. could justify military or economic intervention in the region, perhaps claiming the region as part of its strategic defense needs or economic interests.

To safeguard Canadian sovereignty over the Arctic, it is crucial that Canada establish a stronger military and industrial presence in the North. Strengthening its military capabilities in the Arctic region would allow Canada to assert its authority and deter any foreign encroachment, particularly from the U.S. By investing in military infrastructure, such as air bases, naval stations, and radar systems, Canada can better defend its Arctic borders and ensure that it is not left vulnerable to foreign military expansion. In addition to the military build-up, Canada must bolster its industrial capabilities to develop the Arctic's economic resources and ensure that the extraction of oil, gas, and minerals remains under Canadian control.

Developing infrastructure that supports resource extraction, energy production, and sustainable industries in the Arctic could help create long-term economic opportunities for Canada while preventing other powers from taking control. Canada must prioritize establishing energy independence by developing domestic capabilities to exploit Arctic resources and ensuring the infrastructure to transport and refine these materials. By building strong economic partnerships with European countries, Asian powers, and other nations, Canada can shift some of its trade interests away from the U.S., making it less reliant on its southern neighbor for economic survival.

Additionally, Canada needs to address its Arctic policies proactively, particularly regarding the Northwest Passage, which holds significant geostrategic importance. By enforcing Canadian laws and regulations over the passage, Canada can better defend its claims to the Arctic and prevent external actors, particularly the U.S., from asserting jurisdiction over key routes. The U.S. has previously indicated interest in using the Northwest Passage for military and commercial purposes, so Canada must stand firm in maintaining exclusive control over this vital trade route.

Rebuilding Canadian Culture and National Identity

Dismantling U.S. cultural dominance is an essential step for Canada to regain its cultural sovereignty and foster a more independent national identity. The heavy influence of American culture through media, entertainment, and social media platforms has eroded Canada's cultural uniqueness, often leading Canadians to consume more American-produced content than their own. While American media dominates Canadian airwaves and the digital space, Canada has tools at its disposal to counter this influence, particularly through legislative measures and investments in independent media.

Canada should consider enforcing stronger media protections, such as expanding CanCon (Canadian Content) regulations, to support the revival of domestic television, film, and news industries. CanCon was designed to ensure that a percentage of the content broadcast in Canada is created by Canadians, but over the years, the influence of American media conglomerates has weakened its effectiveness. In the era of streaming platforms like Netflix, Amazon Prime, and Disney+, many Canadians are consuming large amounts of content produced outside of the country, much of it from the U.S. To counter this, Canada could update and expand CanCon policies to require streaming platforms to support Canadian programming, provide funding for local filmmakers, and ensure that Canadians are not only consumers of culture but also active producers. These measures would help revitalize the Canadian film, television, and news industries, create local jobs, and reduce Canada's cultural dependence on foreign (primarily American) content.

American Big Tech companies, such as Google, Facebook, and Twitter, have an outsized influence on the information Canadians receive, controlling news dissemination, shaping public opinion, and defining digital discourse. The algorithms these platforms use prioritize content that often aligns with American political, economic, and cultural interests, further reinforcing U.S. dominance in the information space. Canada should consider limiting the influence of U.S. social media, particularly by enforcing regulations that require these platforms to prioritize Canadian content and news outlets. The Canadian government could also mandate that social media giants pay for the use of Canadian news content or contribute to Canadian journalism funds, thereby ensuring a more balanced representation of national issues and reducing reliance on foreign corporations to shape public discourse.

Additionally, Canada's independent media has been under significant strain in recent years, as corporate consolidation and foreign investment have led to the monopolization of the news industry. The rise of American-owned media conglomerates such as CNN, Fox News, and The New York Times has contributed to the growing Americanization of the Canadian media landscape. To prevent U.S.-style corporate monopolization of news, Canada must reinvest in independent media outlets, both print and digital, to ensure a diversity of voices and narratives. This could involve subsidizing local journalism, offering grants to independent news outlets, and ensuring fair competition by restricting foreign ownership of key media assets. By promoting independent journalism, Canada can strengthen its media landscape and ensure that public discourse is shaped by Canadian voices, rather than a handful of American corporate giants.

Strengthening education and civic engagement is crucial to restoring and solidifying Canada's national identity and ensuring that future generations are equipped to engage with the complexities of governance, sovereignty, and global influence. The educational system plays a central role in shaping how citizens understand their history, values, and political system, and it can serve as a powerful tool to foster a deeper connection to Canadian sovereignty and a sense of pride in the nation's achievements.

A nationalist education curriculum could indeed help rebuild pride in Canadian history and sovereignty. Currently, many aspects of Canada's historical narrative, particularly in relation to Indigenous peoples, colonialism, and the struggles for independence, are either glossed over or minimized in the mainstream curriculum. By adopting a curriculum that emphasizes the unique aspects of Canadian history, from Confederation to the Canada Act of 1982, students could develop a greater appreciation for the country's journey toward self-governance and the challenges it has faced in asserting its independence from foreign powers, including the British Empire and the U.S. A strong, nationalist approach would also provide a more balanced understanding of the country's past, acknowledging both the achievements and the injustices, and could instill a sense of national pride rooted in the country's distinct identity.

Incorporating Canadian history in a way that stresses sovereignty, unity, and self-determination would allow students to see their nation as an active agent in shaping its future, rather than a passive participant in a globalized world dominated by larger powers like the U.S.. This could be particularly important in countering the American cultural dominance that has permeated Canadian society, encouraging Canadians to reclaim their cultural narrative and understand the importance of preserving national values in the face of external pressures. A curriculum that focuses on Canadian heroes, nation-building, and independence movements could deepen students' connection to the country and its ongoing role in the world.

Mandating civics courses focused on Canadian law, history, and self-governance could play a pivotal role in creating a more politically engaged population. At present, many Canadians may lack a deep understanding of their legal systems, their rights and responsibilities as citizens, and the functioning of Canadian democracy. Civics education would equip students with the knowledge necessary to become informed voters, active participants in local and national governance, and advocates for the preservation of Canadian sovereignty. This could be particularly crucial for fostering political literacy, ensuring that Canadians are not easily swayed by populist rhetoric or foreign influences.

Moreover, teaching Canadian students about the constitutional structure of the country, the rights of citizens, and the role of provincial and federal governments could increase their political awareness and encourage them to actively engage with the country's democratic processes. A population that understands the importance of self-governance and the mechanisms that protect Canadian democracy is more likely to defend its sovereignty and resist external pressures that might seek to undermine the nation's autonomy.

Civics courses could also incorporate critical thinking exercises to encourage students to debate and discuss important national issues, ranging from economic policy to environmental protection and national security. Such discussions would not only raise awareness of Canadian issues but also allow young people to develop their own political views based on fact-driven analysis rather than partisan narratives. This would create a more informed electorate, prepared to actively participate in democratic decision-making and protect Canadian sovereignty.

A well-rounded education that emphasizes both Canadian history and civic responsibility can help to create a nation of citizens who are not only proud of their heritage but are also fully equipped to shape the future of their country. This approach would contribute to a culturally confident and politically engaged populace, one that understands its national heritage and the ongoing struggle to maintain sovereignty in the face of external influences.

Restoring a sense of national pride and self-sufficiency in Canada requires a deep commitment to cultivating a distinct national identity that stands apart from the influence of the U.S. and global homogenization. This can be achieved through a combination of reclaiming cultural symbols, reaffirming the country's historical roots, and fostering a collective sense of unity that includes regional identities. Canada is a diverse country, and the challenge lies in weaving these regional identities into a cohesive national fabric while maintaining respect for local distinctions.

Reviving Canada's constitutional monarchy and national symbols could play a significant role in distinguishing the country from the U.S. and emphasizing its unique heritage. The Monarchy, as Canada's head of state, represents a continuity of tradition that ties the country to its British colonial roots while embodying its modern, independent status. While some view the monarchy as outdated, it still provides a clear symbol of Canadian identity distinct from the U.S. presidential system. Reaffirming the Monarchy's role could underscore Canada's unique constitutional structure and remind Canadians of the country's foundational ties to the British Commonwealth, while also illustrating that Canada is not a republic modeled on the U.S. system.

Incorporating and reinforcing national symbols—such as the Canadian flag, national anthem, and official languages—also plays a crucial role in promoting a sense of unity and pride. These symbols help solidify a national identity by encouraging citizens to feel a collective connection to the country, irrespective of their regional or cultural differences. Fostering a deeper appreciation for Canadian symbols can counter the pervasive influence of American culture and provide a sense of belonging that goes beyond mere geography or economic ties. For example, creating public spaces that celebrate Canadian achievements, history, and diversity—whether through art, monuments, or educational programs—could help connect Canadians to the history and heritage of their nation and cultivate pride in being Canadian.

However, the country's diverse regional identities, such as those held by Quebecois, Albertans, and Atlantic Canadians, present both a challenge and an opportunity. The rise of regional separatism—particularly in Quebec, but also in Western Canada—threatens Canada's unity and can often be seen as a response to cultural and economic frustrations. Instead of allowing these differences to divide the nation, regional identities can be reframed as vital components of a unified, sovereign Canada. Canada's strength lies in its diversity, and each region contributes something unique to the nation as a whole, whether it's the cultural richness of Quebec, the economic power of Alberta, or the heritage and natural beauty of the Atlantic provinces.

Quebec, with its distinct language and culture, has long grappled with its place within Canada. However, rather than viewing Quebecois identity as a source of division or a rationale for separatism, it can be framed as a core part of Canada's national fabric. Quebec represents a unique aspect of Canadian identity—French language, Catholicism, and distinct social values—that offers a counterpoint to the Anglophone majority and enriches the national conversation. Celebrating the distinctness of Quebec while reinforcing its essential role in the larger Canadian context can strengthen national unity. Rather than seeing separatist movements as a threat, Canada should leverage Quebec's cultural heritage as a point of pride and engagement with other regions. The challenge is ensuring that Quebecois citizens feel respected and understood within the broader Canadian narrative.

In Western Canada, particularly Alberta, where there has been growing frustration over perceived economic neglect and the country's handling of oil and gas industries, the emphasis should be on unity rather than division. The Alberta identity can be celebrated as an essential component of Canada's economic strength and resource development, while also promoting greater national cohesion in policy and economic direction. Rather than framing regional grievances as a reason for separation, these identities should be viewed as strengths that contribute to a more robust and diversified Canadian economy. By finding ways to bridge divides between the Western provinces and the rest of Canada, especially in terms of resource management and economic development, Canada can avoid the pitfalls of regional separatism and forge a more unified vision of the future.

Atlantic Canada, with its rich history, fishing industry, and unique maritime culture, should also be celebrated as a vital piece of the Canadian mosaic. Strengthening regional ties with Atlantic Canada can foster a sense of shared pride and belonging among the provinces while emphasizing the interconnectedness of the entire nation. Building infrastructure and encouraging investment in the Atlantic provinces can help address economic disparities, allowing these regions to contribute more significantly to national development while maintaining their unique identities.

To truly achieve unity while respecting regional identities, Canada must embrace its diversity and ensure that every region feels empowered and represented. Regional identity doesn't need to be a force for separation; it can be a tool for strengthening the national bond when each region sees itself reflected in the Canadian narrative. Self-sufficiency, both economically and culturally, can be enhanced when Canada builds upon its differences and celebrates its regional strengths, thereby creating a unified, sovereign Canada that reflects its diverse, complex identity.

Rejecting Globalism and International Interference

Breaking away from American-led globalist institutions such as NATO, the IMF, and the WEF is a challenging but potentially essential step for Canada in preserving its sovereignty and protecting its independent policy-making. While these institutions have historically provided benefits, such as military security through NATO, economic stability through the IMF, and global cooperation through the WEF, they are increasingly seen as platforms where U.S. interests dominate, often at the expense of Canadian priorities. To reduce American influence and reassert its autonomy, Canada must evaluate whether continuing its involvement in these entities is in its best interest or if a recalibration of foreign relations is necessary.

First, Canada's role in NATO has long been seen as a security anchor within the Western alliance. While collective defense is a cornerstone of NATO, the reality is that NATO operations are heavily influenced by the U.S. military, with the U.S. providing the lion's share of funding, resources, and strategic direction. This has meant that Canada's military is often aligned with U.S. priorities rather than reflecting Canada's own defense interests or foreign policy goals. The U.S.'s geopolitical agenda has increasingly shaped NATO's actions, often without full consideration of Canada's national interests. In some cases, Canada has been involved in military operations that may not align with its own security concerns or diplomatic stance. Reconsidering its involvement in NATO could open up a broader discussion on Canada developing its own military defense strategy, more aligned with its national priorities, instead of relying on American-led interventions that may involve Canada in conflicts outside its scope of interest.

Similarly, Canada's participation in the International Monetary Fund (IMF) and the World Economic Forum (WEF) has often aligned it with the U.S. and Western financial elites. The IMF, for example, has been criticized for enforcing austerity measures and neoliberal economic policies on developing countries, often leading to economic dependency rather than growth and independence. Canada, as a donor nation, plays a role in these programs, yet the IMF's policies are largely shaped by the U.S. and its global financial system. Canada, as an economically advanced country, might benefit from reassessing its commitment to such organizations, considering whether the IMF's policies align with Canadian values such as economic fairness, social justice, and sustainable development. With the U.S. playing a dominant role in the IMF's decision-making processes, Canada could reduce its influence over global financial decisions by continuing its involvement in such institutions.

The World Economic Forum (WEF), with its annual meetings in Davos, Switzerland, serves as a platform for global elites to discuss and influence economic policy, often prioritizing the interests of the wealthiest nations and multinational corporations. Critics argue that the WEF perpetuates a globalist agenda that undermines national sovereignty, particularly in areas such as trade agreements, environmental policy, and labor rights. Canada's participation in the WEF has raised concerns about the growing influence of corporate elites in shaping public policy, often to the detriment of ordinary Canadians. By reevaluating its role in the WEF, Canada could reaffirm its commitment to democratic governance, ensuring that economic policies reflect the interests of Canadian citizens rather than multinational corporations and global financial institutions.

In parallel, Canada could pursue an alternative economic and diplomatic alliance with non-aligned nations to protect against U.S. dominance. As the U.S. continues to shape global economic and geopolitical institutions, Canada has the opportunity to forge partnerships with emerging economies and non-aligned nations in regions like Asia, Africa, and Latin America. By aligning itself with countries that are not beholden to the U.S., Canada can diversify its diplomatic and economic relations, reduce dependency on U.S.-led systems, and cultivate a broader global influence based on its values and interests.

BRICS (Brazil, Russia, India, China, and South Africa), for instance, represents a growing bloc of countries that are challenging the dominance of Western institutions, including the IMF and World Bank. Engaging with BRICS could offer Canada the opportunity to play a constructive role in reshaping the global economic order, moving away from U.S. financial hegemony and focusing on multilateral cooperation and fairer trade policies. By building closer ties with China and India, which are growing global powers, Canada can tap into the emerging economic markets of the future while also reducing its vulnerability to U.S. economic pressure.

Moreover, Canada could strengthen ties with ASEAN (Association of Southeast Asian Nations), which represents a diverse and dynamic group of countries with growing economic influence. ASEAN nations are increasingly asserting their independence from Western-dominated economic structures, and Canada's involvement with these nations could offer mutual benefits in areas like trade, technology transfer, and cultural exchange. By engaging more deeply with non-aligned countries, Canada could further diversify its trade relations, ensuring that it is not overly reliant on the U.S. as its primary economic partner.

Building alternative alliances would require a strategic shift in Canadian foreign policy—one that prioritizes self-sufficiency in both trade and security. Canada would need to engage diplomatically with non-Western countries and reaffirm its commitment to multilateralism and sovereign independence, moving away from the idea that its economic and security interests must align with U.S. priorities. While this shift would require careful management of complex international relationships, it presents an opportunity for Canada to chart a course that better reflects its national interests and values, separate from the influence of the U.S. and its global dominance.

Limiting foreign corporate and government influence in Canada is essential to preserving the country's sovereignty, democratic integrity, and the independence of its policy-making processes. The increasing influence of foreign entities, particularly American corporations and government interests, poses significant risks to Canada's ability to craft policies that reflect Canadian interests rather than those of foreign powers. By banning foreign political funding and strengthening foreign ownership laws, Canada could regain control over critical sectors of its economy and political landscape, reducing the risk of undue foreign influence.

Canada should ban American political funding and lobbying from influencing elections and policies. The U.S. has a long history of influencing Canadian politics, both through corporate interests and government pressure. Political funding from foreign entities is often used to advance the interests of multinational corporations that have significant stakes in Canadian industries. These corporations use lobbying and political contributions to shape Canadian policy on issues ranging from trade to environmental regulations. By banning foreign political donations and implementing stricter lobbying regulations, Canada can reduce the influence of foreign interests on its domestic policy, ensuring that decisions are made in the best interest of Canadians rather than foreign investors or foreign governments.

The U.S. has considerable influence in shaping Canadian policies, particularly in sectors such as energy, trade, and banking, where American corporations have strong investments. These foreign entities often exert influence through lobbying and financial donations to political campaigns, further consolidating their control over critical sectors of the Canadian economy. By restricting foreign political influence, Canada can safeguard its democratic process and prevent outside actors from undermining Canadian sovereignty. This would be a necessary step to ensure that elections are determined by Canadian citizens and political parties and not by the priorities of foreign corporations or foreign governments that seek to sway policy to serve their interests.

Canada must also tighten foreign ownership laws to prevent American firms from owning critical Canadian infrastructure, banking, and real estate. Over the past few decades, there has been a significant increase in foreign acquisitions of Canadian assets, particularly in strategic sectors such as natural resources, energy, agriculture, and real estate. American firms have been among the most aggressive in acquiring Canadian companies, often at the expense of Canadian control over key infrastructure and industries. This growing foreign ownership leaves Canada vulnerable to external pressures and risks undermining the economic sovereignty of the nation.

By introducing strict foreign ownership laws, Canada could limit the amount of foreign influence in its critical sectors. This would involve implementing stronger regulations on the percentage of Canadian assets that can be owned by foreign entities, especially in areas deemed strategic, such as oil and gas pipelines, electricity grids, financial institutions, and real estate. These measures would protect Canadian infrastructure from foreign acquisitions and ensure that critical sectors of the economy remain under Canadian control, allowing the country to shape its economic future without undue external influence.

The banking sector is particularly important in this regard, as the financial system is the backbone of any nation's economic sovereignty. American-owned banks have been acquiring Canadian banks for years, and this foreign control over financial institutions makes Canada's economy more susceptible to U.S. policies. By enacting stronger foreign ownership laws, Canada could ensure that its banking sector remains independent, serving Canadian interests rather than the interests of foreign investors or governments.

Similarly, real estate in Canada has increasingly been targeted by foreign investors, particularly in major cities like Vancouver, Toronto, and Montreal. This has driven up housing prices and led to concerns about housing affordability for Canadian citizens. By restricting foreign ownership of Canadian real estate, particularly in the residential sector, Canada could ensure that housing markets serve Canadian citizens and families, rather than being driven by foreign capital. This would also help to protect the Canadian real estate market from being exploited by foreign entities seeking to make profits rather than contribute to the local economy.

Reasserting national borders and immigration control is essential for maintaining Canada's sovereignty, cultural integrity, and national cohesion. While immigration has historically been a cornerstone of Canada's growth and diversity, the pace and nature of recent immigration trends have raised concerns about long-term social integration and the country's ability to preserve a coherent national identity. By tightening immigration policies and implementing a Canada-first immigration strategy, Canada could better align its immigration policies with the nation's economic needs, ensuring that newcomers contribute to national cohesion and the long-term prosperity of the country.

Tightening immigration policies can be seen as a way to prevent demographic shifts that may, over time, weaken Canada's national cohesion. The rapid pace of immigration, combined with the growing diversity of newcomers, can sometimes lead to challenges in terms of social integration, community unity, and the preservation of Canadian values. While immigration brings economic benefits, including filling labor gaps and supporting an aging population, it is important that these benefits do not come at the cost of national identity or the cohesion of Canadian society. By implementing more selective immigration policies—prioritizing those who align with Canadian values and social norms—Canada can ensure that newcomers can better integrate into the Canadian way of life and contribute positively to the country's social fabric.

A Canada-first immigration policy would prioritize skills that benefit national industries and meet economic needs, rather than simply contributing to globalist labor markets. In recent years, Canada's immigration policies have been influenced by the notion that global labor mobility benefits the economy by filling gaps in labor markets. While this is true to some extent, it often leads to importing workers who may be more aligned with the interests of multinational corporations or foreign economies than with Canada's long-term industrial goals. A Canada-first approach would prioritize the skills and talents needed to build and sustain Canadian industries, ensuring that immigrants contribute to sectors that are vital to the country's future, such as technology, manufacturing, healthcare, and natural resource management. By targeting skilled workers who can fill key positions in these sectors, Canada can strengthen its economy, foster innovation, and reduce reliance on foreign labor that may be better suited to global markets rather than Canada's unique needs.

This approach would also emphasize economic self-sufficiency and national resilience, ensuring that Canada's workforce is highly skilled, diverse, and aligned with the country's long-term goals. Rather than simply responding to global economic demands, Canada would tailor its immigration policies to meet the specific needs of the domestic economy, ensuring that newcomers contribute to building a strong, independent Canada. Prioritizing skills-based immigration would reduce the tendency to import workers who are primarily driven by global labor markets, ensuring that Canada's immigration system is focused on strengthening its own national industries and economic independence.

Additionally, a skills-based immigration policy could address the growing concern that large-scale immigration may be placing undue pressure on Canadian social services, particularly in urban areas where housing, healthcare, and education systems are already under strain. By selectively admitting immigrants who possess the skills needed to contribute to sectors experiencing shortages or high demand, Canada can help ensure that newcomers are better integrated into the workforce and that public resources are more efficiently allocated.

14 |

Conclusion

C anada has certainly seen a gradual erosion of its sovereignty in various areas over the years, particularly as a result of its deepening
economic integration with the U.S., participation in globalist institutions, and the increasing influence of foreign corporations. This loss of
sovereignty has led to concerns that it may be too late to reverse course.
However, while Canada faces significant challenges, it is not beyond the
possibility of reclaiming much of its independence—economically, politically, and culturally. The strategies of tightening immigration policies, reasserting national borders, and limiting foreign influence are all
feasible, but they would require significant political will, public support, and long-term commitment to changing Canada's trajectory.

The idea that Canada has lost too much sovereignty to reverse course
stems from the significant economic dependence on the U.S. and the
globalized systems that shape much of Canada's political and economic
decision-making. For example, trade agreements like NAFTA (now
USMCA) have increased Canada's reliance on the U.S. market, while
military agreements such as NORAD and NATO tie Canada to U.S.-
led defense initiatives. Additionally, the influence of foreign corporations in Canadian industries like banking, real estate, and natural
resources has led to a situation where Canada's sovereignty in these sectors is often undermined by external interests. These factors make it feel
as though the loss of sovereignty is irreversible.

However, it is important to recognize that sovereignty is not an absolute state—there are degrees of sovereignty, and Canada still retains

significant control over its domestic policies, borders, and cultural identity. While Canada may be influenced by foreign powers and global economic forces, there are still pathways available to reclaim and strengthen its sovereignty, particularly in areas that are more susceptible to government intervention.

Implementing a Canada-first immigration policy that prioritizes skills-based immigration and aligns newcomers with national industries is a feasible strategy. Canada can control who enters the country and can tailor its immigration system to meet its economic needs and social cohesion goals. Immigration has been a vital part of Canada's history, but managing it in a way that benefits the national interest rather than serving globalist labor markets is entirely within Canada's power.

Similarly, tightening immigration controls and reasserting national borders are strategies that Canada can pursue with political will. If Canadians elect governments that are committed to prioritizing national interests over globalization, significant changes can be made in terms of immigration policy and border control without sacrificing Canada's position in the world. The key would be to balance economic independence with the benefits of international cooperation—ensuring that Canada remains an active global player without compromising its sovereignty.

Reasserting control over foreign ownership in critical industries like banking, real estate, and natural resources is another avenue for restoring sovereignty. Canada has the legislative tools to implement stronger restrictions on foreign investments and corporate ownership of key sectors. Though challenging, these changes would require political courage and public support to resist foreign pressure and corporate interests. The country could create more robust regulations to ensure that Canadian businesses remain in the hands of Canadians, reducing the influence of foreign interests over critical economic infrastructure.

Reclaiming cultural sovereignty is also achievable through a stronger media presence and national education policies that prioritize Canadian identity over foreign influence. By revitalizing Canadian media, enforcing CanCon regulations, and introducing national education programs that emphasize Canadian history and sovereignty, Canada can strengthen its cultural cohesion and resist Americanization. While the influence of U.S. culture through media and social media is pervasive, Canada still has the tools to shape its cultural landscape to better reflect its national values.

It is important to recognize that while reversing the tide of economic globalization and foreign influence is challenging, it is not impossible. Many of the strategies discussed—such as tightening immigration policies, limiting foreign ownership, and reinforcing cultural identity—are within Canada's control, provided there is the political will to implement them. These strategies are not without obstacles, such as global pressures, trade relations, and the political establishment that may be invested in maintaining the current system. However, these challenges are not insurmountable. Canada has faced significant historical challenges to its sovereignty, from British colonialism to U.S. expansionism, and has navigated them with resilience.

The question of whether any Canadian government would be willing to take the political risk of pursuing true independence from the influence of foreign powers, particularly the U.S., is a complex one. Canada's historical relationship with the U.S., its involvement in globalist institutions, and its reliance on economic integration with the U.S. have all shaped the country's policy-making approach. In many ways, Canada has made strategic decisions based on the need for economic stability and geopolitical alignment rather than full independence. That said, while the risks of pursuing true independence are high, there is also significant potential for reclaiming sovereignty if a government were willing to challenge the status quo.

For any Canadian government to pursue true independence, it would require a substantial shift in political priorities. Canada's dependency on the U.S. is multifaceted—spanning trade, defense, and cultural influence—which makes any push for true independence an inherently complex and risky proposition. Political elites, whether within the Conservative, Liberal, or NDP parties, have generally maintained policies of cooperation and integration with the U.S., seeing this as a route to economic growth, security, and international influence. There is a general reluctance to challenge the economic and military stability that comes with being closely tied to the U.S. and to take actions that could disrupt trade relationships, military alliances, or global partnerships.

For example, trade agreements like NAFTA (now USMCA), which have integrated Canada deeply into the U.S. economy, are seen by many as vital to Canada's economic prosperity. Reversing course on these agreements could provoke economic backlash, lead to job losses, and risk the loss of market access to the U.S., which remains Canada's largest trading partner. In this context, even governments with strong nationalist inclinations have been hesitant to pursue policies that might jeopardize economic stability or international trade relations.

Furthermore, Canada's military ties to the U.S. through NATO and NORAD also make it difficult for any government to drastically reframe its defense policy without alienating a key military ally. The U.S. is Canada's primary defense partner, and the U.S. military infrastructure plays a critical role in Canada's national security. With the global security climate continually evolving, and the growing military challenges posed by other powers like China and Russia, the idea of severing ties or pursuing true independence could be seen as a risk to national security.

However, political will and public support are key factors that could drive Canada toward greater independence. While the political elites may remain cautious, the Canadian public could play a significant role in pushing for a reassertion of sovereignty. If public sentiment shifts towards a more self-sufficient Canada that focuses on domestic economic interests, cultural identity, and political autonomy, a government would face increased pressure to adopt policies that reflect these values. This could involve strengthening domestic industries, limiting foreign influence, and pursuing independent trade agreements. In such a climate, a government might be more willing to take the political risk of breaking away from the U.S.-dominated status quo.

Moreover, the emergence of populist movements and rising discontent with globalist policies in many Western democracies could create an opening for true independence in Canada. As seen in other countries, a shift towards nationalism or sovereignty movements has led to political realignments, particularly as concerns about economic inequality, immigration, and cultural preservation grow. If these sentiments gain more traction in Canada, it could create the political climate necessary for a government to pursue more independent policies, despite the risks involved.

It is important to note that pursuing true independence would not necessarily mean isolating Canada from the world or ending all relationships with the U.S.. Canada could still maintain strong trade relationships, diplomatic ties, and security arrangements with the U.S. and other countries while focusing on reasserting sovereignty in key areas such as defense, trade policy, and cultural identity. The focus would be on reducing dependency on foreign entities and prioritizing Canada's own interests, while also strengthening regional alliances and multilateral cooperation with countries that share Canada's values.

If Canada fails to take decisive action now, full absorption into the U.S. could become an increasingly likely outcome within the next few decades. While it's impossible to predict the future with absolute certainty, there are several key trends that suggest that Canada's economic, cultural, and political integration with the U.S. is deepening to a point where maintaining full sovereignty will become increasingly difficult without significant policy changes and a renewed focus on national independence.

First, the economic integration between Canada and the U.S. is overwhelming. The U.S. is Canada's largest trading partner, and Canadian industries are highly dependent on U.S. markets, particularly in sectors such as energy, manufacturing, and technology. With NAFTA (now

USMCA) and the growing influence of American corporations in Canadian industries, it is evident that Canada's economic interests are increasingly aligned with the U.S. at the expense of a more diverse and independent trade policy. The expansion of multinational corporations, many of which are U.S.-based, has led to corporate control of critical sectors of the Canadian economy, including banking, real estate, and natural resources. American capital flows into Canadian industries, and Canadian resources are often directed to the U.S., further embedding Canada in the U.S. economic sphere. If this trend continues without efforts to diversify trade partnerships and reduce dependency on U.S. markets, the eventual economic absorption of Canada into the U.S. could be seen as a logical extension of the current trajectory.

Second, Canada's military and defense integration with the U.S. through NATO and NORAD has contributed to the erosion of Canadian sovereignty in defense matters. Canada's military policy and defense infrastructure are increasingly tied to U.S. interests, meaning that decisions about national security are often influenced by U.S. priorities. While Canadian forces are capable and independent, they are often aligned with U.S. military objectives, and Canadian defense policies are largely shaped within the framework of U.S. strategies. This relationship has made it more difficult for Canada to assert independent defense policies and maintain its military autonomy. If Canada continues to remain tightly aligned with U.S. defense initiatives without a clear vision of an independent defense strategy, it may eventually find itself militarily absorbed into U.S. defense structures, with decision-making power further eroded.

The influence of American culture is another critical factor. Over the last several decades, the dominance of American media, entertainment, and social platforms has led to the Americanization of Canadian society. The influence of Hollywood, U.S. social media, and corporate culture has blurred national boundaries, making Canada's cultural identity more susceptible to U.S. values. The decline of CanCon (Canadian Content) regulations and the increasing reliance on American platforms like Netflix, Facebook, and Google have made it harder for Canada to cultivate and protect its distinct cultural narrative. Without proactive steps to revitalize Canadian culture and limit foreign influence, Canada risks losing its cultural sovereignty entirely, with Canadian values, norms, and interests being eclipsed by those of the U.S..

Finally, political integration between Canada and the U.S. is becoming more evident in the form of policy convergence. The liberalization of trade, harmonization of environmental regulations, and shared concerns over national security have led to the alignment of policies between the two countries. The pressure for closer cooperation in areas such as immigration, border control, and intelligence sharing makes it increasingly difficult for Canada to maintain fully independent policies that diverge from those of the U.S. The ideological and political alignment between U.S. administrations and Canadian leadership often facilitates this process, even if the Canadian public remains wary of too much political integration. If this alignment continues, and if Canada's political leaders continue to prioritize cooperation with the U.S. over sovereignty, the idea of full political absorption could become more palatable, particularly in times of crisis or economic instability.

If Canada fails to act now, focusing on reasserting its sovereignty, diversifying its trade partners, independent defense policies, and cultural preservation, full absorption into the U.S. could eventually become a foregone conclusion. Without a deliberate strategy to reassert national autonomy and resist U.S. influence, the trends of economic integration, military collaboration, and cultural assimilation could solidify the process of Canada becoming increasingly indistinguishable from its southern neighbor, eventually leading to a de facto annexation—not necessarily by military force, but by political and economic coercion.

Canada has the resources, political agency, and capacity to resist full integration, but it will require bold leadership, public engagement, and commitment to sovereignty to ensure that Canada can maintain its distinctiveness and independence. The time for decisive action is now, before the country's national identity and independence are permanently compromised by forces beyond its control.

If Canada fails to take decisive action now, full absorption into the U.S. could become an increasingly likely outcome within the next few decades. While it's impossible to predict the future with absolute certainty, there are several key trends that suggest that Canada's economic, cultural, and political integration with the U.S. is deepening to a point where maintaining full sovereignty will become increasingly difficult without significant policy changes and a renewed focus on national independence.

First, the economic integration between Canada and the U.S. is overwhelming. The U.S. is Canada's largest trading partner, and Canadian industries are highly dependent on U.S. markets, particularly in sectors such as energy, manufacturing, and technology. With NAFTA (now USMCA) and the growing influence of American corporations in Canadian industries, it is evident that Canada's economic interests are increasingly aligned with the U.S. at the expense of a more diverse and independent trade policy. The expansion of multinational corporations, many of which are U.S.-based, has led to corporate control of critical sectors of the Canadian economy, including banking, real estate, and natural resources. American capital flows into Canadian industries, and Canadian resources are often directed to the U.S., further embedding Canada in the U.S. economic sphere. If this trend continues without efforts to diversify trade partnerships and reduce dependency on U.S. markets, the eventual economic absorption of Canada into the U.S. could be seen as a logical extension of the current trajectory.

Second, Canada's military and defense integration with the U.S. through NATO and NORAD has contributed to the erosion of Canadian sovereignty in defense matters. Canada's military policy and defense infrastructure are increasingly tied to U.S. interests, meaning that decisions about national security are often influenced by U.S. priorities. While Canadian forces are capable and independent, they are often aligned with U.S. military objectives, and Canadian defense policies are largely shaped within the framework of U.S. strategies. This relationship has made it more difficult for Canada to assert independent defense policies and maintain its military autonomy. If Canada continues to remain tightly aligned with U.S. defense initiatives without a clear vision of an independent defense strategy, it may eventually find itself militarily absorbed into U.S. defense structures, with decision-making power further eroded.

The influence of American culture is another critical factor. Over the last several decades, the dominance of American media, entertainment, and social platforms has led to the Americanization of Canadian society. The influence of Hollywood, U.S. social media, and corporate culture has blurred national boundaries, making Canada's cultural identity more susceptible to U.S. values. The decline of CanCon (Canadian Content) regulations and the increasing reliance on American platforms like Netflix, Facebook, and Google have made it harder for Canada to cultivate and protect its distinct cultural narrative. Without proactive steps to revitalize Canadian culture and limit foreign influence, Canada risks losing its cultural sovereignty entirely, with Canadian values, norms, and interests being eclipsed by those of the U.S..

Finally, political integration between Canada and the U.S. is becoming more evident in the form of policy convergence. The liberalization of trade, harmonization of environmental regulations, and shared concerns over national security have led to the alignment of policies between the two countries. The pressure for closer cooperation in areas such as immigration, border control, and intelligence sharing makes it increasingly difficult for Canada to maintain fully independent policies that diverge from those of the U.S. The ideological and political alignment between U.S. administrations and Canadian leadership often facilitates this process, even if the Canadian public remains wary of too much political integration. If this alignment continues, and if Canada's political leaders continue to prioritize cooperation with the U.S. over sovereignty, the idea of full political absorption could become more palatable, particularly in times of crisis or economic instability.

If Canada fails to act now, focusing on reasserting its sovereignty, diversifying its trade partners, independent defense policies, and cultural preservation, full absorption into the U.S. could eventually become a foregone conclusion. Without a deliberate strategy to reassert national autonomy and resist U.S. influence, the trends of economic integration, military collaboration, and cultural assimilation could solidify the process of Canada becoming increasingly indistinguishable from its southern neighbor, eventually leading to a de facto annexation—not necessarily by military force, but by political and economic coercion.

Canada has the resources, political agency, and capacity to resist full integration, but it will require bold leadership, public engagement, and commitment to sovereignty to ensure that Canada can maintain its distinctiveness and independence. The time for decisive action is now, before the country's national identity and independence are permanently compromised by forces beyond its control.

You said:

• Does Canada need a radical shift in leadership and national consciousness, or is slow decline inevitable?

ChatGPT said:

ChatGPT

Canada stands at a critical juncture in its history. Whether the country needs a radical shift in leadership and a renewed sense of national consciousness, or if slow decline is inevitable, depends largely on the actions taken by the government and the Canadian public moving forward. The forces shaping Canada's future are complex, involving economic dependency, military integration, and cultural assimilation with the U.S. While the slow erosion of sovereignty is a very real concern, Canada still holds the power to regain control over its destiny—but only if there is a collective shift in how the country views itself on the world stage.

The current trajectory suggests that if Canada continues on its present path, particularly with its increasing economic dependence on the U.S., military alignment with NATO and NORAD, and the overwhelming cultural influence of American media and tech companies, a slow decline into cultural homogenization and political subordination is indeed a possibility. The country has become deeply intertwined with U.S. systems, and the loss of sovereignty in key areas like trade, defense, and cultural identity could continue to erode the foundations of Canadian independence over time. This would lead to a scenario where the gradual loss of political autonomy could culminate in Canada's absorption into a broader North American Union or simply becoming a de facto extension of the U.S., whether through economic pressure, cultural influence, or military cooperation.

However, it is not inevitable that Canada will succumb to slow decline. The country still possesses the institutional strength, democratic frameworks, and cultural resilience to initiate a radical change—if there is the political will to do so. A shift in leadership that prioritizes national sovereignty, economic independence, and the preservation of Canadian culture could break the cycle of increasing dependence on the U.S. and return Canada to a position of autonomy in the global order. This would require political leaders who are committed to national renewal, not just through policy changes, but by engaging in a broader cultural and ideological reawakening that emphasizes Canadian distinctiveness and self-determination.

A radical shift in leadership would involve politicians willing to stand up to the U.S. on key issues, whether it be trade policy, military alliances, or foreign influence. It would require leadership that challenges the status quo, stepping away from globalist agendas that prioritize corporate interests or international alliances over national sovereignty. This could involve policies that limit foreign ownership, curb immigration in ways that prioritize national cohesion, and reassert control over

Canada's resources and industries. It would also require a renewed commitment to Canadian values, including a stronger emphasis on localism, regional autonomy, and cultural preservation in the face of pervasive American cultural influence.

Equally important would be a shift in national consciousness—a widespread reawakening of the Canadian identity and a deepened sense of pride in the country's history and sovereignty. Canada's education system, media, and public discourse could play key roles in fostering this national awareness. Canadians need to be reminded of the unique nature of their country, the sacrifices made to build the nation, and the importance of maintaining a distinct cultural identity that is not easily absorbed into the American model. A renewed focus on Canadian history, the struggles for independence, and the foundational principles that make Canada unique—such as multiculturalism, peacekeeping, and social welfare—could provide the necessary foundation for rebuilding national pride.

Moreover, activating public engagement through grassroots movements, civil society organizations, and political reforms could create the kind of political momentum needed to push for sovereignty-centered policies. Canadians must feel empowered to demand policies that prioritize their economic, cultural, and political well-being, even if it means confronting powerful interests that seek to undermine Canadian autonomy. If Canadians can develop a strong sense of national unity around shared values and objectives, there is the potential for mass mobilization to take action on these critical issues.

THE END

www.ingramcontent.com/pod-product-compliance
Lightning Source LLC
Chambersburg PA
CBHW062131040426

42335CB00039B/1956